INDUSTRIAL MEGAPROJECTS

INDUSTRIAL MEGAPROJECTS

Concepts, Strategies, and Practices for Success

Edward W. Merrow

WILEY

John Wiley & Sons, Inc.

Published by John Wiley & Sons, Inc., Hoboken, New Jersey.
Published simultaneously in Canada.

For general information on our other products and services or for technical support, please contact our Customer Care Department within the United States at (800) 762-2974, outside the United States at (317) 572-3993 or fax (317) 572-4002.

Wiley also publishes its books in a variety of electronic formats. Some content that appears in print may not be available in electronic books. For more information about Wiley products, visit our web site at www.wiley.com.

Library of Congress Cataloging-in-Publication Data:

Merrow, Edward W.
   Industrial megaprojects : concepts, strategies, and practices for success / Edward W. Merrow.
      p. cm.
   Includes index.
   ISBN 978-0-470-93882-9 (cloth)
   ISBN 978-1-118-06748-2 (ebk)
   ISBN 978-1-118-06749-9 (ebk)
   ISBN 978-1-118-06750-5 (ebk)
   1. Project management.   I. Title.
   HD69.P75M47 2011
   658.4'04—dc22

                                                                    2010054037

Printed in the United States of America

10 9 8 7 6 5

CONTENTS

FOREWORD

Will your megaproject be a success or a failure? Data from more than 300 global megaprojects shows that 65 percent of industrial projects with budgets larger than $1 billion in 2010 U.S. dollars failed to meet business objectives. In some industrial sectors the failure rate was as high as 75 percent. Most of the failed projects were unprofitable, but not all. Some made money due to a serendipitous increase in forecasted product prices or other unanticipated windfalls. Unfortunately, these projects support some people's belief that "it is better to be lucky than good" at what you do. However, if this isn't how you want to manage your business risks on very large investments, there is some really good news. For more than two decades, Independent Project Analysis, Inc., has been exploring what makes projects succeed and fail, and the results of their research on megaprojects are now available in this book.

Industrial Megaprojects is a primer on what to do and what not to do as part of end-to-end megaproject management. This book provides the necessary information for you to establish a decision and execution framework that allows you to be in control of your project's outcomes, not "just hope to be lucky." It is structured in a way that those who sponsor, direct, or work on large projects can gain a functional understanding of how best to achieve the most business-effective results. It also enables business executives who are genuinely in charge to make better decisions about how the project should be developed, governed, and executed. Most important, it lays out ways to overcome the largest challenge in successful implementation of megaprojects—enabling the business and technical professionals to work together collaboratively as a fully integrated team.

Now back to the critical question: Will your megaproject be a success or a failure? The answer is . . . it depends. It depends on whether you can positively answer these key questions:

- Will it be built and started up without injury to anyone involved, or will people be hurt or killed?
- Will the total cost be in line with the amount authorized, or will it exceed the estimate by more than 25 percent?
- Will it be completed on the original schedule, or will it slip by more than 25 percent?
- Will it start up and deliver the promised production, or will there be an initial or permanent shortfall?

How confident you are that you can accurately answer these questions depends on several things. The critical ones are: (1) Have you put the concepts, strategies, and practices—proved to deliver successful megaprojects—in place? and (2) Have you integrated them into a disciplined project management process? In addition, I would like to call to your attention what I, as well as the author, believe is the most important and almost unique requirement for a successful venture: the need to assess and then shape the opportunity into a reasonably stable platform from which to manage the project. Opportunity shaping is a process involving both the business and the technical professionals who would be assigned to the project. To be successful, it must be led by the senior business executive accountable for the financial performance of the business unit proposing the venture. It allows the sponsors to evaluate the key attributes of a potential project, gather information that is needed to guide venture level decisions, and then allocate the value to the various stakeholders. This will make the project environment stable enough for successful execution, while holding enough of the project's value for the sponsors to make the venture worthwhile. In this book, the opportunity shaping process is discussed from the perspective of the business and the project professionals who are working for the leading stakeholder-investor. Both the information that needs to be developed to make good shaping decisions and how to devise a successful shaping strategy are detailed. I believe this part of the book is a must-read for business and technical professionals charged with the accountability of developing and successfully executing a megaproject. When business and technical professionals do not understand and then apply opportunity shaping concepts and strategies, the risk of their project being one of the 65 percent failures is extremely high.

After more than 40 years working in the capital project arena, I remain mystified by the extreme reluctance of very intelligent business and technical leaders to pay attention to validated past experience. It is my opinion that failing to accept that there are project best concepts, strategies, and practices that, when executed in a disciplined manner, deliver predictably good results makes no business sense. Over the course of my career, I have struggled to find the right way to communicate this and show that the business value was so obvious that the use of the proven approaches should be a no-brainer. But, until now I have been woefully unsuccessful, even on projects for businesses that have experienced failures in the past. I had begun to fear that we were all destined to continue to validate the observation expressed in this quote from Douglas Adams, English humorist and science fiction novelist:

Human beings, who are almost unique in having the ability to learn from the experience of others, are also remarkable for their apparent disinclination to do so.

However, knowing that the knowledge contained in this book is now available to everyone makes me cautiously optimistic. I am truly hopeful that this book will become the "megaproject handbook" and be required reading for all business and technical leaders currently working on or contemplating a venture that would include a large capital investment. Looking to the future, I recommend this book become the primary text for all college and professional development courses on venture and project administration and management. This would contribute significantly to current and future business and technical leaders being much better prepared to plan and execute successful projects regardless of size.

I know as business and technical professionals there is always a great demand on your time, but now that you've read this far, I strongly encourage you to read all of this book. The key concepts, strategies, and practices are described in actionable terms, and their business value is supported by actual project examples. I'm certain you'll agree that your investment of a few hours reading this book and discovering how you can potentially save billions in project costs will have a huge return.

—James B. Porter, Jr.
Chief Engineer and Vice President (Retired)
Engineering and Operations
E.I. DuPont & Company

ACKNOWLEDGMENTS

My first and deepest thanks must go to the megaproject teams that patiently answered thousands of questions about their projects. Without their time and candor, there would be no data to examine and no stories to tell. I also thank my colleagues at Independent Project Analysis, Inc., who asked the questions, probed the responses, and evaluated the individual projects. I hope they will see the fruits of their fine efforts reflected in the book. My special thanks go to my research colleagues Kelli Ratliff and Luke Wallace. Kelli worked closely with me several years ago in the development of the first megaprojects course for the IPA Institute. Luke did a remarkable job providing me with needed data as I wrote the book; his timeliness was essential to the schedule.

While writing the book, I was very fortunate to have a splendid set of reviewers. My IPA colleague, Paul Barshop, read and commented on most of the chapters and provided an insider's expertise while commenting on the analysis. I also had five external reviewers who gave of their time and expertise to review and comment: Joseph Brewer, megaproject manager extraordinaire at the Dow Chemical Company; Drew McCullin, Director of DuPont Capital (ret.); Jim Porter, Chief Engineer and Vice President (ret.), DuPont Company; Iain Smith, formerly Director of Capital Projects, Imperial Chemical Industries, Ltd; and Maggi Walker, Vice President, Engineering Solutions and Technology Centers, Dow Chemical Company. Each reviewer provided a distinct point of view and improved the book at every turn. Mike Loulakis, a very rare lawyer who deeply understands projects, provided a great review of Chapter 11, which deals with contracting. Any mistakes likely resulted from my not heeding their good advice.

It is to my most important reviewer, critic, and friend, my wife, Loretta, that I dedicate this book in thanks for her unstinting encouragement.

INTRODUCTION

WHY MEGAPROJECTS FAIL SO OFTEN
SEVEN KEY MISTAKES

By way of introducing you to the strange world of megaprojects, I am starting by discussing seven critical mistakes that I have seen most often in my 30 years of studying these projects, first at The Rand Corporation and then for the past 23 years at Independent Project Analysis (IPA). If you are responsible for a megaproject right now, try to ask yourself, "Am I now in the process of making one of these whopper blunders?"

After outlining how to do large projects well to the executive committee of a large company, the chief executive officer (CEO) asked me an obvious question: "Given that all of this is rather straightforward," (he actually said "smashingly banal"), "why can't we do it?"

The answer was one he anticipated and feared: "Because you are incapable of generating the kind of deep cooperation within the company that is necessary to do these projects well."

Most of the big mistakes that companies make in developing and executing these projects stem from a basic lack of being able to pursue a common goal with clarity and good behavior.

This book is mostly about mistakes, often masked with the bravado of "taking daring risks," but in the end just plain mistakes. So I thought it appropriate to start our discussion of megaprojects with seven whopper mistakes that doomed too many of these projects from the start. For the most part, the engineers on these projects tend to make little mistakes, although some of them occasionally cascade into disaster. Most big mistakes are made by senior business managers in the sponsoring firms. The reason they make most of the big mistakes

1

is because they have control of the things that matter most: strategy, money, and people. In most megaproject developments, the most important single relationship among the many thousands of relationships involved is the one between the business director for the project and the project manager, often called the project director.

So here are my top "Sorry Seven":

1. **I want to keep it all!**

   In days of yore, greed was considered a bad thing, even in business, because greed was liable to get us into trouble. I am pleased to report that in megaprojects, greed still works that way. When companies approach these projects with a view of trying to take as much of the pie as they possibly can, they lose sight of an essential element in making the project succeed: the allocation of the project's potential value in a way that provides a stable foundation on which the project can be executed. This will be a primary subject of Chapters 4 and 5. Working a deal that will be seen as essentially unfair to other stakeholders will tend to backfire. Greed generates an imbalance in the distribution of costs and rewards of the project.

   Most commonly, a project with a greedy lead sponsor falls apart in the development (shaping) phase, so we end up with nothing rather than all of it. In other cases, the project proceeds, but those who believe they have been treated unfairly never let go of their opposition. They then add turbulence to the project environment, giving project directors more trouble than they can manage. By their nature, megaprojects often struggle with turbulent project environments. Adding to that turbulence is a recipe for failure.

2. **I want it *NOW*!**

   Schedule pressure dooms more megaprojects than any other single factor. When there is pressure to move a project along quickly from the outset, corners get cut and opportunists have a field day.

   A classic case was a group of difficult deepwater petroleum developments that was put on a fast track when the CEO mentioned in a meeting with the financial community that the projects would go into production on a particular date. The project community's reaction within the company was, "It can't be done!" But that didn't deter an ambitious vice president who saw an opportunity to ingratiate himself with the boss. He then set up a "daring and ambitious" program with an inexperienced contractor to deliver the projects in 70 percent of industry average time at 70 percent of industry average cost. The result was a program overrun of numerous billions of dollars, and a full four-year delay on the company's largest and most important project.

No project should ever be deliberately slow. (If it really doesn't make any difference when the project is completed, you probably shouldn't be doing the project now anyway.) But taking risks with megaproject schedules is a fool's game. Every megaproject has an appropriate pace at which the project can be developed and executed successfully. Furthermore, that pace is known with a fair degree of confidence early on if good practice is followed. If the economics of the project require an accelerated schedule, then the appropriate conclusion is that the project is uneconomic and should not be done. Unlike smaller projects, megaprojects cannot be used to "fill in a gap" in your production or "meet a market window." When the calendar rather than the needs of the project drives the schedule, the project fails. We return to the issue of fast-tracking megaprojects in Chapter 5.

3. **Don't worry; we'll work out the details of the deal later.**
   As a megaproject director friend of mine likes to say: "The deal drives the project; the project can't drive the deal!" I would add that the project *can* drive the deal, but it never turns out to be a *good* deal. The business deal and the project have to develop together and inform each other, but the deal governs. The deal establishes the parameters and the priorities for the project. The deal determines the relative importance of capital cost versus operating cost and cost versus schedule. The deal also determines how big the scope can be.

   Many megaprojects center around a deal between a resource holder (e.g., petroleum, minerals deposit) and a company with the technical expertise to develop that resource and sell the product. The basic contours of the deal between the resource holder

and the resource developer must be decided quite early in the front-end development of the project. The deal is what will ultimately shape how money will be made, as well as how it will be divided. In the absence of the deal, the project is directionless. If project development continues without the deal informing its shape, the chances that the deal will never be struck increase. Furthermore, if the potential partners cannot agree fairly quickly on the shape of the deal, there may be something terribly amiss. Let me cite an egregious example.

A European company was developing a large project (~$7 billion) in the Middle East with a resource holder. The idea was that the resource holder would provide the feedstock at a discounted rate to promote industrialization and job creation; while the project was busy being developed and defined, the negotiations over the formula for this went nowhere. When we challenged the rationality of this situation with the company executive driving the deal, we were brushed aside with a "You don't understand the Middle East." Finally, the invitations to bid were issued and more than $250 million of the company's money had been spent and the board of directors finally required a deal or no authorization. When there was no deal forthcoming, the company was forced to cancel the project and eat the loss. What was going on? The resource holder didn't actually have the feedstock, and exploration efforts were coming up empty. Not wanting to lose face (and make their resource situation known to the world), they dragged their feet until the sponsor quit. They then publicly blamed the sponsor for killing the project and being an unreliable and untrustworthy company! And who is it exactly that doesn't know the Middle East?

4. **Why do we have to spend so much up front?**

Every project professional worthy of the title knows that skimping on the front-end definition of a project is stupid. So when it comes to the biggest and most important projects that we do, we routinely skimp on the front end. Megaprojects—with so much at stake—are routinely less well defined at authorization than smaller, less important projects. The primary reasons are time (see Mistake 2) and money (see Mistake 1).

Depending on the specifics of the project, doing a thorough job defining and planning an industrial megaproject takes 3 to 5 percent of eventual total capital cost. Let's be clear; on a megaproject that is a lot of money. The cost, however, of *not* spending the money is much, much more.

Senior managers are understandably concerned that if they spend, say, $100 million and the project is canceled, they are stuck with the bill. Even worse from their perspective, the $100 million is expense, not capital, and is therefore deducted immediately from earnings. However, when senior managers are faced with this situation as a realistic possibility, it is symptomatic of other problems.

Sometimes managers find themselves in this risk of loss position because the resource holder has deliberately set them up. Some resource holders want no decision points between the initial "memorandum of understanding" (which has no binding effect) and the full-funds authorization of the project. This is a simple bargaining ploy: The resource holder believes that if they can get the sponsors to spend enough money, the sponsors will be locked into the project whether or not they really want to be. This is a psychological example of the forward-going economics trap—that is, "throwing good money after bad."

At other times, senior managers can find themselves in this dilemma because the cost of the project was not understood at the necessary and appropriate time. As we discuss at some length in Chapter 4, the eventual cost of the project should be known with a fair degree of assurance when only about 1 percent of total cost has been expended, not 3 to 5 percent. If management doesn't have the stomach for spending 1 percent as pure risk money, they should not play the game. Spending that front-end money well is the subject of Chapter 10.

5. **We need to shave 20 percent off that number!**

One of the most counterproductive exercises in megaprojects is the "cost reduction task force" responding to management's admonition to significantly reduce the cost of the project, usually within a few months of full-funds authorization. I have literally heard a vice president say, "You guys [meaning the project team] need to sharpen your pencils and get a billion dollars out of that estimate!" Those must be magic pencils, because in the real world, the cost of a project is inextricably linked to its scope, which in turn is a reflection of its intended functionality. Unless I change the scope, which means that some functionality has to give way, I cannot really change the cost estimate. But to change the scope would require another year or two before we are ready to authorize the project, which is, of course, unacceptable because of Mistake 2.

So project teams in this situation do one of two things: they change the assumptions underlying the estimate such as the cost and productivity of labor, prices for equipment, and so on, or they actually cut the scope knowing that it will all have to come back later to achieve the needed performance of the project. Either way, they are headed for a big overrun, and the savviest among them will be preparing to post their resumes so as not to be caught up in the scapegoating that will surely occur later.

6. **The contractors should carry the risk; they're doing the project!**

A majority of megaprojects in most parts of the world are executed on some form of fixed-price contracts between the sponsors and one or more prime contractors. Rather than project professionals, the preference for fixed-price (lump-sum) contracting almost always comes from the business leadership or from the banks financing the projects. Their belief is that the contractual form will transfer the cost (and often schedule) risk from the sponsors to the prime contractor(s). And every once in a while, it actually does! Most of the time, however, relatively little risk is actually passed, but a substantial premium is paid nonetheless.

There is a simple and unavoidable problem with wholesale risk transfer from sponsors to contractors: the contractors cannot actually carry the risk on a megaproject. The firms that engineer and construct industrial projects are variable-cost firms with very little in the way of fixed assets. Their balance sheets are not loaded with capital assets, and generally the cash they have on the balance sheet is needed for working purposes. They earn by selling the services of people rather than via the production and sale of products. This simply means they cannot possibly carry the kinds of losses that can and do occur on megaprojects. As a consequence, given the preference of business leaders and banks for lump-sum contracts, the engineering and construction firms have become very adept at taking on lump-sum contracts with loopholes or bidding so high that the risk is manageable.

Most of Chapter 11 takes up the issue of how to match the contracts to the situation rather than the situation to the contracts. However, the belief that lump-sum contracts establish a ceiling on what sponsors will pay for a project is to completely confuse a ceiling and a floor. No sponsor has ever paid *less* than the value of the lump-sum contract, but many, many a sponsor has paid much more.

7. **Fire those #$@$^! project managers who overrun our projects!**

Beating up project managers who overrun capital projects is a blood sport that certainly dates back to the Great Pyramids. However, it's a bit of fun that comes with a very high price tag for the business.

I have been looking at capital projects now for more than 30 years. I have met hundreds of project directors and managers of all sorts and descriptions. I have yet to meet one who starts the day by asking, "What can I do today to screw up my project?" I have met some project directors who struck me as hopelessly incompetent, but very few of those were working on megaprojects. Large cost overruns on major projects can almost never be honestly laid at the door of the project director.

I will never forget a very long morning I spent with the CEO of a large international oil company. Much of our discussion that morning focused on why it was inappropriate and counterproductive for him to personally browbeat project managers who overran their projects. I finally concluded the discussion this way: "If you beat up the project managers for overruns, they will find ways to hide money so you can never find it. If they don't, you have hired a bunch of morons. And morons don't do projects well either!" As I walked down the corridor after the meeting, the vice president responsible for exploration and production turned to me and said, "Ed, now you see what we're up against." I left that day knowing that I had lost the argument, and 15 years later, the company's engineering department, led by a former contractor, focuses most of its effort on finding where the project directors have hidden the money.

The previous seven megamistakes are not mutually exclusive; they can and do show up together in many combinations. However, any one is usually sufficient to doom a project to failure.

PART ONE

UNDERSTANDING THE PROJECTS

CHAPTER 1

MEGAPROJECTS—CREATORS AND DESTROYERS OF CAPITAL

If you have spent much time hiking in the woods, you have probably had that uncomfortable occasion when, after walking for several hours, perhaps chatting with a friend along the way, you suddenly realize you have absolutely no idea where you are or how long it has been since you knew where you were. Many a megaproject director has encountered that same feeling while trying to bring a large and complex project safely home. This book seeks to explain how and why we so often find ourselves lost when trying to develop and execute very large industrial projects. If we can understand how and why we tend to get lost, we will better recognize when we are leaving the trail, find our way back if we do get lost, or at least know when to plead for directions.

Industrial corporations create their capital assets primarily through projects. The first decade of the twenty-first century has seen more very large and complex projects executed by the process industries— oil, chemicals, minerals, and power—than any comparable period in human history. These projects satisfy the world's demand for energy, metals, chemicals, and other products. Without them, modern society as we know it could not exist.

Projects have increased in size and complexity for a number of reasons: easily accessed resources close to markets have largely been depleted; international oil companies must venture into deep water and other difficult environments because national resource holders control more easily developed oil and gas; and chemical companies seeking lower-cost feedstocks need to exploit economies of scale to compete globally and often must go to the source of the feedstocks to make the project viable. The need for extensive infrastructure development means that many projects will have to be very large to spread the infrastructure costs over a wide enough base of beneficial production to be economic.

As the projects have increased in size and complexity, they have become much more difficult to manage. Cost overruns, serious slips in completion schedules, and operability problems have all become more common. Many of these very large projects end up being disappointing to their sponsors; a fair number turn out to be massive destroyers of shareholder wealth; and a few are horrendous with respect to anything and everything involved—the investing companies, the local population, and the environment. When megaproject disasters become public knowledge, which is rarely the case, they damage reputations and even jeopardize continued existence.*

The research program of Independent Project Analysis, Inc. (IPA) on megaprojects over the past five years shows clearly that virtually all of the poor results of these projects constitute self-inflicted wounds. The sponsors are creating the circumstances that lead inexorably to failure. *And that is profoundly good news!* Problems we cause ourselves, we can fix.

WHO SHOULD READ THIS BOOK?

Anyone with responsibility for large, complex, or difficult capital projects will find things of interest in the pages that follow. My particular goal is to help those who sponsor, direct, or work on large projects guide the projects to safe and successful outcomes. My special focus is on what I call "industrial megaprojects"—very large projects sponsored by the petroleum, chemicals, minerals, power, and related industries.

---

*The failure of BHP's Hot Briquetted Iron Project in 1999 contributed to the company losing more than half of its market value. The $10-plus billion overrun of Shell Sakhalin-2 Project damaged Shell's reputation and created an excuse for the Kremlin to nationalize a large portion of the project. The structural failure of BP's Thunder Horse semi-submersible platform in 2005 in the U.S. Gulf of Mexico was an important element in a series of stunning setbacks for the company. Most megaproject disasters, however, remain carefully private—while sometimes wearing a very different and well-contrived public face.

Anyone interested in complex projects, even if they fall far short of megaproject status, will find the story of these projects informative to their situation. Most of the basic principles of doing megaprojects well are the basic principles of doing all projects well. Megaprojects display some attributes that are common to megaprojects and uncommon in smaller projects, and we will focus our attention on those. But if the reader is interested in projects, megaprojects will always be fascinating.

I very much hope that members of boards of directors of companies that sponsor megaprojects read this book. To be blunt, when it comes to the governance of large projects, most boards strike me as brain dead. They are not asking the right questions, and they are not asking questions early enough in the process to deter bad decisions.

Those who finance major projects should find a great deal of interest (forgive the pun) in the book. In many respects this book is all about large project risk, which is a key concern for banks and others involved in project finance. It is my observation that bank financing often increases cost while doing nothing whatsoever about project risk.

Those who are concerned about the management of the modern publicly owned industrial corporation and teach others about how it should be done will also find this book interesting, and perhaps very disturbing. The failure of these projects is symptomatic of the core problems of the modern firm: too much outsourcing of key competencies, poorly informed decision making, a woeful lack of accountability for results, and a pathological focus on the short term at the expense of the long-term health of the corporation and its shareholders.

WHAT IS AN INDUSTRIAL MEGAPROJECT?

The projects that are the subject of our research are a subset of all projects and even a subset of large projects. We focus on *industrial* megaprojects. By *industrial,* we mean projects that make a product for sale, for example, oil, natural gas, iron ore, nickel, gold ingot, diamonds, and high-volume chemicals. All of the projects under scrutiny were intended to make an economic profit, at least eventually, for some if not always all of the sponsors.* By confining ourselves to industrial projects, we have excluded several classes of important projects: military developments, purely public works and transportation projects, monuments, works of art, and so forth. By excluding these sorts of projects we have excluded some megaprojects from our analysis. We have a couple of reasons for doing so:

- Confining ourselves to projects that are intended to make money simplifies the task of assessing outcomes, not necessarily simplifying the range and complexity of objectives in the projects. Although it is true for almost all of our projects that *someone* wanted and expected to make money on the result, it does not follow that *all* of the sponsors expected to make an economic profit. Some were motivated by jobs creation, political ambition, general economic development, and other "public" goals. These "mixed motive" projects as we call them are an interesting class and pose challenges for for-profit sponsors.
- Having some economic profit motive disciplines and constrains the objectives of the projects in important ways. Some public works projects have objectives that are hard to fathom by mere mortals. Some military acquisition programs appear to continue almost solely on the strength of political patronage long after the military rationale has become obsolete or discredited.[†] And some "prestige projects," such as the Concorde supersonic transport, have objectives that must forever be in the eye of the beholder. Who is to say whether prestige has actually been enhanced, and was it by an amount sufficient to justify the opportunity cost of the project? Industrial projects tend to have at least some nicely tangible objectives.

---

*A few of our projects were undertaken with the explicit expectation that they would make little or no economic profit but would facilitate highly profitable projects later. These projects bear the dubious title "strategic," a subject to which we return in Chapter 4. The term *sponsor* is reserved for those organizations that claim formal ownership of a project by virtue of their economic investment in the project. Those investments could occasionally be in-kind or deferred but usually indicate monetary investment in the cost of the project.

[†]For example, long after a superior option had emerged, the U.S. Air Force B-1 Bomber program continued due entirely to political influence. "B-1 Problems, if reparable, could cost $3Billion," the *Boston Globe,* February 13, 1987. The V-22 Osprey aircraft program not only overran its budget colossally, but it also suffered repeated crashes . . . but continued anyway. "Assessments Needed to Address V-22 Aircraft Operational and Cost Concerns to Define Future Investments," GAO-09-482, May 2009.

What makes an industrial project an industrial *mega*project? Megaprojects, as the name implies, are very large. To provide a simple and simply applied definition, we are defining a megaproject as any project with a total capital* cost of more than $1 billion (U.S. dollars) as measured on January 1, 2003. In 2010 nominal dollar terms, that would amount to about $1.7 billion due to the effects of rapid escalation in project costs in the last decade. One can reasonably object that this definition is simplistic; it totally disregards the effects of complexity (however measured) and the project environment on whether the project is a megaproject. The objection is noted but must be dismissed. If we include consideration of aspects other than size in our definition, we forfeit the ability to examine the effects of those aspects on the outcomes and management of our projects. One can also most certainly object that the $1 billion criterion is completely arbitrary. Why not $500 million or $2 billion? Yes, the $1 billion figure is arbitrary, but it is somewhat less arbitrary than it may seem. In the neighborhood of a billion dollars is where we see project outcomes begin to deteriorate sharply.

WHY STUDY THESE PROJECTS?

There are four compelling reasons to study and understand megaprojects:

1. There are many more of them than in times past, and this will continue for decades to come.
2. These projects are important. They are important to the societies in which they are being done; they are important to the health of the global economy; they are important to the sponsors and others putting up huge amounts of money.

---

*By capital we mean the costs for materials, engineering, and construction labor associated with completing a project. We exclude venture costs associated with setting up the permanent operating organization at the site or in some cases for the new company. In frontier environments, these venture costs can be quite substantial, in some cases more than 20 percent of the capital costs of the venture. We also do not explicitly evaluate operating costs, although we do keep track of when operating costs end up substantially higher than expected in these projects. The sponsors should, of course, be looking at total costs of the venture and should do so on a life-cycle basis to the extent that the data permit.

3. These projects are very problematic. They are failing at an alarming and unsustainable rate.
4. There is not much published that speaks directly to the types of projects considered here.

I will discuss each of these reasons to worry about megaprojects in turn.

Increasing Numbers

Industrial megaprojects have become much more common. For much of the 1980s and virtually all of the 1990s, there were few very large projects, even in the petroleum industry. The Norwegian and UK North Sea had been home to a number of megaprojects in the 1970s. These projects had a very difficult go, and without the rapid rise in crude oil prices in the wake of the overthrow of the Shah of Iran, almost none of the megaprojects in the North Sea would have been profitable ventures.[1] Most of the megaprojects that had been in planning stages in the late 1970s died abruptly when commodity prices fell in the early 1980s.

However, a number of factors have converged to make megaprojects much more common in the first decades of the twenty-first century, and these factors give every indication of being enduring drivers of very large projects. The first factor driving the current wave of megaprojects has been the rapid rise in the demand for almost all major commodities; iron ore, coal, copper, and petroleum have all experienced very rapid increases in demand (and therefore price) since 2003. Previously, most prior commodity price fluctuations had not been synchronized; prices might rise for one or two metals, oil and gold prices might rise for political reasons, but not all at the same time. The underlying common driver this time was the rapid industrialization of China and India in the context of reasonable overall global growth. None of the major commodities are actually facing imminent global depletion; however, most are facing upward sloping long-run marginal costs.

The different commodities have had somewhat different drivers for large projects:

- Opening up a new major mineral ore body has long been expensive. Most major new mines today are in places that require major infrastructure development to be practicable. When a good deal of infrastructure is needed, the production volume must be very large to spread those infrastructure costs across a broad enough base for the venture to be profitable. This makes large size the only avenue to development.

- Crude oil is a special case, at least partially. A large portion of oil that remains relatively inexpensive to produce is held by state companies.[2] To stay in the oil business, international companies have been pushed quickly into places where oil is difficult and costly to develop, usually deep water. International companies also have gained access when reservoirs are difficult to produce, for example, offshore heavy oil production in Brazil, very heavy oil onshore in Venezuela, the very sour oil and gas reservoirs in the Caspian area, the very harsh climate off western Russia, or in inaccessible areas such as central Africa. As a consequence, the marginal capital costs of production have increased very rapidly for these companies. This translates into a dramatic increase in the number of international oil company megaprojects.

- Finally, rapid changes in the global economy have driven basic chemical companies to shift more of their manufacturing to fast-growing Asian economies. They have also sought to gain feed-stock cost advantage by moving manufacturing to countries offering feedstock below world open market average prices to attract production facilities, mostly in the Middle East.*

IPA's projection of industrial megaproject activity excluding power is shown in Figure 1.1. The graph shows the number of dollars spent each year from 2000–2009 on megaprojects in the oil, chemicals, and minerals industries outside China. The pace of megaproject activity in the middle of the first decade of the twenty-first century was so brisk

---

*High natural gas prices have pushed a good deal of basic chemical manufacture out of Europe and the United States. Natural gas prices control the prices of ethane and propane, which are feedstocks for building block commodity chemicals such as ethylene and propylene. The situation in the United States may be stabilized by the advent of shale gas, which has substantially lowered natural gas prices. It is even possible that we will see some reversal of the decline in commodity chemicals in the United States if prices remain low. The situation in Western Europe shows no signs of reversal anytime soon, as natural gas is largely imported and relatively expensive.

Figure 1.1
IPA Forecast of Industrial Megaproject Activity, 2000–2013

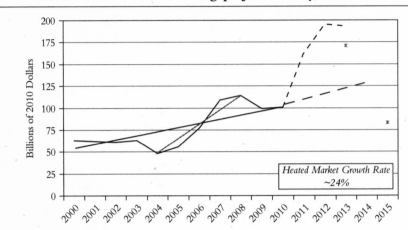

that it triggered rapid global escalation in EPC* services and equip-ment markets. From 2004 until the boom ended in 2008 with the global financial crisis, the megaprojects market expanded at a rate of 24 percent per year. IPA's forecast for the next four years exceeds that growth rate even in constant U.S. dollar terms.[†] By 2012, we expect to be spending at a rate of nearly $200 billion per year on industrial megaprojects outside China and excluding the electric power genera-tion sector.

Megaprojects Are Important

Without the industrial megaprojects in the extractive and manufac-turing sectors, global competition for resources, which is already very intense, would become unmanageable. Although one can reason-ably question whether extractive projects have been a net boon for less developed economies that hold large supplies, one cannot doubt

*EPC is shorthand for engineering, procurement, and construction. It refers both to the activities and to the industry that supplies these services to the megaprojects marketplace.
[†]IPA's forecast is based on projects in development by our clients that we are highly confident will be authorized for execution. This is then extrapolated to nonclient companies based on 2009 capital spend. This forecast was completed in May 2010; major economic changes between then and publication may perturb the forecast in either direction.

that the overall megaproject effect on global economic growth has been substantial. Megaprojects are responsible directly and indirectly for millions of jobs around the world, and without the many megaprojects we have seen over the past decade, global prices for virtually all major commodities would be much higher with all the attendant economic dislocation.

For the sponsors of megaprojects, success or failure of the project can mean the success or failure of the company. For all except the largest oil companies, a serious failure of a megaproject puts the company's future in jeopardy. Megaprojects are increasingly seen as essential to being competitive, but in many cases the skills needed to effectively develop and control these projects have not developed in tandem with the need.

It is also important to remember that the success or failure of these projects is often critical to the societies in which they are developed. Megaprojects place a good deal of stress on local communities. When they fail, and especially when they fail completely, the local communities suffer irreparable damage.

Megaprojects Fail Too Often

Megaproject results are frequently seriously short of the expectations of the sponsor-investors. Their cost overruns are often so significant that the whole project becomes NPV negative.* Their schedules often slip, and early-year operability, which has a disproportionate effect on profitability, is frequently very poor. Occasionally, the projects produce environmental disasters as well. As we will show, these results are not inherent in the nature of the activities. They are instead, caused by human decisions, ignorance, and uncontrolled, but controllable, human failings. These projects can be fixed.

The Literature Is Sparse

This book is needed because, despite the many thousands of pages written on the management of projects, very little of the literature addresses the peculiar nature of very large and complex projects as a class.

---

*NPV, of course, refers to net present value, which is a measure of the economic returns from an investment with future profits discounted for the effects of time.

There are some notable exceptions. Morris and Hough explored a set of eight very large public and private projects in 1987.[3] Like us, they concluded that the success rate is quite disappointing. We build on their path-breaking work. Miller and Lessard[4] and their colleagues explore what they call "large engineering projects," focusing on the development of new institutional arrangements. Their discussion of the process by which turbulent project environments might be settled is a key starting point for our own discussion of the shaping process in Chapter 4. We focus much less on the creation of new contractual forms, such as build-own-transfer (BOT), simply because we have seen very few of these "new institutional arrangements" actually function as advertised. Our data, which are considerably deeper than that found in Miller and Lessard, flatly contradict the effectiveness of certain arrange-ments, such as incentivized contracts, which they tout as successful.

Flyvbjerg, Bruzelius, and Rothengatter make the most recent major contribution to the megaprojects literature, focusing primarily on very large infrastructure projects executed by the public sector around the world.[5] Although we share some of the same conclusions about these projects, public infrastructure projects are in many respects quite different than the projects explored in this research. Public infrastruc-ture projects share many of the pathologies common in other publicly funded projects, such as military acquisition. They are frequently beset by a phenomenon known as "buy-in and hook," in which low costs are promised early, knowing full well that the eventual costs will be much higher. Although this sort of deception is not unknown in pri-vate sector ventures, it is not very common, simply because there is usually no taxpayer available to foot the bill later.

THE ORGANIZATION OF THIS BOOK

I have organized this book in three parts. Part One introduces the IPA megaprojects database and describes the research process that underpins this book. I seek to provide enough about methodology to satisfy the methodologically oriented reader without boring others to a stupor. I then present the track record of industrial megaprojects, summarizing the 300-plus large and complex projects we have studied to date.

Part Two deals with corporate decisions that relate to megaprojects and the behavior of senior management as it affects megaproject outcomes. This section deals extensively with what Miller and Lessard[6] call the "shaping" of megaprojects. It focuses on some brilliant examples of business leaders making an inherently unstable environment strong enough to permit a successful megaproject to be executed. But it also focuses on the decisions that corporate managers make that have devastating consequences for their projects without their ever fully understanding what went wrong. Business professionals who touch capital projects need to read Part Two to avoid being the root cause of trouble and to see what has worked well in situations similar to those they face. Project professionals need to read Part Two to understand how they got into this mess and what they might do in the future to elevate problems when mischief is being created by their bosses. Part Two will also be of interest to those concerned with how industrial corporations are being managed and mismanaged.

Part Three is written more for the project professional. It focuses not just on what needs to be done to make these big projects successful but on *why* those things are crucial. Many of the practices required to generate successful megaprojects are resisted by business management because they are apparently expensive and time-consuming. When the project team understands why certain practices are critical based on the actual history of megaprojects, they are better able to persuade reluctant managements to do the right things. The first chapter of Part Three addresses one of the most common root causes of megaproject failure: inaccurate or incomplete Basic (technical) Data. As I was tallying up the causes of failure in these projects, I was surprised to see the number of times that Basic Data problems occurred. Because the Basic Data development often needs to start long before the project gets fully going, the Basic Data chapter should be read by the business professionals, who often control the funding for Basic Data development, and by the research and development (R&D) and technical specialist community that often do not consider themselves part of "project management" but who usually do the Basic Data development.

RESPECTING CONFIDENTIALITY

Some of the readers (I sincerely hope) will have been directly involved in the megaprojects that underpin the conclusions of this research. When I have offered examples, I have tried to select cases that are not unique and in some cases I have masked the cases enough to ensure that no individual project for which we have conducted a closeout evaluation can be identified conclusively. This is necessary to meet our obligations of confidentiality to the people and companies involved. When any project is mentioned by name, it is based solely on publicly available information.

If you are certain that I am discussing your project in a particular example, let me offer this caveat: several years ago, I wrote a volume of 20 case studies of new technology projects for the DuPont Company. Many of the projects had disastrous outcomes, but some were brilliant successes. In the introduction, I carefully explained that *none* of the projects summarized in the volume were DuPont projects, because the DuPont new technology projects would be covered in a separate volume. Nonetheless, for the next six months I had DuPont business and project professionals stop me in the hall while I was visiting the company and comment something like this: "You did a pretty good job summarizing my project, but you got a couple of the details wrong. . . ." This reflects a well-known fact: We humans have been making a hash of projects for a long, long time.

CHAPTER 2

DATA AND METHODS

$\mathbf{R}$esearch on capital projects, especially in the private sector, is sorely hampered by the researcher's lack of access to data and the people who created those data. In these regards, IPA is enormously fortunate; we have access to both the written record of projects and the people who developed and executed the projects as part of our normal project evaluation work. In the course of a year, we evaluate 700 to 800 capital projects in the process industries. There are typically 40 to 60 megaprojects in that set of evaluations.

THE TIMING OF DATA ACQUISITION

IPA's data collections are synchronized with a company's staged and gated project work process. The typical arrangement of such a work process is shown in Figure 2.1. The usual work process is arranged into three to five phases prior to full-funds authorization (sanction) of the project. The three-phase front-end arrangement, which is the most common, is shown in the figure, along with the various names that are widely used by different parts of the industry.* The first row of names below the figure are those used mostly by the oil industry; those listed in the second and third rows are those used commonly by the chemicals and minerals industries, respectively.

---

*Occasionally, companies have a formal and systematic "Phase 0" during which background work is performed for potential projects. Megaprojects in locations new to a company benefit greatly from such a "FEL-0" process because it is an opportunity to familiarize the company with the peculiarities of the locale. We discuss country advance teams in more detail in Chapter 4. Some companies also divide the scope development phase into two parts: the first selects the general scope or "concept" that will be employed for the project, and the second part refines and completes that scope. We believe the two-part Phase 2 is a best practice.

Figure 2.1
Three Phase Front-End Loading Model

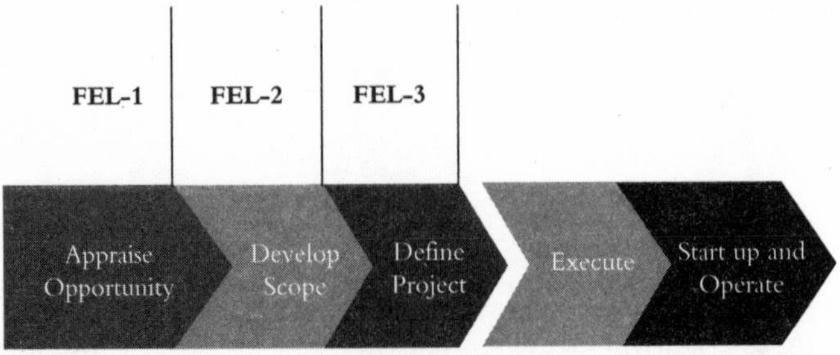

FEL-1	FEL-2	FEL-3		
Appraise Opportunity	Develop Scope	Define Project	Execute	Start up and Operate

Also Called	Appraise	Select	FEED	**Oil and Gas**
	Business Planning	Facilities Planning	Execution Planning	**Chemicals**
	Concept Study	Prefeasibility Study	Feasibility Study	**Minerals**

For the most part, the meanings of the stages are very similar, even if the names are not.

We call the period prior to sanction of the project front-end loading, or FEL. We provide a quick overview of the "stage-gated" project work process now in order to ground the reader. The subject recurs multiple times in much greater detail in other parts of the book.

FEL-1 is devoted to the development of the business case and sorting out the basic feasibility of a capital investment. Among more disciplined (read "better managed") companies, the paramount issue for this phase is whether the type of investment contemplated in the locale envisioned is consistent with the company's overall business strategy. FEL-1 should be used to winnow down the range of possible projects to a manageable few to be explored in the next phase. The issue of whether a particular project is consonant with the company's strategy is very important for megaprojects. To be successful, megaprojects require much deeper corporate support than do smaller projects. Sometimes this is in the form of technical support; sometimes it is in the form of senior management's willingness to intervene on behalf of the project when difficulties arise.* Companies sometimes have IPA evaluate the completeness of the business case package as the FEL-1 phase is drawing to a close.

The gate monitoring passage from FEL-1 to FEL-2, scope development, is the least well managed of all the gates. In too many companies, what would constitute an acceptable package for this gate is not well established. Too often, the businesses that staff the gate do not hold themselves to particularly high standards. This weakness in the FEL-1 stage foreshadows the weakness we see in the shaping process for megaprojects, which is a greatly expanded and enriched version of the FEL-1 work process.

FEL-2 is the scope selection and development phase of a project. If it was not already commissioned during FEL-1, a core technical team is now formed. The team seeks to translate the proto-project as envisioned in the business case into a real project with a physical scope, albeit all on paper (or in electrons) at this point. The definition of all elements of the scope with completed flow diagrams for all facilities marks the end of the FEL-2 phase. This is a critical juncture for the project because it is now, for the first time, that a reliable cost estimate for the project can be developed. The reliability of that estimate hangs heavily on the completeness of the scope developed.

IPA usually evaluates a project at this point to assess whether the scope is actually closed and to benchmark the competitiveness of the cost estimate and preliminary execution schedule.

The third phase of the front-end process, FEL-3, involves advancing engineering to a point where detailed design can be fully mobilized and advancing the execution planning to the point that execution can proceed without changes. This final phase of FEL is expensive for any project and very expensive for megaprojects. As a

---

*Some companies take pride in being "highly entrepreneurial," which often translates into every business unit for itself. Such companies, even if they are very large, often find it difficult to develop and execute megaprojects successfully because they lack a center strong enough to provide deep support to their very large projects. The tendency to organize the company in a highly decentralized fashion is normative in minerals and now typical in many oil and gas companies as well. Decentralization makes most aspects of megaproject management and control more difficult.

consequence, very few projects are halted once they begin the FEL–3 phase. IPA typically conducts a full evaluation of a project at the end of FEL–3 just before full-funds authorization.

Each of the IPA front-end evaluations is designed to support the management decision about whether a project should proceed to the next phase; continue in the current phase; or be stopped, shelved, or canceled. The final IPA evaluations of a project occur after the completion of commissioning and startup of the project and then 12 to 18 months later to assess production performance. If an evaluation is not performed at any point, we collect the data that would have been collected at the skipped stage at the next evaluation point.

THE DATA COLLECTION PROCESS

We collect all data except production information with a series of face-to-face interviews with members of the extended project teams augmented with a large number of documents. We employ a set of standardized electronic data collection protocols and train project analysts on the use of the protocols and interpretation of the questions in an extensive classroom and on-the-job program. By the time a project is complete, depending on the complexity of the project, we will have collected the answers to between 2,000 and 5,000 questions about the development, execution, and startup of the project facilities.

The training programs for project analysts are key to ensuring the greatest possible consistency of data. Trained analysts can explain what the questions mean to those providing the answers. We train analysts for particular types of projects, for example, minerals mining and processing, petroleum production, chemical process facilities, and so on. Senior and highly experienced analysts evaluate the megaprojects, which often pose significant data collection problems. Unlike smaller projects, megaprojects are frequently highly political in the general sense of that term. Careers can be made not only by bringing a megaproject to a successful conclusion but by merely getting a megaproject successfully to authorization. Because of the political nature of the projects within the companies, we are more likely to encounter gamesmanship in the data collection process for megaprojects than other types of projects.

Table 2.1

Breakdown of Industrial Sectors in Database

Industrial Sector	Number	Percent of Sample
Oil and gas production	130	41
Petroleum processing and refining	66	21
Minerals and metals	47	15
Chemicals	31	10
Liquefied natural gas (LNG)	24	8
Power generation	8	3
Pipelines	7	2
Other	5	2
Totals	**318**	**100[1]**

[1]Does not add up to 100 percent because of a rounding error.

The IPA Megaprojects Database

The IPA database consists of 318 megaprojects. The industrial sectors involved are shown in Table 2.1. About 40 percent of the projects are oil and gas production projects. Just over two-thirds of the oil and gas projects have their primary production facilities offshore, often in deepwater areas. Many of the offshore projects also had a substantial onshore component. This is important because the construction of onshore facilities and offshore projects present different challenges. Offshore environments heavily penalize failure to complete work in the fabrication yards. If far from land, they pose significant logistics challenges. However, offshore projects benefit from being out of sight and therefore not constantly in public view. The second largest group of projects involves the processing of hydrocarbons. These include both petroleum refining projects and large oil or gas processing facilities that were not executed in conjunction with a new production project. Minerals and metals projects constitute about 15 percent of the sample. Most of these include both a mining and a processing facility. In general, those that involve only mining and transportation of the ore to shipping are technically easier than those that also process the material. Basic chemicals, liquefied natural gas (LNG), long major pipelines, and power generation round out the set. The

Figure 2.2
Geographical Breakdown of Projects

Regional Distribution

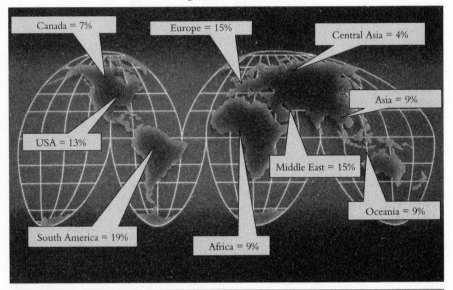

"other" category consists of terminals and projects that defy easy classification.*

Locations of the projects are shown in Figure 2.2. The projects are fairly well distributed around the globe. The sample in Central Asia (including Russia) is relatively small, but the projects themselves tend to be very large and are centered around the Caspian Sea. The U.S. projects are primarily oil and gas developments in the Gulf of Mexico and Alaska. We have a very good sample of South American projects drawn both from a number of national companies and the private sector. All of the industrial sectors are represented in the South American sample.

The only area that could be described as seriously underrepresented is China. Although there are a good many Chinese projects in the dataset, almost all are joint ventures with Western companies rather

---

*We also draw on a number of projects that never went forward. These projects are very instructive. Sometimes their not going forward was a major success because the projects would have been disastrous.

than Chinese firms acting alone. The sample of projects in Africa includes oil and gas developments from both North and West Africa and predominantly minerals projects from the southern area. Similarly, the Australia/Papua New Guinea sample is split between minerals and petroleum development.

The projects range in size from about $1 billion to almost $20 billion, measured in 2010 U.S. dollars. The average project cost about $3.2 billion and took 43 months to execute, which is measured as the time from full-funds authorization to completion of all facilities. The average cycle time, measured from start of scope development through the startup, averaged 66 months and took more than 10 years in a number of cases. In the case of petroleum production projects, the first phase of drilling may not have been complete when we stopped the clock on the project.

Company Representation

The companies represented in the sample are a good cross section of the process industries. The sample is described in Table 2.2. The oil, chemicals, and minerals industries are very well represented, with both national and international oil companies in the mix. Eight companies were represented by more than 10 projects. Not surprising, the companies in the best represented groups include almost all of the leading companies in their particular sectors. Not shown are a number

Table 2.2
Types of Sponsoring Companies in Database

Industrial Sector Category	Number of Companies Represented
Integrated international oil companies	10
National oil companies	13
Nonintegrated petroleum producers	10
Regional refiners	5
Chemicals companies	18
Mining, minerals, and metals	14
Electric power companies	4
Pipeline companies	3

of single-project joint venture companies. Perhaps quite surprising to some, company size in no way predicts success and failure of projects. Large and powerful companies fail at least as often as smaller firms. Of course, that may reflect the fact that a failed megaproject can be the end of a smaller firm, whereas it merely wounds the largest companies.

USE OF NEW TECHNOLOGY

Our most general scale describing the degree of technological innovation embodied in a project is shown in Table 2.3.* Almost half of the projects in our sample employed technology that had been used before in similar applications, which we dub off-the-shelf. To describe technology as off-the-shelf does not imply that the project was in any sense a clone of another. Only a handful of projects were approaching clones. And being off-the-shelf does not imply that the technology is simple. Many of the standard technology projects employed the technology at a scale that had never been attempted before. However, using technology with a track record of successful application does remove one source of risk and challenge for the project teams.

Another 15 percent of our projects used standard technology but in a mix that was novel. These new integrations increase the engineering challenge associated with the projects, but they are not otherwise a major source of risk.

Table 2.3
Comparative Innovations

Degree of Technological Innovation in Core Technology	Megaprojects (%)	Other Projects (%)
Off-the-shelf	49	76
First-time integrations of known technology	15	14
Minor process modifications	20	6
Major process modifications	9	2
Substantially new technology	6	3
Total numbers of projects[1]	**318**	**12,849**

[1]Due to rounding, the percentages do not add up to 100.

---

*Testing for whether the greater use of technology in megaprojects is statistically significant, we find $P > |2| < .0001$.

The remaining 35 percent of the projects introduced at least some element of technology that had never been applied before. We call an innovation minor if it affects only a single step in a process and the step is not core to the functionality of the technology. Minor modifications are genuine improvements, but with relatively little risk attached because they are isolatable.

The projects in the last two categories took on substantial new technology risk. Major process modifications involve a change to the core technology, whereas "substantially new" is reserved for cases in which a wholesale change of the technology is involved. For example, the first use of a petroleum platform concept, such as a tension leg platform or spar production platform, would be considered substantially new. In processing technology it would involve the introduction of a new chemical process or the processing of a particular type of feedstock for the first time.

The last column in Table 2.3 shows the degree of innovation in non-megaprojects in IPA's databases. What it tells us is that megaprojects are much more innovative than smaller projects. In the right-hand corner we show the probability that with repeated tries we would get this degree of difference in innovation as a matter of chance.

METHODOLOGY

The methodology used for this research was quite straightforward and contains two significant parts: statistics and case study root cause analysis. We discuss each in turn.

Statistical Analyses

For more than two decades, IPA has been exploring what makes projects succeed and fail. That research provides the conceptual framework from which we proceed to establish and test hypotheses about the relationships between project characteristics and project development practices on one hand and project outcomes on the other. The overall purpose of the effort is to provide our customers with the basis for using statistical process control as the primary method with which to manage their capital project systems. Almost from the beginning of our research,[1] we have explored the relationships between project size and complexity and project outcomes, noting that outcomes tend to deteriorate as a function of size and complexity.

The conceptual understanding as it exists at any point in time guides our statistical analyses. Most of our "aha!" moments come not from statistics but from seeing something occur in an individual project, recognizing a pattern with other projects, and only then checking our supposed insight with the data.

The testing of hypotheses is one key role for statistics. The other is building statistical models that enable us to compare project outcomes in a meaningful way. If one seeks a reasonably high degree of precision, comparing projects is actually quite difficult. No two projects are exactly the same, and across any large database of projects, the projects will usually be very different along a number of dimensions that are important to project results. Statistical models facilitate valid comparisons, even for quite disparate projects. Using statistical controls we can control for key characteristics such as size, technical complexity, the degree of technological innovation, process type, and so forth, while comparing cost, schedule, operability, or even construction safety. Statistics enable us to "hold constant" inherent project characteristics while exploring the effects of practices, including both business and project management practices, on project results.

A variety of statistical techniques have been used to test and demonstrate that various relationships are not likely to have been generated randomly. We use ordinary least-squares regression, t-tests, logit and probit regression when binary dependent variables are involved, Pearson product-moment correlation, and the Pearson chi-square for testing differences in tabulation tables.

Table 2.4 shows how the various test results will be noted in the text and footnotes as we proceed. We show the results of the statistical test that supports a statement and indicate the type of test performed. For example, "$P > |t| < .001$" means that the probability of generating the result randomly with repeated tries is less than 1 in 1,000 based on a t-test or coefficient t-ratio from a regression. This enables the methodologically sophisticated reader to judge the basis on which the conclusion is reached. Fortunately, in most cases, common sense works as well as the statistics. Following standard procedure, we call

Table 2.4
Statistical Test Used in Analysis

Technique	Test Statistic	Notation
OLS or t-test	t-ratios/t-test	$P > \lvert t \rvert < .0XX$
Logit or probit regression	z-ratio	$P > \lvert z \rvert < .0XX$
Pearson correlation	r	$P > \lvert r \rvert < .0XX$
Tabulation	Chi-square (χ^2)	$P > \lvert \chi^2 \rvert < .0XX$

results statistically significant only when the probability (using a two-tailed test except where noted) is less than or equal to 0.05.*

Root Cause Understanding from Cases

The typical megaproject in our database has thousands of variables that have been coded from our completed interview protocols and supporting project documents. These supporting documents often include the "lessons learned," developed by the project team. The strengths and weaknesses of those lessons learned are discussed in later chapters.

The preceding information is augmented and fleshed out by our analysts in case study write-ups, done for every project collected, large or small. For megaprojects the case studies are quite extensive and focus on what happened and why. These case study notes are based on in-depth and wide-ranging discussions with members of the project teams and the business leadership of the projects. Much to our continual surprise and delight, project directors and managers are overwhelmingly forthcoming and forthright about their completed projects. Without their cooperation, this book could not have been written.

SOME METHODOLOGICAL NOTES

Escalation Adjustments

Unlike many project researchers, IPA measures capital cost and cost growth in costs in constant currency terms. If the effects of inflation on costs are not removed, it is impossible to really understand

---

*In many cases the argument for using a one-tailed test would be persuasive. Most of the hypotheses being tested have very strong priors. However, we almost always elect to use a two-tailed test anyway.

project results. When it comes to measuring cost and cost growth, most project researchers fail to follow basic sound practice.

A simple example will clarify how important this is. Let's say a natural gas processing facility is estimated and authorized on January 1, 2004, for exactly $1 billion. Included in the cost are $50 million for inflation. The project is completed on schedule on January 1, 2008, for a cost of $1.4 billion—a massive 40 percent overrun of the costs, right? Well, yes and no. In the period between 2004 and the beginning of 2008 the costs of the items going into a gas plant increased by 52 percent on average around the world. The cost of the equipment, the pipe, the engineering, and in most places the craft labor increased quite rapidly during this period. Was the estimator's inclusion of "only" $50 million for inflation the problem? Yes, but the $50 million was entirely reasonable; for the 15 years prior to 2004, project inflation had been averaging only a percent or two per year. When measured correctly, the project actually came in just about where it should have. On the other hand, if the price of the product being sold from this gas plant has not escalated along with the cost of the plant, the sponsor is going to earn a significantly lower return than expected. From a methodological viewpoint, the problem of reporting our gas plant as having suffered a 40 percent overrun is clear: there is absolutely nothing that the project team could have done differently to prevent an overrun. In the same vein, there is no reason to think that those making the decision to invest in the facility should have been able to anticipate the sudden change in the projects marketplace. Therefore, if we are trying to explore the relationships between investment decisions and project practices and outcomes, failing to correct for escalation will leave us forever bewildered. It is very unfortunate that too many researchers studying capital projects do, in fact, fail to do so.

In addition to adjusting cost for the effects of inflation (usually called escalation in the project business), we also adjust for the effects of location when we are measuring cost-effectiveness. For example, building a plant in China is generally cheaper than building the equivalent plant in the United States or Europe. Not only is craft labor less expensive, almost all items that are purchasable in China will be less expensive than the same items in the United States or Europe. Specialized equipment that must be imported is not subject to extraordinary taxes in China and can therefore be purchased on the world open market. Only the costs of any expatriates sent by a foreign sponsor will add to costs in China relative to most other parts of the world. Therefore, to make apples-to-apples comparisons of cost, we adjust the various input costs up or down depending on the location in which they must be purchased. We are careful not to overadjust either. If the decision is made to purchase items locally that can be purchased for less on the world open market, that added cost is not adjusted unless the local purchases are formally mandated.

Finally, we correct for changes in foreign exchange relationships as they apparently change the cost of a project. Almost all megaprojects buy things from all over the world. When the final estimate before authorization is prepared, a set of assumptions must be made about the value of the different currencies in which things will be purchased. Unexpected changes in foreign exchange can make a project substantially more or less expensive unless the currencies are hedged, which is an uncommon practice.* Like escalation, however, currency fluctuations are notoriously difficult to predict.

SAMPLE BIAS

Is our sample of 318 industrial megaprojects really representative of all industrial megaprojects executed over the past 15 years? That question is important in some contexts and less important in others. If we are discussing what all recent industrial megaprojects look like, then the question is very important and the answer, alas, is "no." We are not particularly concerned about any potential effects of the mix of industrial sectors represented for a very simple reason: the industrial sector in and of itself appears to have little, if any, effect on how the projects turn out. Differences between sectors can be accounted for by differences in practices. However, we have a couple of reasons to suspect that our sample of megaprojects is on the whole *better* in terms of outcomes and management than industrial megaprojects as a whole.

---

*The sponsors could also seek to "fix" the currencies by passing all foreign exchange risks to the vendors and contractors. As discussed later, however, this approach is highly problematic.

First, companies that subject themselves to systematic benchmarking are generally more capable project companies than those that do not. We can infer this in many ways. For example, we know that the companies that benchmark their projects with IPA suffer about one-tenth the number of construction accidents as the overall construction industry norms. We know that companies first starting benchmarking have project outcomes that are significantly poorer than those that have benchmarked for more than a few years.

Second, we know that even the companies with which we have worked for many years will sometimes find excuses not to close out a project that had particularly horrid outcomes. The excuses range from the specious "That project really isn't representative!" to the lame "We fired all the people on the team, so there is no one to talk to." Conversely, we are aware of no megaprojects whose final data were withheld from us because the projects went abnormally well!

The fact that we have a known positive bias in the data should make the outcomes presented in the next chapter all the more sobering because, even with the assistance of the bias, we are not doing very well.

CHAPTER 3

PROJECT OUTCOMES

In the world of normal-sized projects, how well the projects turn out distributes in the usual way: there is a big group of mediocre projects in the middle, a smaller group of good projects, and a slightly larger group of poor projects. When we first started examining very large projects as a separate group, we almost immediately noticed an odd phenomenon. The projects seem to fall naturally into exceptionally good projects and exceptionally poor projects, with only a very few in the middle, where the bulk of smaller projects would be found. For this reason we separate our mega-projects into two groups: successes and failures.

To separate the wheat from the chaff, we use the five dimensions of project effectiveness, shown in Table 3.1. Also included are the thresholds to establish what would constitute failure.

If a project fared more poorly than our threshold on any one of these five dimensions, we classified the project as a failure. However, very few projects failed on only one dimension. If they did fail on only one, it was overwhelmingly likely that it was the most economically important criterion: production versus plan.[1]

If a project does not experience one of the serious problems listed in Table 3.1, we call it a success. By success, we mean that the project basically performed as promised at the time of authorization or better. It was built close to budget and close to on time, it was reasonably competitive on cost and schedule, and it made on-specification product as intended.

Success, then, is defined as a lack of failure. Although this may seem rather unsatisfying, it works for these projects because very few were merely mediocre; overwhelmingly the successes are outstanding projects in every respect. The very small mediocre group could easily have

37

Table 3.1
Thresholds for Failure

Type of Outcome	Threshold for Failure
Cost overruns[1]	> 25 percent
Cost competitiveness[2]	> 25 percent
Slip in execution schedules[3]	> 25 percent
Schedule competitiveness[4]	> 50 percent
Production versus plan	Significantly reduced production into year 2

[1]Cost overruns are measured as the ratio of the actual final costs of the project to the estimate made at the full-funds authorization (sanction) measured in escalation-adjusted terms.

[2]Competitiveness measures how much the project spent (in constant dollars adjusted to a common location) relative to other projects with similar scopes.

[3]Execution schedule is measured from the start of production (sometimes called detailed engineering) until mechanical completion of facilities. Slip is defined as the actual schedule divided by the schedule forecast at full-funds authorization.

[4]Schedule competitiveness is the length of the execution relative to similar projects.

been great projects: they were planned and executed well. However, they set conservative targets and then executed on lump-sum contracts that locked themselves into mediocre results. Most of these projects were sponsored by government-owned companies in regions where failure to be predictable is heavily penalized.

We were sometimes missing one or two of the measures on any particular project. For example, many of the projects do not yet have enough operational history to judge whether they have failed or succeeded in that dimension. Some of the projects are so peculiar in scope that we could not measure cost competitiveness. Whenever we are missing a measure, we assume the project succeeded on that measure. What this means is that a few more projects will end up in the failure category when the final data become available.

COST

The thresholds for success and failure are less arbitrary than their round numbers would suggest. If you overrun a project by more than 25 percent in real terms, the project manager and project team will likely be considered a failure (and may well receive a career-limiting

flogging).* A 25 percent overrun substantially damages the economics of many megaprojects.† If you overspend in competitive terms by
25 percent or more, the business is spending itself into oblivion. As
we look back over the past 23 years at IPA customers that have disappeared, all but one of them grossly overspent for their capital assets.‡
(The exception was a large oil company that could never seem to find
any oil.)

One of the ironies of large projects around the world is that most of
them are executed on fixed-price (lump-sum) contracts. And yet many
of those so-called fixed-price contracts end up anything but fixed. (I
discuss the merits and demerits of lump-sum contracting in Chapter
11.) The reason that lump-sum contracts offer only the weakest insur-
ance against cost overruns is that changes are often made after the contract is agreed on. It doesn't make much difference where the change
comes from; if there is substantial change, the cost of the project will
go up. Sometimes, we can point to new technology as the source of
change, but that just begs the question of why the technology was
not ready when the project was sanctioned. And many large overruns,
some up to 350 percent, are in projects with entirely standard technology. Sometimes the source of change is lack of sponsor familiarity
with the region, although again we will have to ask why. Some of the
large overrun projects were caught up in a downward labor productivity spiral. (I discuss how and why these collapses of progress in the
field occur in Chapter 12.)

---

*It is also true that the original business director of the project will probably not suffer adverse conse-
quences of that overrun. It is very likely he or she will have moved on to another, usually higher, position
and any connection with the project will have been forgotten. The tendency in most companies to move
business directors rather quickly (three years is a long stay) fosters a lack of business accountability for
project results. This is especially true for megaprojects because their gestation and execution periods are
so long.

†This anticipates an issue that we take up in Chapter 5: the relative importance of cost versus schedule for
the typical large project.

‡Too many senior business decision makers in commodity industrial sectors fail to realize the disastrous
effects of overspending on projects. When a company overspends on its capital projects relative to the
competition, even by a relatively small amount, it is systematically disadvantaging itself. The effects show
up when a serious downturn hits their industry. In commodity businesses, cycles are a fact of life. Part
of the reason for business indifference to capital effectiveness is that the effects are insidious and long-
term rather than dramatic and immediate. Some, I fear, understand the effects but simply do not care—
because the effects are long term and their personal horizons are not.

SCHEDULE

The execution schedule is the forecast of the time that will be required from full-funds authorization until the project is ready to start up. If the schedule was developed properly, the time requirement is intimately linked to the scope and therefore the cost of the project. If you slip your schedule by 25 percent, you are usually a year late, which is very damaging to the economic value of the project. Being late in execution is associated with stretching out the period in which you are heavily invested in the project (most of the money is already spent) with no revenue stream to show for it. We set the threshold on being slow at a higher level (50 percent) because if you *plan* to be slow, the economic damage is less because the spending is back-end loaded and you tend not to plan to be slow in the construction portion of the project. However, there are limits to that strategy, and we set them at 50 percent over industry average time.

Large schedule slips are a little less common than large overruns and some of the projects with large cost overruns had only modest schedule slippage. The underlying reason that schedule performance looks somewhat better than cost is also one of the core pathologies of very large projects: they are frequently highly schedule-driven from the earliest point right through to startup. Because we end the execution time when the facility is, in principle, ready to operate, we are not capturing with this measure whether the project operated successfully. Executing a project rapidly that also operates is much more compelling than merely executing a project rapidly. Startup and operability are captured separately.

Some very extended construction schedules had their proximate cause in engineering. As mentioned in the previous chapter, industrial megaprojects are very engineering-intensive. For a typical project, 25 percent of the total cost will go to engineering and project management services. A good many of the projects with severe slips and cost growth in construction suffered from late and/or shoddy engineering. Late and poor-quality engineering make the construction in the field or fabrication in the yard much less efficient. Late engineering and poor-quality engineering tend to happen together; as engineering gets late, it gets progressively rushed and quality control is bypassed to get engineering to the constructors. When engineering work is slow to mobilize early in the project, it drives late and out of order equipment and engineered bulk materials, such as pipe spools. Construction/fabrication then waits until the right materials arrive. Engineering problems were common in the failed projects, but they were usually proximate causes, not root causes of failure.

Some of the large schedule slips occurred when the projects got crosswise with the host government. One of the time-honored ways politicians have of intervening in large projects is to withdraw a permit on a technicality. For example, the Russian government withdrew the construction permit for the Sakhalin-2 Project when it was deep into construction knowing that the project was very vulnerable economically at that point because the investment is large and irreversible—you can't get your money back!

A few of the large slips in schedule occurred when the sponsors acknowledged that the project was going so poorly that it needed to be slowed down while errors were corrected. That is a very painful, difficult, and courageous decision to make, which is why it is made so rarely. Ironically, two of the successful projects were rescued by running into government trouble. Both projects were about to be authorized but were nowhere near ready for execution; their failure was ordained when government delays in approvals held them up for 18 months in one case and two years in another. They used the time to get ready for execution. Both project directors said they could never have succeeded otherwise. Their good fortune was to encounter government trouble early rather than during the middle of execution.

PRODUCTION

Finally, production versus plan is the most economically leveraging outcome. When we assessed operability, we did not penalize a project if there was insufficient demand. (One could justifiably argue that is the worst outcome of all. I built a great project that nobody wanted! Lack of demand, however, is not something on which project management per se can have much effect.) We classified a project as a failure in this dimension only if it was experiencing severe technical problems that continued well into the second year after startup.

We did not set an absolute production threshold because the importance of poor operability is different for different projects. For example, for an oil production project, production of 70 percent of plan is not terrible—the industry's average is just over 80 percent of plan.* By contrast, 70 percent of plan for liquefied natural gas (LNG) is abysmal. LNG is very capital-intensive, which exacerbates the effects of poor operability. LNG is almost always forward-sold, and if you cannot produce the LNG, you have to go into the merchant market and buy it from competitors to fulfill your contractual commitments. The result is that you hemorrhage money. The actual production of the projects that failed in this dimension averaged a miserable 41 percent of plan in the second six months after startup.

Even worse, however, when a project suffers significant production shortfalls, a great deal of money is spent trying to rectify the problems. Although we lack the systematic data we would like, my guesstimate based on limited data is that 25 to 50 percent added cost over the initial capital is common. Most of this is not actually capitalized, and in many cases there are no reliable records of the amount spent at all—because nobody actually wants to know.

Production shortfalls in petroleum production megaprojects were common. Almost half (47 percent) of all the oil and gas production projects in our database had significant operability problems. A few were caused by facilities that did not operate properly or facilities that were incorrectly matched to the characteristics of the oil and gas being produced. The most common problems were associated with reservoir surprises that limited the production from the intended wells.† This almost always resulted in additional wells that were often more complex than the original wells planned. We almost never were able to capture the cost of these additional wells. So once again, we are perforce underestimating the true economic costs of production shortfalls.

The effects of production problems can be debilitating for a business. One global chemical company client had a $9 billion per year

---

*Yes, that does raise the question about why the industry as a whole is so optimistic, but that is not an issue for us here.

†As we discuss in Chapter 7, the reservoir problems often could have been anticipated and addressed before the start of the project if the basic technical data development had been better.

business earning 22 percent return on capital employed (ROCE)—a very nice commodity business. A single megaproject that failed to produce as planned reduced the ROCE from 22 percent to 16 percent for the five years after the project was supposed to have started up. They ended up divesting the business. Another example is a metals project that was to debottleneck and expand a major processing complex by 90 percent. After a 39 percent overrun (76 percent nominal) and an 85 percent schedule slip, the complex actually produces 10 percent *less* than before the project. This project managed to achieve the unachievable: negative production!

When megaprojects fail, the results are rarely publicized unless the failure is spectacular. When the failures do make the press, they are damaging to a company's reputation. Large overruns and delays in cash flow due to schedule slippage or production shortfalls jeopardize the sponsor's ability to fund other projects in its portfolio. Megaprojects are by nature lumpy investments. Only a handful of companies in the world are large enough to be able to support a genuine portfolio of these projects to spread the risk internally, which is why most industrial megaprojects are joint ventures.

TRADING OUTCOMES

Making trade-offs among cost, schedule, and quality (measured by operational performance in our case) is as old as projects and a feature of everyday life. How trade-offs are made tells us a lot about how decisions around major projects are made. I find the patterns in megaprojects interesting.

First, cost-effectiveness and schedule effectiveness are not being traded overall, although they clearly are for some projects. In fact, lower cost and faster schedules correlate very strongly ($P > |t| < .0001$). Projects that are slow relative to industry standards also are expensive relative to industry standards and vice versa. This means that cost and schedule in megaprojects need not compete. Expensive projects were projects that slipped their schedules and overran their costs—no surprise there ($P > |t| < .0001$). Expensive projects correlate, but less strongly, with operational failures ($P > |t| < .02$).

There is *no* relationship between being schedule competitive and overrunning costs. One strategy for megaproject execution is to stuff additional contingency into the authorization estimate. That money then helps keep the projects on schedule and renders them relatively fast. This is a reasonable strategy for projects with very robust returns, but it does, of course, lead to projects that are at least somewhat more expensive.

There is also little relationship between cost growth and schedule slippage $(P|t| < .08)$. What this tells us is that we can have projects that trade cost growth for adherence to schedule (19 percent of projects), projects that slip in schedule to prevent costs from overrunning (22 percent), projects that grow in cost and experience schedule slippage (40 percent), and projects that meet or underrun both cost and schedule targets (19 percent).

Projects that slip in schedule, however, have a strong tendency $(P|z| < .003)$ to be operational failures. This result is important. Projects slip for two kinds of reasons, which often end up being related: (1) the schedules were set far too aggressively at the outset, and (2) a large number of major changes occur during execution. When the schedules are set too fast at the beginning of the project—it almost always happens long before authorization—corners are cut leading up to execution. Those cut corners ultimately translate into production failure.

Projects that grow in cost also have a tendency to suffer production failure $(P|z| < .04)$, but when schedule slippage is controlled, the effect of cost growth on operational failure disappears entirely $(P|z| < .51)$.

WHAT ABOUT CONSTRUCTION SAFETY?

Normally, when IPA evaluates a project, the first outcome discussed is whether the project was completed without seriously hurting anyone. We have three basic safety statistics for about 70 percent of the megaprojects:

1. The recordable incident rate, which measures the number of injuries and work-related illnesses that require assistance beyond first aid

2. The number of DART cases—injuries and work-related illnesses that require **D**ays **A**way from work, **R**estricted work duties, or job **T**ransfer
3. The number of fatalities

I have elected not to incorporate the safety results in the assessment of success and failure for a very simple reason: Too many of the safety numbers for megaprojects are simply not credible. Some of them are ridiculous on their face: we had one project with 36 recordable injuries in over 20 million hours . . . and every one of those recordable injuries was a fatality. And we obtained the fatality number only because we had monitored the local press.

Injury rates in construction follow a reasonably predictable pattern: There are many more recordables than DART cases, and many more DART cases than fatalities. This is referred to as the "safety pyramid." For megaprojects, that relationship *appears* not to work. In particular, there are a lot of fatalities and too few recordables. This leads us to believe there is a reporting problem; fatalities are generally very hard to hide.

The third reason to doubt the data makes us sure that underreporting is going on: There is a very strong regional bias to the numbers and that regional bias is completely counterintuitive. Projects with higher skilled, more experienced, and higher productivity workforces will on average experience fewer accidents. The higher productivity effect alone helps greatly because it reduces the number of laborers on site. Congestion is a known safety hazard. However, as one can see in Table 3.2, for megaprojects none of this appears to hold.

Table 3.2
Safety by High-Wage versus Low-Wage Regions

Incident Type	Europe and North America	Middle East, Central Asia, Asia, and Africa
Recordables[1]	1.20	0.43
DART rate	0.50	0.12
Fatal incident rate	0.009	0.006
Projects with fatalities	18%	39%
Field hours per million dollars	7,300	21,500

[1]The rates in the first three rows are calculated per 200,000 field hours. For readers familiar with the per million hour formulation, multiply by 5.

If we believe the numbers, which we do not, megaprojects in Europe and North America, where skill levels and productivity are high, are about three times more dangerous than those in areas where the average skill level is much lower. They even have more fatalities per 200,000 hours worked, even though the probability of having at least one fatality is much higher in the second group. What we also know about Europe and North America is that there are substantial penalties for underreporting injuries and that the legal systems are geared to ensuring that reporting occurs. Those safeguards are much weaker in many other areas.

There is one final clue that the safety numbers are not legitimate. For North American and European projects, the DART rate is correlated with the thoroughness of the project execution planning, just as it is for projects generally. (This is a subject we take up in Chapter 10.) For projects in the regions in the second column in the table, there is no relationship whatsoever.

In low-productivity environments, keeping track of safety and getting reporting done accurately are much more difficult. Each million dollars of investment (based on 2003 U.S. dollars) in North America and Europe consumes about 7,300 hours in the field. In the low-productivity regions, about three times as many hours are needed and the projects in those regions are among the largest in our database. Furthermore, the labor force is often drawn from numerous nationalities and cultures, so language and custom must be overcome as well.

Nonetheless, the underreporting is systematic. The problem starts at the craft level. The workers know that when injuries are reported, they will get into trouble. Sponsors try to fight against the problem (although sometimes not too much), but the problem is deeply endemic from the craft labor and foreman level up. The pattern of safety results from the regional difference paints a clear picture of underreporting.

It is very unfortunate that construction safety numbers in some parts of the world are underreported. Honest reporting is necessary for creating genuinely safe projects because it provides the incentive structure for strong safety systems to be viewed as good business. It also must be disheartening to those project professionals who have driven genuinely safe projects in places where the numbers are suspect. Their accomplishments tend to get denigrated along with the liars and the cheats.

There are things that sponsors can do to improve safety reporting even when the governmental apparatus does not support honest reporting. The first and perhaps most important step is to discontinue all monetary incentives to contractors and subcontractors for meeting safety goals. For projects as a whole, there is absolutely no relationship whatsoever between safety-based monetary incentives paid to contractors and better safety performance. That result is only logical: If a contractor has strong safety systems and culture, they will always carry them to the job. If they lack the systems and culture, there is no chance they can acquire them in time to be of any use on your project. Safety incentives paid to contractors encourage underreporting whenever and wherever it is feasible to do so. Safety incentives to contractors were so ubiquitous on the megaprojects in our sample that we cannot even prove our point with the data here. It is a mindless and counterproductive practice.*

Having eliminated bonuses to contractors for meeting safety targets, sponsors need to recognize and reward incident reporting when incidents could have been made to disappear. Modern safety programs all center on positive reinforcement; this is just another application of that approach. There should be no penalties for safety outcomes— and this includes no penalties allowed by contractors to subcontractors. The penalties must be centered on failure to cooperate fully with the project's safety program. In this area, as in so many others in projects, it is impossible and counterproductive to try to manage by results rather than practices.

THE JEMIMA PRINCIPLE

Most of us in the English-speaking world grew up with a nursery rhyme by Henry Wadsworth Longfellow, the first verse of which goes like this:

> *There was a little girl who had a pretty curl*
> *Right in the middle of her forehead.*
> *When she was good, she was very, very good*
> *And when she was bad, she was horrid!*

---

*Properly structured recognition awards at the craft level can be quite effective in promoting safety. Where it is easy to hide accidents, however, even these incentives can encourage underreporting.

Figure 3.1
Contrasting Successful and Failed Projects

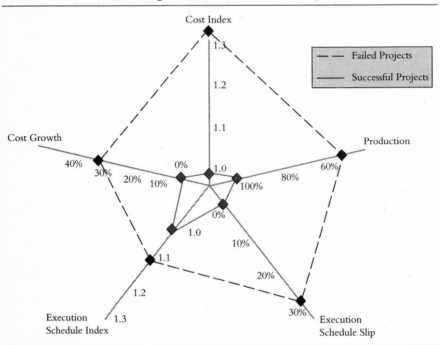

Like Longfellow's "little girl with the pretty curl," whose name was Jemima, megaprojects are rarely mediocre; they tend to be either very, very good, or they are horrid. Figure 3.1 tells the story: The 35 percent of the projects that succeeded were genuinely excellent projects. On average, they underran their budgets by 2 percent while delivering highly competitive (96 percent of industry average) costs. They were completed on time with schedules that were only slightly (4 percent) slower than the long-term industry average. Their average production was well ahead of the plan.

By contrast, the failures are truly miserable projects: they averaged a 40 percent constant currency overrun while being very expensive in absolute terms. They slipped their execution schedules by an average of 28 percent while being 15 percent slower than a competitive schedule. Worst of all, after they were completed, they averaged only 60 percent of planned production in the first year. Sixty-five percent

of the failed projects for which we have operating data available suffered long-term operational problems. Three were abandoned completely as hopelessly inoperable.

Most of the failed projects were unprofitable, but not all. In particular, some bad projects producing crude oil made money despite themselves. Sometimes increases in oil prices enabled poor projects to make
money; in other cases the manner in which the operator was compensated by national resource holders made it possible to make money even
with massive cost overruns or large shortfalls in promised production.

The oil and gas production sector fares the worst; 78 percent of
megaprojects in this industrial sector are classified as failures. Of the
failed oil and gas projects, cost overruns averaged 33 percent and cost
competitiveness was almost 40 percent more spent than the industry
average. They fared better on execution schedule, which is not surprising given that many were schedule-driven (only to end up not
producing). Nearly two-thirds of the petroleum development failures
suffered severe operability problems. Despite the fact that the oil production sector had the worst results, this does not tell us that oil projects are inherently more difficult. Rather it tells us that the practices
followed were poorer than those used in most other sectors. I discuss
the underlying causes of the extraordinary difficulties in petroleum
development projects in Chapter 9 in conjunction with team organization and in Chapter 10 in conjunction with front-end loading.

Minerals megaprojects failed about 70 percent of the time and had
failure patterns similar to those seen in petroleum development: poor
operability and very high cost growth. Unlike oil and gas projects,
however, minerals project failures tended to be slow and have significant schedule slippage as well.

The only industrial sector with more successes than failures in our
database was LNG. We explain this result in part by the fact that most
of the LNG projects in our sample were trains being added on to an
existing complex, rather than greenfield projects. Although not all of
these expansion projects were successful, most of them were and were
often fairly straightforward projects to execute. We also note that the
failure rate is higher among more recent LNG projects.

If we compare the two groups—successes and failures—shown in
Figure 3.1 against a pro forma 15 percent real internal rate of return

base, what results? The returns of the successful projects increase to almost 18 percent, whereas the returns of the average failure fall to 5 percent, which is significantly less than the cost of capital.

So what is the Jemima principle? The Jemima principle is that large capital projects are by their nature either quite good or quite bad. This sort of bimodal distribution of outcomes is quite unusual; most phenomena tend to center around a typical ("modal") result and then gradually vary away from that result in both directions. Most smaller projects follow this single mode character with a skew toward poorer outcomes.*

The strange pattern of results for megaprojects is produced by one of the most important characteristics of megaprojects: their fragility. Instead of tending to go slightly wrong, they tend to fall apart. Understanding that this happens and the mechanisms by which it happens are keys to managing these ventures successfully.

The Jemima principle tells us that very large projects are fragile. They do not tend to simply degrade toward poor outcomes; they tend to collapse instead. Most of these projects must be very tightly integrated to achieve economic success. If one of the many parts fails, the whole effort fails. So we have a lot of failed megaprojects, even if many of the failures are carefully covered up.[2] As you will see as we move forward, this is not a necessary outcome. It can be fixed.

---

*The skew is to be expected: There are more ways for things to go poorly than to go well. Good outcomes tend to be strictly bounded, whereas poor outcomes (except operability, which is bounded at zero) are not.

PART TWO

MAKING THE RIGHT BUSINESS DECISIONS BEFORE YOU COMMIT

CHAPTER 4

THE OPPORTUNITY-SHAPING PROCESS

After looking at hundreds of megaprojects in the process industries over the past three decades, I am convinced that most business executives and project teams do not fully understand what they are signing up for when they start a megaproject. For most, this will be their first megaproject and very likely their first project that closely resembles this one. It is very unlikely they will have been specifically trained to deal with the peculiar problems posed by megaprojects, even if they are seasoned and well-trained business and project professionals. If they or their bosses expect the project to be easy, they may be about to destroy their careers.

Because they are unprepared, the executives, project directors, and project managers often fail to ask a series of key questions at the earliest points in project gestation, the answers to which should shape their assessment of the desirability of proceeding and their fundamental strategy if they elect to proceed.

In this chapter we deal with the one requirement for a successful venture that is almost unique to megaprojects: the need to assess and then shape the opportunity into a reasonably stable platform from which to manage the project. I discuss this process from the perspective of the business and project professionals working for the leading stakeholder-investor in the project. This chapter focuses on what information needs to be developed to make good shaping decisions. The next chapter focuses on devising the shaping strategy for your project.

WHAT IS OPPORTUNITY SHAPING?

Opportunity shaping[1] is a business-led process by which sponsors evaluate the key attributes of a potential project, develop and gather information that is needed for key decisions, and then allocate the value of the project to the various stakeholders to make the project environment stable enough for successful execution while holding enough of the project's value for themselves to make the venture worthwhile.

Money spent on and during the shaping process is not capital investment; it is *not* project money and must not be perceived as such by those concerned. Money spent in shaping is for purposes of information acquisition only, not capital investment. One must be prepared to walk away from a bad deal without any negative repercussions. Think of it this way: You were engaged in information acquisition and you acquired enough information to understand that this deal was not going to benefit the company. That is a good result; now move on. One of the keys to a successful opportunity-shaping process is to be looking for reasons to *kill* a project, not reasons to continue. The more clearly one can view the process as information gathering for decision making, the less likely you are to become so personally invested in the project that you are unable to negotiate successfully and are able to extricate yourself (and your company) only at considerable personal loss. During this same period, the project management team will be busy developing the scope for the project in tandem with the business' shaping efforts. Those expenditures also are for purposes of information development only. All money and effort up to the shaping closure point, which we discuss in Chapter 5, are not capital investment!

Megaprojects don't come ready-to-go right out of the box from any perspective—technical or business. A good many megaprojects are not even the result of a systematic corporate search for opportunities. The exceptions to that rule are oil and gas development projects, which generally result from a corporate exploration strategy. Even then, I often get the clear impression that the company was not really prepared for the success of that exploratory process, especially in regions that are new to the company.

In an ideal world, megaprojects would be the result and expression of corporate strategies with respect to sustaining and growing the corporation.[2] Extensive analysis would have preceded a search for opportunities that fit with the comprehensive vision.* However, there are distinct limits to how far eschewing opportunism will carry companies in the current environment. International petroleum companies are facing rapid depletion of opportunities for new black oil developments. Similarly, minerals companies have long since discovered and developed rich ore bodies in easily accessible venues. European and American commodity chemical company assets are mostly far from rapidly growing markets and far from low-cost feedstocks. Repositioning requires gaining access wherever an opportunity arises. And repositioning often requires megaprojects because large size is an essential element in cost-effectiveness when opening up new areas.

The result is that we are often, perhaps usually, facing challenges in our large projects for which we are ill prepared. Shaping is an essential response to that reality. We must take the project opportunity that has arisen and subject it to enough scrutiny that we understand the implications in terms of risk, resources, reputation, and preoccupation that will be involved in trying to turn this possibility into an asset. The shaping process requires an open-minded approach because so many aspects of the process will be new.

Shaping must not be confused with the project work process prior to full-funds authorization. That process, which we call front-end loading, partly overlaps shaping in the project timeline and both is informed by shaping's progress and informs the shaping process. Shaping and the project work process must be aligned, which we discuss in Chapter 5. Shaping never substitutes for front-end loading; the two processes are symbiotic, not substitutes.

WHY IS SHAPING ESSENTIAL?

Project management is the science of project planning combined with the art of reacting to surprises during execution. I describe planning as a science because we know how to do it and what needs to be done. It is a repeatable process. If the planning is thorough, the project is

---

*There are notable exceptions. For example, the Kerr-McGee Corporation, now subsumed by Anadarko Petroleum Corporation, systematically searched for petroleum development opportunities that suited the deepwater development technology, production spars, which they had perfected.

appropriately staffed, *and the project environment is stable,* surprises will rarely overwhelm the ability of project managers to react appropriately. If the planning is inadequate, or if the owner staffing is too lean to identify problems, or the project environment is unstable, the art of project management almost always fails for complex projects.

As the name implies, the role of shaping is to configure a project in such a way that it is profitable for the stakeholder-investors and at the same time has stabilized the project environment. These two objectives— profitability for the investors and a stable project environment—generally compete. The bigger the piece of the pie that you as the leader of the shaping process attempt to keep for yourself, the less likely you will be to have a stable platform from which to execute the project.

Unlike project planning, shaping remains substantially an art at this point. Although there are many common elements from case to case, each megaproject poses its own shaping challenges. The effective management of large projects requires a stable environment. The requirement to make major changes in the objectives, scope, precise location, or any other major element after the start of the detailed definition phase* can result in an unmanageable project. Turbulence in the project environment translates to changes and disruptions in execution that render projects failures. We often blame the project managers for these failures, but actually it was a failure of opportunity shaping, not project management.

THE FIRST FIVE STEPS IN THE SHAPING PROCESS

Whatever the underlying source of the possible opportunity, in the beginning the project is nothing more than that—a possible opportunity.

---

*We call this phase of the front-end work front-end loading phase 3, or FEL-3. It is also often called FEED—front-end engineering design. I don't like the term FEED because much more than engineering design is involved in the phase. In particular, the execution plan must be perfected in this phase, and that is a major activity. In the minerals world, this project phase is often called the feasibility study. I like that term even less. The economic and other dimensions of whether a project is feasible should have been largely settled before the beginning of FEL-3. FEL-3 is expensive, consuming 2 to 3.5 percent of eventual total cost. We cannot get to the full-funds authorization point at the end of FEL-3 and then decide the project is not feasible.

In the usual case, 6 to 12 years will pass from the first identification of a potential project until something of value is produced, and sometimes no project ever results from the effort. Sometimes, the company that was the potential lead sponsor is not even part of the sponsor group when the project starts up.

What determines how often a company ends up with the prize, and whether that prize is valuable or a booby prize, is the company's skill at shaping a raw opportunity into a valuable project. We are not aware of any company in the process industries that has developed a work process specially designed to meet the challenges of the shaping process for megaprojects. There is no standard practice here within the industry, which helps explain the considerable variation in the practices and procedures followed. Only a handful of companies in the process industries have sought to develop and train a cadre of personnel who are particularly skilled and trained in the activities needed to shape a megaproject. Whether these efforts have succeeded is an open question. These factors contribute to the failures of shaping that later result in failed projects.

The steps I describe in this chapter and the next are normative rather than empirical. These are things you should do, not necessarily the things that have been done in the past. The order of the steps is important because each builds on the prior steps. It is important to remember that shaping is an artificial construct, not a naturally occurring process that we are observing.

STEP 1: UNDERSTANDING THE CONTEXT

When thinking about what makes megaprojects especially difficult, the first consideration is the project context, which is to say the environment in which the project will have to be executed. It is the interaction between the context and whether it is relatively robust or fragile and the size and characteristics of the project that determine whether this will be "just another big project" or a project of considerable difficulty.

The interactions between the project size and the context might be considered this way: If the project is a rock and the context is a body of water into which that rock will be dropped, then what happens when the rock hits the water is a function of three things—the size of the rock, the size of the body of water, and who is standing nearby when the splash occurs. A very small rock will rarely cause anyone to get wet, even when dropped in a small puddle, and a large rock dropped into the ocean will usually disappear without a trace. However, even a medium-sized rock dropped into a puddle with lots of people standing around will cause a fair amount of distress to those getting soaked.

Like every other organization, all projects have a context, an environment, a milieu.[3] That context may be relatively stable and robust with respect to the things that affect capital projects, such a regulatory regime, labor relations, and so on. The context may be stable but fragile, which is to say unaccommodating of major changes. The milieu may be turbulent and even chaotic. The relationship and interaction between the context and the project help us decide whether a project is merely large or a true megaproject. One of the key tasks of the shaping process is to assess the context, decide whether the intended project will be feasible in that context, and then seek to fashion the project and the distribution of its value in a way that will render the milieu stable enough for the project to be successfully completed.

The context for a project should not be conceptualized as merely or even primarily local, although the local project context is important. The context includes the global markets for project inputs: materials, engineering and project management resources, and finance. The context includes what is happening regionally and finally the nature of the local situation.

The context is also subject to change over time. A context that was very difficult to deal with when the first megaproject was introduced may become progressively more benign and hospitable to projects over time as local players adjust to the presence of the projects. Contexts that have been stable and accommodating for many years can suddenly become extremely turbulent. Examples include the UK North Sea regulatory context for petroleum production immediately after the Piper Alpha disaster. At present, the deepwater U.S. Gulf of Mexico's regulatory climate is highly uncertain in the wake of the BP Macondo blowout.

The context does not cause project failure. Failure results when the context is not adequately or correctly assessed or when major changes are unanticipated. In the past decade, the most important change in the global context for megaprojects was the turn in the contracting market in 2003–2004 from a generation of being a buyers' market to a decidedly sellers' market. That change, which we discuss in Chapter 11, caused a good deal of disruption and some significant cost overruns. After correcting for the effects of escalation, however, we cannot point to a single project in our database for which the turn in the market was the root cause of failure. Many projects weathered the market change with discomfort but without major damage. The projects that were hurt seriously had other crucial vulnerabilities that were exacerbated by the market chaos.

If the context does not cause failure, what it does do is outline the magnitude of the task that lies ahead. If the context presents major challenges, the sponsor's strategy for shaping should be different. The need for staff resources may increase substantially. The amount of time that sponsors expect for both development and execution should increase.

An ever-present danger in the early days of shaping is an abundance of optimism. We humans are always quick to believe what we wish to. When we are ignorant of the difficulties because they are new and unappreciated, optimism is easy. Sponsors must establish clear objective criteria in advance to keep realism in play.

Country Advance Teams

The assessment of the project's context needs to start as soon as the project possibility arises—or even earlier.* If the project is in a new venue for the company or if the company has worked on a project in this location for several years, a country advance team needs to be formed immediately.† The team should consist of specialists trained

---

*Companies with an FEL-0 phase are exploring the context before any particular project has been identified. It is an excellent practice.
†The need for an advance team is equally pressing if the project is in a new region of a large country, such as the United States, Russia, China, or Brazil. Local governments are routinely very important in geographically large countries.

to assess the 10 context areas described in the following section. This prescription applies equally to companies doing their first offshore oil and gas project in a country. The country advance team provides critical information about the context for any project.

The country advance team should include marketing and sales, supply chain, purchasing and logistics, public relations and government affairs, and human resources. At least one experienced megaproject director should always be on this team. It can be a great job for an experienced senior person who will retire within a year or two and is therefore unable to take on a new major project.

An effective advance team will consist of 12 to 15 members plus locals who speak the language and can assist in introductions. *In most cases the lead sponsor should not depend on a local partner to do this work.* A local partner may be very helpful in the process of investigating the context, but the local partner may not share the same objectives or concerns as the lead sponsor. The local partner may be anxious for the project to proceed regardless of whether it makes sense for other partners. *In far too many examples, the local partner lacked the needed expertise or objectivity to assess and weigh the issues.* The local partner may not know what to look for, especially if that partner has little megaproject experience.

Sometimes a sponsor makes the classic mistake of relying on the FEED contractor to supply the needed expertise in the local setting. There are a number of reasons why a contractor's expertise cannot substitute. First, it is usually far too late in the project's evolution when the contractor is brought on board to be discovering how much of a mess you are getting into. Second, the contractor looks at projects from a distinctly different viewpoint than an owner. The contractor's focus will be on execution issues, whereas the sponsor's needs to be on whether the project is a good idea. Finally, contractors and owners have different interests, and putting the contractor in this role is a conflict of interest. Owners need to do this work.

The Physical Location

The physical location comes first, and the first question to ask in regard to the location is, What's the weather like? It is surprisingly difficult to take a proven technology and design and move it from an area of temperate climate to a harsh climate. This is true both onshore, where it should be obvious, and offshore, where sometimes it is not. For example, the first projects executed west of Shetlands off the UK coast encountered ocean conditions that have battered one of the vessels almost to pieces, leaving it with a serviceable life of about half what was expected. For many process-type facilities, including liquefied natural gas (LNG), the ambient temperatures are extremely important and have a dramatic effect on facilities cost. Facilities being designed for a very cold environment for the first time are prone to high levels of cost growth because the difficulties with design and construction tend to be underestimated. Process projects being placed in very warm climates have to be able to deal with much greater cooling requirements than the "standard design." And projects in or near desert areas will have to design for blowing fine sand, which is quite difficult. Four of our megaprojects failed solely because the weather implications were not accounted for correctly. One failed because of the cold, and three failed because of the heat! The weather may be obvious, but that doesn't make it easy.

The second element of the location is remoteness, which affects infrastructure, logistics, human resources, and the supply chain. If a site is remote or otherwise requires significant infrastructure development, the prize involved in the development of the project must be much larger than in semiremote or nonremote locations. We call an onshore project remote if it is more than 150 km from a population center and there is little or no project-related infrastructure at the location. For projects labeled "remote," the average distance from a population center was more than 400 km. Offshore, a project is considered remote if the project opens a new province. For example, Foinaven and Schiehallion would be considered remote projects because they opened the area west of Shetlands in the UK Atlantic margin. A project is considered semiremote if it is among the first projects in an area and the infrastructure is still in development. About 17 percent of our samples were genuinely remote, 36 percent were considered semiremote, and the remaining 47 percent were nonremote.

Table 4.1 shows the relationships between remoteness of location and key project outcomes. The first row shown—the proportion of

Table 4.1
How Outcomes Vary with Remoteness of Site

Outcome Factor	Nonremote	Semiremote	Remote
Successful (%)	33	42	26
Cost overruns (%)	20	27	26
Schedule slip (%)	17	17	22
Operability failures (%)	34	32	58[1]
Median production in second six months (% of plan)	78	71	45[2]

[1]Statistically significant at .05 (χ2).
[2]Statistically significant at .01 (*t*-ratio).

projects in each group that was successful—may surprise some readers, although it probably won't surprise many project managers. Although the result does not quite reach statistical significance, semiremote projects fared better than nonremote projects. If being in a genuinely remote location is really difficult, and the paltry 26 percent of successful projects would support that, being in a more heavily populated area can also present some serious challenges. When you are close to population centers, projects are very visible and more likely to become politically difficult. There also may be a tendency to relax a bit when one should not. This is borne out by the fact that nonremote projects are not as well front-end loaded (defined) at authorization as semiremote projects are. There were no statistically significant differences in cost overruns or slips in execution schedules, although directionally remoteness tends to make both worse.

The big difference is in the rate of operability failures and the production rates among the remote projects. Remote projects really suffered with operability problems. Almost 60 percent of the remote projects are classified as operational failures, and their production in the second six months after startup was only 45 percent of planned production. Most of the operability problems with these projects stemmed from errors in the Basic (technical) Data, the subject of Chapter 7.

A project may need infrastructure additions whether it is remote or not. In fact, we know one example of a project in a nonremote location that will require at least $8 billion in infrastructure additions. When substantial additions must be made to infrastructure for a project to be practicable, substantial new risks are added. If the infra-structure being added serves only the project, the project usually pays the cost. However, paying the cost does not always translate into con-trolling the infrastructure projects. If the infrastructure will be used by others and over a long period of time, the central or local government may be responsible for paying the cost and is often responsible for controlling the infrastructure project. This now means that your proj-ect depends on the timely and successful completion of a third party's project. Consider this a major risk because governments are notori-ous for being late with projects and there isn't a great deal you can do about it.

Not being in a remote location should not encourage complacency, even about a simple thing such as access. One of our failed projects was in the middle of a populated area teeming with construction workers; however, it failed when the authorities decided to start reconstruction of the superhighway that was the only convenient access point for the project. Craft workers became disgusted with their 60- to 90-minute wait to get into the site and quit the project in droves. The highway construction had been planned for some time, but nobody thought to check.

History of Prior Projects in the Area

Megaprojects can be quite disruptive to the daily lives of those in the immediate area. Suddenly many more people are in the area, some of whom may be deemed peculiar, if not downright undesirable. If yours is not the first project in an area, it is important to discover how the previous projects were received. If they were greeted pos-itively or at least indifferently, the shaping process is likely to be considerably easier than if they were met with continuing hostility or, perhaps worse, if they generated considerable hostility during con-struction or operation. If a prior project has "fouled the nest," it will be very important to clearly differentiate yourself from that project. Differentiation, however, will always cost something.

Understanding the local reaction to a new megaproject absolutely requires local presence and local presence for a substantial period of time, not just a few weeks. As a sponsor who may be bringing huge amounts of money to a local area, what you are told by the community boosters, who are often the first ones you meet, and what is actually true can be very different. Local presence is required.

The Nature and Perceived Value of the Physical Environment

If your project involves disruption to an area that is considered to have substantial value from an environmental standpoint, be prepared for a long shaping process that must be carefully orchestrated. Being in such an area does not necessarily doom the project. After all, the Chevron-led Gorgon project in Western Australia is building three LNG trains on Barrow Island, which is a nature preserve. That said, the shaping process was long and tortured for the project. Success in such cases hinges on genuinely accepting that the environmental value of the area will have to be carefully, if not fully, maintained. Remember that the environmental value of an area is always, to some extent, in the eyes of the beholder. Appreciating how the local population views the area is also not enough. How the area is viewed more broadly in the society is often what counts. In the United States, for example, many residents of Alaska strongly support opening the Arctic National Wildlife Refuge to oil and gas exploration and development. But national environmental groups almost uniformly oppose it.

Where prior projects have done considerable environmental damage, the shaping road is likely to be a bumpy one. It is likely that a tightening of environmental regulations will take place or is under way. You can deal with tight regulations; dealing with changing regulations is a real problem.

The Political and Institutional Environment

The strength of the institutional environment is measured by the extent to which business in the country, including projects, is controlled by rules that are clear, codified, agreed to by all key players, and enforced by the appropriate authorities. One simple measure is the extent to which the political authorities are controlled by the rule of law. If laws can be bent or ignored to suit the wishes of those currently in power, the institutional framework that will surround your project is weak.

No institutional environment is perfectly predictable and under control. Officials can drag their feet on your requests or expedite them in the most rule-bound of societies as they see fit. However, if the institutional environment is weak, the shaping process is both much more difficult *and much more important to the success or failure of* your project. One way of thinking about the shaping process is that it is intended to shore up, from the project's perspective, those areas where the institutional environment does not provide much assistance. In a strong institutional environment, most stakeholders in your project will be bound by the institutional rules not to renege on promises they have made. Contracts have clear and enforceable meaning. In a weak institutional environment, players in your game have to be bound in noninstitutional ways. Usually, this means they must be bound by self-interest to meet the commitments they have made.

Consideration of the political environment should inform the sponsor's basic strategy regarding investment in the country. The most important political consideration is whether the political authorities are controlled by the courts or vice versa. If the politicians control the courts, the value of the project is never fully secure at any point. The project will always depend on the sufferance of the political authorities and whether they see your presence as beneficial to their interests, which may or may not coincide with the country's national interests.

Sponsors have tried to hedge or lay off political risks in a number of ways, but none of them are entirely satisfactory. As Exxon learned with its Chad experience, even World Bank involvement in the financing, which was seen as the gold standard of reducing country risks, doesn't always work.

Sponsors also need to remember the late U.S. House Speaker Tip O'Neill's admonition that "Politics is always local." It is not sufficient in most cases to have the central government on your side if local officials are not. As many a company moving into China has learned the hard way, the local mayor may be more important to your project's prospects than the premier in Beijing. Access to land, water, power, and people may be controlled locally, even in countries that appear to have strong central control.

Political instability is an obvious source of significant risk, and again both the national and local levels need to be reviewed and understood.

Political instability is not a problem confined to the so-called Third World. When a project becomes politically contentious, even orderly changes of political party in charge can spell serious trouble for the shaping process or execution in the worst case. Even in orderly political climates, politicians will weigh whether killing your project will buy or cost votes. How one is treated may depend on where you are from and therefore how many votes you have. For example, in "resource development–friendly" Queensland, Australia, the state premier had no trouble throwing a bone to Greenpeace by killing an oil shale development venture sponsored by Americans. Welcome to Queensland; now go home!

If there is substantial political opposition to a project, the greatest virtue is often patience. Trying to push forward in the face of serious opposition will be costly and usually ends up being futile. Smart companies will keep a constant eye on project opportunities in areas with political opposition because times do change.

Regulatory Climate and Stability

The regulatory climate is defined by whether the regulations are clear and strict and strictly enforced. The regulatory climate in the state of California, for example, is widely viewed by industry as being very difficult. But from the viewpoint of planning a project, the climate is stable and reasonably predictable: it's going to be difficult. Problems are most likely to occur when the regulations are unclear or in transition. (Of course, if the regulations are not thoroughly investigated by the sponsor, they will be unclear.)

About one megaproject in five encounters a significant permitting problem. We define a problem as when one of the following occurs:

- A permit is seriously delayed or withheld such that it causes slippage in the overall schedule.
- Permitting requirements change repeatedly during front-end loading.
- Permits are made contingent on non–permit-related issues, such as allocation of ownership rights.
- Permits are withdrawn for non–permit-related reasons.

Table 4.2
Permitting Problems Degrade Outcomes

Success Factor	No Permitting Problems	Permitting Problems
Cost overrun (%)	16	67
Execution schedule slip (%)	15	30
Serious operability problems (% of projects)	32	56

Although only 20 percent of our projects encountered such problems, those that did really suffered. Permitting problems were most common in Russia and the Caspian area. Nearly three-quarters of projects in that area encountered difficulty. Asian and African projects encountered more problems than average, whereas permitting problems were less common in North America (United States and Canada) and Europe. Permitting problems were almost nonexistent in the Middle East.* Permitting problems were also more common among projects in remote areas; 40 percent of projects in remote areas suffered permitting problems, twice the overall average.

The effects of permitting problems are shown in Table 4.2, but with a caveat: in some of the cases in which permits were withheld, it was because the sponsor-investors did not understand the permit requirements. Simply put, permitting problems were occasionally caused by sponsor sloppiness and nothing else.

Projects with permitting problems suffered crippling cost overruns. Some of these cost overruns can be attributed directly to the permitting problems, but a good deal can be attributed to the problems that were only indirectly related to permitting. These projects were much more likely to have problematic relationships with the host government on a range of issues, not just permits per se. There were disputes over local content, contracting, importation of equipment, and movement of labor.

Permitting problems also correlate strongly with measures of corruption of government officials. Transparency International[4] has developed a measure of reputation called the Corruption Perceptions Index (CPI). The 2009 CPI for most countries of the world is shown

---

*This result may be affected by the fact that the governments in the Middle East were partial or complete owners of almost all the projects.

in Figure 4.1. Every country is given a rating based on a series of surveys, and the countries are divided into 10 groups. Low numbers indicate that corruption is perceived to be worse. We assigned the CPI value to our projects based on the CPI measured in the year of authorization of the project. The CPI correlates with permitting problems as well as problems with the host government.* Even more starkly, 37 percent of the projects in countries that fall in the worst three categories experienced serious permitting issues, versus only 12 percent in the remainder of the sample. A CPI rating of 3 or less is associated with a tripling of the probability of a significant permitting issue.

When there is serious political unrest in a country, permits may be at risk even when granted. Political opponents often view the actions of current officials as inherently illegitimate and subject to reversal if political power changes hands.

Permitting problems are symptomatic of a turbulent project context. The shaping process for these projects can be said to have failed fundamentally. A primary purpose of the shaping process is to calm the turbulent environment sufficiently to execute the project without serious damage from the project's environment. Careful attention to the permitting situation can alert the potential sponsor to what kinds of challenges are going to be faced. Projects to be executed in such environments need better teams, better definition, and less aggressive targets. In fact, however, projects in turbulent environments often had weaker teams, poorer definition, and more aggressive targets. This suggests that those leading the shaping process fundamentally did not know what they were doing.

Local Content Requirements

Virtually everywhere in the world where capital projects are executed there are formal or informal requirements that some portion of the procurement for the project will come from local vendors, contractors, craft laborers, or whatever. No country is exempt from these practices—no matter how vehement their protestations of being adherents of open market principles. For example, in the U.S. Gulf

---

*Using logit regression, $P > |z| < .02$ for permitting problems and $P > |z| < .0001$ with problems with host government.

Figure 4.1
Measuring Corruption Problems

CORRUPTION
PERCEPTIONS
INDEX 2009

highly clean

9.0–10.0
8.0–8.9
7.0–7.9
6.0–6.9
5.0–5.9
4.0–4.9
3.0–3.9
2.0–2.9
1.0–1.9
0.0–0.9
no data

highly corrupt

© 2009 Transparency International. All rights Reserved.

TRANSPARENCY
INTERNATIONAL

CORRUPTION PERCEPTIONS INDEX 2009

of Mexico, only U.S. flag carriers are allowed to operate in the off-shore oil fields. Sometimes, the local content requirements are entirely informal but very substantial. For example, in the UK sector of the North Sea, platform fabrication has historically been entirely within the UK or more recently the European Union, despite the simple fact that fabrication elsewhere is much cheaper, with at least as high of quality. There are no written rules to that effect, but the unwritten rules are at least as powerful.* Sometimes there are no local content rules, but the authority's actions have the same effect. For example, in Alberta, Canada, there are no requirements for the use of only Canadian craft labor. But actually getting foreign workers into the country is so difficult that very few projects have even tried. For some projects, the financing approach includes purchase requirements, such as when government credit facilities are used.

In some countries, mostly in the developing world, the local content requirements are formal, and that draws a lot of criticism. The requirements are, of course, intended to encourage the development of local industry. There is a great deal of misunderstanding about local content requirements beyond the pretense of developed nations that they don't have them. As most megaproject managers will attest, securing local content is often just plain good business. The local content is often less expensive than material procured in the world open market, and the use of local content is an important part of building a local supportive constituency for the project that pays dividends all the way through execution and into operation. Nonetheless, local content requirements are viewed very negatively by many sponsor-investors and are almost universally disliked by international contractors.

So when you are exploring the project context, what aspects of local content requirements should worry you and what aspects should not? The answer depends in part on the relationship between the magnitude of the local content requirements and the current capabilities of the local industry. If the local markets are strong in the areas required by your project, local content requirements should not be a big concern. Second, it makes a great deal of difference if the local content requirements are specific rather than general. The more exactly

---

*Written rules would likely encounter an unwanted World Trade Organization challenge.

the local content requirements tell you what must be procured within the country, the more the business is being directed to specific in-country firms and they know it. These cases will trigger sizable risk premiums in bids from international contractors for the work. Their concern is understandable: In these situations, the local suppliers are notorious for being late and providing work of low quality. When work is in effect guaranteed, one does not have to be good to be successful. (We return to the issue of contractor risk premiums in Chapter 11 when we discuss contracting.)

Sometimes local content requirements are little more than vehicles to expedite bribery. There is more than a full 2-point difference in the CPI between countries that have formal local content requirements and those that do not.* The use of local "consultants" will satisfy the requirements, or in some cases the local content requirements may not be enforced in exchange for "consideration." These situations too, are fraught with difficulty.

Your country advance team needs to be careful and nuanced as it assesses local content requirements and free of ideological bias. Yes, local content requirements can complicate the shaping process, and if not properly dealt with, they can cause projects to fail. However, the development of local industry is a normal and legitimate aspiration of governments. The danger in local content is worst when the rules are murky and enforced in seemingly random ways.

Local content can be a huge advantage for a project. Local content helps build project support both in the short and long term. Politicians who might be tempted to jeopardize your project will be much more careful if there is strong local support generated by a successful local content program.

Social, Religious, and Cultural Considerations

Over the past 15 years or so, companies sponsoring megaprojects have focused sharply on not running afoul of cultural differences as they

---

*The mean CPI for countries with formal local content requirements is 5.1, versus 7.1 for countries without local content requirements. Lower numbers indicate more perceived corruption. The difference is significant at less than 1 chance in 10,000 of being random using a z-score on a logit regression predicting formal local content requirements.

execute their projects. This awakening to cultural issues followed a series of notorious projects in sub-Saharan Africa and Asia Pacific that justifiably damaged the reputations of both sponsors and contractors.

After reviewing the records of several hundred recent megaprojects, I am pleasantly surprised to say that this focus on understanding the importance of social and cultural differences appears to have paid off. Few in our project sample got into serious trouble in this area. Of course, this doesn't mean that we should not worry about such things. It simply means that when we pay attention, it makes a difference.

The one area that was problematic for our projects was dealing with cultural and religious issues of craft labor. The juxtaposition of imported and local labor caused serious difficulties in the field for some of the projects, particularly in Central Asia. In areas in which imported labor was the norm and expected, such as the Arabian Gulf area, relatively few issues were reported. The combination of substantial amounts of relatively unskilled local labor with imported labor is a difficult mix to manage. It is also very difficult to have in-country national laborers who are managed at the foreman level by foreigners. Wherever possible, foremen should have the same ethnic, cultural, and national background as the labor they directly manage.

Local Labor Availability and Quality

When in-country labor is going to be used for construction, its availability and quality are one of the most important shaping issues. These situations are usually ones in which the mass importation of labor is forbidden or actively discouraged by the host governments. This issue is so important that it should often prompt decisions not to proceed with projects or to proceed very carefully.

The megaprojects in northern Alberta, Canada, during the past decade suffered from a thin labor market and found that even the slightest imperfections in their development and definition led to enormous problems. Thin labor markets are most damaging to megaprojects under two conditions: (1) the labor requirement for the project and particularly the labor peak were underestimated and (2) the schedules were too aggressive. These two conditions are not entirely unrelated: projects with resource-loaded schedules prior to authorization tended to get the labor requirements right and generally had longer schedules than those without resource loading. Even if they had been in a benign labor market, the projects in Alberta that suffered the worst overruns would have still all underestimated the base labor requirements.

Megaprojects fail in a fairly small number of ways. One of those ways, however, is the downward labor productivity spiral. This occurs when engineering deliverables are late and/or incorrect, which in turn causes field construction to fall behind and get out of sequence. When field management responds incorrectly, which is quite easy to do, a collapse of labor productivity results. Problems with the availability and quality of local labor almost always accompany this scenario. We discuss this failure process in considerably more detail in Chapter 12 as we discuss project execution.

Competing Projects

Part of the context assessment should be real or likely projects that will compete for resources. Competing local projects exacerbate potential labor shortages discussed previously. One must be very cautious about assumptions that a neighboring project will provide labor for your project as it ramps down. Neighboring projects often slip.

The crucial engineering services component of megaprojects is a global, rather than local, marketplace. When that global market is overheated, as it was in the 2004–2009 period, megaprojects are more prone to fail, but the overheated market *does not cause* failure. Rather, the overheated market renders the project more sensitive to errors. The market increases fragility of the project, and if the shapers of the project do not understand that, the projects fail.

Again, the competing projects themselves do not trigger failure; the root causes are found elsewhere. The competing projects render the projects more vulnerable to mistakes and errors of omission. When the global megaprojects market is hot, there is very little resiliency. Contractors will not have the personnel "on the bench" that can be brought in to help rescue a project experiencing difficulties. Similarly, sponsors usually find themselves understaffed in a hot market environment as they attempt to do too many large projects.

STEP 2: ASSESSING THE POTENTIAL VALUE

The potential value of a project is the total net gains that could be developed as a product of the project if it goes forward and is developed and executed well. The potential value of the project should not be confused with the value that may accrue to your firm. Furthermore, the potential value should not be confused with just immediate short-term economic returns. For example, the number of short- and long-term jobs created by the project may be considered a prime benefit by the host governments. Downstream or secondary employment should also be assessed. In addition to the cash costs associated with the development of the project, social costs associated with the project should also be assessed. In other words, a full cost-benefit analysis of the venture should be developed.

One may legitimately wonder why a private sector firm should go to the trouble and expense of doing a full cost-benefit analysis of a project when its only interest is in immediate economic returns. There are several compelling reasons:

- Megaprojects that survive the shaping process to sanction will almost always appear to be very lucrative ventures at the start of the shaping process. Projects that appear economically marginal at the outset are likely to look submarginal quite quickly. Does the venture offer enough possible value to make it worth the effort?

- The shaping process is all about the allocation of the project's value out to various claimants, also sometimes called stakeholders. If you do not understand the value that can be produced, you lose control of the process very quickly. If, for example, the government doubts the value of the project and you are in a position to counter with the number of primary and secondary jobs to be created, your bargaining position is much better. If environmental or other social cost objections are raised, you are in a position to respond. If you are going to be the lead sponsor of a complex megaproject, you must be in a position to control the conversation about the project's worth. If you surrender that position to another stakeholder, your interests will suffer.

- The potential value needs to be weighed against the assessment of the project environment. If the environment looks difficult, the project is not nearly as valuable as it may first appear. For example, if there are infrastructure requirements, the non–value-adding portion of the project's cost will balloon. If the geography is environmentally valuable and fragile, the costs will increase dramatically, and so forth.
- The potential value will also have to be weighed in light of the other stakeholders. If there are a large number of claimants on the project's value, there may not be enough left to justify proceeding.
- A thorough cost-benefit analysis strengthens the negotiating position of the lead sponsor enormously. When you come to the negotiating table with all the facts, can articulate other stakeholders benefits, and honestly acknowledge their costs, you are much more likely to come out with a valuable result. Being surprised when opponents point out unacknowledged costs is a good way to lose.

Making even a rough assessment of a project's potential value is much more difficult at the outset of shaping than it will be when shaping is complete. The standard tools for value calculation, rate of return and net present value (NPV), are likely to be very misleading at this point as they depend on inputs that are not remotely knowable at this time. Among the barriers to assessing value is that the cost of the endeavor is quite uncertain at this point.

Coarser but more robust measures are needed. For example, in petroleum development we often have a first assessment of reservoir size at the beginning of shaping, even though the appraisal process is not complete. We may also have analogous geology from which to work the key issue of recoverability. We will know enough about the context, based on the first step of shaping, to develop rough figures of merit such as capital cost per barrel in the ground. In minerals development we will have our first guess as to the size and quality of the ore body. Again, using analogs we arrive at a range in terms of dollars per ton.

Standard bottom-up approaches to cost estimating, which are essential later on, are of little or no value at this point. At this point in project evolution, if we ask a cost estimator to develop a standard estimate of the project, we are in effect asking the estimator to fake it, to imagine a concept and fill in so much missing information that the result is utterly worthless. Despite the thousand caveats that the good estimator puts on the number, if the number is treated as if it is the "real" and correct number, we are already on the path to failure. (We address this problem of bogus cost estimates later.)

In chemicals, it is both easier and more difficult than in natural resources to come up with a good early figure of merit for a venture. It is easier in that there are no unknowns in the reservoir or ore body and in that addressing the cost of the main processing units can be done with little more than a product slate and capacities. It is more difficult in that the costs outside the main processing units can be highly variable depending on the circumstances and there is no simple way to address these costs.

However, a few things are clear in chemicals. A megaproject commodity chemicals venture will have to make a product that is cost-competitive at the bottom of the cycles. This means the operating costs need to be low and the capital charges must either be as low as any in the company's system or must be offset by, for example, advantaged feedstock costs. If low-cost feedstock is the draw, the process of calculating what feedstock cost would be required to make a venture attractive needs to begin and the securing of the feedstock cost advantage should become a primary focus of the shaping process.

These coarse measures of project potential value can tell us whether we want to further consider this venture or pass it by. They can also be used to look at the project in the context of the company's project portfolio. If the project does not look attractive relative to other ventures on these coarse measures, it will probably not look appealing when more information becomes available. It is time to withdraw.

While assessing the project's value, you must also ask whether the project fits with basic corporate culture, commitments, and strategy. If it does not, you will probably fail in the shaping process, and if you are unlucky enough to get the project sanctioned, it is likely to fail during execution.

Let me provide some real examples. Your company has a strong and deep-seated safety culture, but your strategy to keep project costs low is to have the locals, who have a terrible safety culture, control the project. Your company is genuinely committed to Responsible Care* or some other set of promises vis-à-vis environmental protection, but you would like to follow weaker local codes. Your business is built around a strong intellectual property position, but you would like to put your flagship technology in a country that practices routine technology theft. In the last example, we saw something that is almost unknown in project circles; the project team rebelled against the business because a substantial portion of the team was convinced the project would destroy the global business by ceding their leading technology to competitors.

With respect to company strategy, if your project is to be located in an area that had not been targeted for entry by the company, you have a problem that must be addressed immediately. Entering a new geography is a basic strategic decision for a company. It implies a major corporate commitment of money and leadership resources. If your proposed megaproject is not an outgrowth of the corporation's regional strategy, it will be very difficult to win support as the project moves toward authorization. Even worse, when the inevitable difficulties arise, you will not have easy access to additional corporate resources to push through the problems. If your project would expand a business from which the company is beginning to withdraw, you will likely encounter headwinds all the way. Even if the chief executive officer (CEO) supports your efforts on a project that is running counter to strategy, others will actively seek to undermine your progress by starving you for resources and withholding information whenever possible.

STEP 3: ASSESSING COMPARATIVE ADVANTAGE: THE BASIS FOR BUSINESS OBJECTIVES

One of my favorite questions to ask the business director on a megaproject is, "Why do you want to do this project?" "To make a lot of money" is a common but meaningless answer. Some megaprojects,

---

*Responsible Care is a program of the Chemical Manufacturers Association that promises to maintain the highest environmental standards regardless of location of facilities.

usually at the smaller end of the spectrum, are extensions of normal business. The development of another oil reservoir in a province in which you are already active is an example. It does not mean, by the way, that the project will be easy, but other things being equal, it should be easier than, say, opening in a new area. Many megaprojects, however, are path-breaking ventures for the lead sponsor in at least some dimensions and sometimes in a number of ways at once.

When considering whether to entertain a path-breaking project, there are some key questions to be addressed:

- Why is this project fundamentally better than alternatives? For example, does it provide an enduring low-cost basis for the product? How?
- If this is a new geography for the company, do we really want to be here for a long time? Is the long-term political outlook stable? Is there really enough enduring business or resource base to make the area interesting long term? For example, when international oil companies undertook the first petroleum development project in the nation of Chad, I have to wonder whether the sponsors asked themselves these questions, and, if they did, how they came up with affirmative answers.
- What are the characteristics of the eventual venture and project that will be important to success? For some projects, maintaining or developing a strong relationship with the local community is as important as designing the project correctly. Some projects depend on keeping a very low profile, whereas others are best served by prominence.

Unfortunately, in too many cases the question of why the company wants to do this particular project in this particular place and time is never fully addressed. When we lack convincing reasons, we often label a project "strategic." Strategic in this context is another way of saying, "We are going to lose money, but I want to do it anyway."

I was once in China evaluating a megaproject one of my Western clients wanted to do there. At the end of the first day with the business team, I could not see any way that the venture could be profitable. When I said that, they immediately shot back, "This project is strategic!" So I quizzed them about what that really meant, and it finally came down to this: "Yes, we may lose some money on this project, but the Chinese will be grateful and it will pay dividends later." So I asked them two questions: (1) "Who exactly are 'the Chinese,' as it is a country of 1.5 billion people, and (2) are you aware of a single instance in 4,000 years of recorded Chinese history in which 'the Chinese' had been grateful to a bunch of Westerners for losing money in China?" They built the project, they lost money, and they have never done another project in China.

Comparative Advantage Defines Business Objectives

Comparative advantage exists when a company can uniquely do something of value better than others and can hold that position over time. The key reason for defining comparative advantage is that comparative advantage is what will come to define the business objectives for the project. If we gain comparative advantage with the project because the long-term prospects for business are excellent and we are in first, then the objectives will need to mirror the permanent presence in the area by, for example, including objectives around community relations and community development. If comparative advantage is generated with low feedstock costs, the objectives must be consistent with maintaining a low cost of goods sold (COGS) throughout the supply chain for the project. Otherwise, the low-cost feedstock advantage will be lost in other areas. If comparative advantage is to be generated by being the first to develop in this geography, this will ultimately translate to a time objective for the business objectives and a schedule objective for the project and a larger program of projects will need to be developed and followed through realization of the full advantage.

Comparative advantage becomes the core of a bundle of business objectives that will ultimately translate to project objectives into the complexion of the finished project. If you are not clear about what generates the comparative advantage, the business objectives will not reflect all that is important or the priorities among the many objectives that make up a project.

Clear and coherent business objectives are one of the principal drivers of megaproject success. Clear business objectives drive project

Figure 4.2
Clarity of Objectives Drives Success

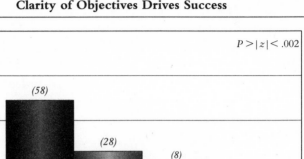

success in a number of ways. The relationship between the clarity of the business objectives as laid out to the core project team is shown in Figure 4.2. As shown in the first bar, clarity of objectives does not guarantee success, but the lack of a high degree of clarity almost guarantees failure.

Figure 4.2 is generated from project directors' answers to a request to rate the clarity of the business objectives from which they were developing the front end of the project. The numbers in parentheses indicate the percentage of the sample in each group. Of the 58 percent of projects in which the project directors rated the objectives as "very clear," almost half of the projects were successful. As soon as the objectives were not rated best, the percentage of projects succeeding drops off dramatically. The probability that the pattern shown would occur randomly is very low.*

Business Objectives Drive the Project

Unclear business objectives trigger a cascade of pathologies in the project. Unclear objectives are strongly associated with the project

---

*Using a z-score probability based on logit regression for dichotomous dependent variable.

Table 4.3
Clear Business Priorities Improve Team Functionality

Is Condition Below Met? Percentage Answering "Yes"	When Trade-Offs Are Clear	When Trade-Offs Are Unclear
All needed functions are on the team	68	43
Target dates have been established	88	64
Roles and responsibilities are defined for team	82	69
A documented schedule exists	93	78

team not understanding project priorities regarding cost versus schedule versus operability. When business objectives were rated as very clear, 80 percent of the project teams said they basically understood the priorities among cost, schedule, and operability. When any fuzziness was noted ("fairly clear"), the percentage of project teams understanding the trade-offs desired dropped to 59 percent, and when the business objectives were described by the project director as "somewhat clear," only 25 percent thought they knew how to set priorities.*

Understanding the trade-offs among outcomes is essential for effective project management. How much money should we spend to gain a month of time? How valuable is flexibility in production rates? These trade-offs guide key focus areas and the building of an effective project team. Lack of clarity around business priorities cripples project management. Table 4.3 shows the relationship between understanding business priorities and some very basic measures of team functionality.†

A team is much less likely to have all of the needed functions represented on the team during front-end development when the trade-offs are unclear. Actually, the causality flows the other way: Teams that are missing key functions—usually the business and/or operations function—are much less likely to understand the trade-offs because those functions are essential to articulating the trade-offs. When

---

*The relationship between the rating of business objectives and clarity of the outcomes trade-off is significant (x^2) at less than .0001.
†All differences are statistically significant (x^2) at .05 or less.

priorities are not clear, the team has difficulty establishing target dates for key activities and is less likely to have established team roles and responsibilities—the most basic of team development activities.

The Business/Project Team Interface Requires Attention

Successful megaprojects require an extraordinary degree of trust, cooperation, and communication between the business sponsoring the project and the technical functions developing and executing the project. Too often, we encounter the exact opposite. Project team entreaties to fully understand what the business is trying to accomplish are treated as a challenge to business prerogatives. Requests for the economic model of the project are sometimes treated as a threat to confidentiality. And protests that the objectives appear blatantly conflictive are classed as whining. The all-too-frequent result is that project teams are attempting to meet business expectations they do not fully understand.

The interactions between the business and the core project team, especially the project director and direct reports, are critically important during the shaping process. Too often the business professionals pursue the commercial aspects of the venture, the project team pursues the engineering aspects of the venture, and the two streams fail to align. The business leadership and project leadership need to be inseparable until the shaping process is closed and the scope development is complete. Good alignment means full and complete access to business information by the core project team and project information by the core business team. It means models are shared, progress and setbacks are honestly shared, and at the end of the day success is shared. It means that the business director and project director report project progress and problems up the ladder together without any possibility of shifting blame.

Team Development Depends on Clear Objectives

We must not overlook the psychological dimension to the relationship between clear business objectives and high-performance teams. If the objectives are unclear, the project leadership's task of building a strong

Figure 4.3
Strong Teams Require Clear Objectives

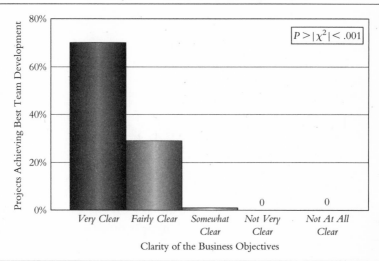

team is hopeless. Figure 4.3 tells a stark story for our megaprojects. When objectives were clear, projects achieved a "best" rating on IPA's team development index (TDI) 70 percent of the time.* When there was any fuzziness around the objectives, the chances of developing a strong team were very poor indeed.

We should not be surprised by this result. Consider the situation from the prospective team member's point of view. I am being asked to spend a large portion of my career on this project, move at least once, and possibly leave my family for several years and the project leadership can't even explain what the objectives are much less why I should consider them important! The relationship between clear goals and team effectiveness is echoed in virtually every study of team development. Of course, the exact same dynamic applies to the business team.

So if comparative advantage gained via the project is understood and clear business objectives are communicated to the project team, then the next step in the shaping process—identifying the stakeholders and defining the boundaries of the project—can proceed.

---

*The TDI is a weighted index composed of the documentation of project objectives, team composition, a set of questions around assignment of roles and responsibilities to team members and the availability of a structured and documented project work process.

STEP 4: IDENTIFYING AND UNDERSTANDING THE STAKEHOLDERS

We define a stakeholder as any organization or person (in the odd case) that asserts or may assert a claim on the value of the project. Asserting a claim on the value of the project does not necessarily mean that a stakeholder is an owner in any normal sense of the word. When an environmentalist objects to a project's potential effects on the natural environment, he or she is in effect staking a claim on the value of the project. The person wants at least some of the project's value spent on mitigating the effects of the project on the environment. When a community group demands funding for a hospital from the project, they are doing the same. When a politician sees an avenue to votes or support by becoming a claimant on the project, he or she has become a stakeholder. Even the corrupt public official demanding a bribe is a stakeholder and, like any other stakeholder, will have to be addressed, like it or not.

We define a stakeholder as a claimant on value because we see the shaping process for a megaproject as a process of allocating value in a way that renders a project feasible. Stakeholders must be bought in or bought off. Either way, a piece of the value is allocated because nothing is free. Some stakeholders are unable to make a successful claim. Usually, that will be because they are not strong enough politically. However, the sponsors of a project need to understand that anyone who is affected negatively by a project is likely to assert a claim. Furthermore, we live in an age in which information moves so easily that claimants who would have had no voice in the past may be able to find that voice effectively today. The losers will attempt to widen the sphere of conflict until they either fail or create a winning coalition.[5]

It is generally much better to anticipate who the stakeholders are likely to be and devise your approach to them early than to wait until they have developed into implacable opponents of the project. The failure to correctly identify those who will be negatively affected by a project can have tragic consequences, ranging from tens of thousands of cases of bilharzia around African rivers from dam impoundments to destroyed livelihoods in Papua New Guinea due to pollution.[6]

If any third-party projects will be needed for your project, be sure that the sponsors of that effort are included among the stakeholders for your project. Sometimes this will be local or central government bureaus responsible for infrastructure development, such as transportation, water supply, electric power, and the installation of the grid. Sometimes local universities will have a role in the development or certification of part of the scope. They too should be included in the mix. Although it is tempting to try to put these players to the side, it is a mistake.

Identifying all of the stakeholders early and evaluating the size, strength, and realism of their claims in at least a preliminary way are essential steps in sponsor decision making. Knowledge of the stakeholders will inform and guide their strategy toward shaping the project. It may even cause sponsors to withdraw if they believe that the size of the prize cannot justify the number and size of the claims that are sure to be made. Sometimes the strategy will involve passing legislation that defines who is and who is not a stakeholder, or that at least establishes a process in law by which claims can be pursued.*

Many of those making decisions that affect the success and failure of these projects are not acting out of a desire to make the project economically successful. In many cases, that is altogether appropriate behavior given their underlying goals. For example, in some cases (but certainly not all) environmentalists may try to kill a project they believe is too damaging to the environment. Politicians may be interested in maximizing the number of local jobs and economic development at the expense of profitability. Project success is merely instrumental for them; whether sponsors make money is not their concern. In some cases political opposition groups or even nongovernmental organization (NGO) interest groups may want a project to be canceled so that the proceeds of the project will not be available to strengthen the government or provide an avenue for corruption. Non-sponsors often have entirely understandable goals that damage a project's value or even render the project impracticable. That's why

---

*One prominent example of this route was passage of legislation in the United States that made the Supreme Court the court of original jurisdiction for suits opposing the construction of the Trans Alaska Pipeline System, the megaproject that eventually carried oil from the North Slope to market.

sponsors' decision makers need to be very cognizant of the incentive structures of non-sponsor stakeholders.

A final concern: When there is a time constraint for completing the shaping process, one of the stakeholders put that constraint in place for his or her benefit, not yours. Ask yourself, Who controls the rules by which this process will unfold? Obviously, to the greatest possible extent you would like to make the rules, but often that is simply not possible. If you are playing someone else's game, then be sure you understand the rules and carefully assess whether your company can reasonably live with those rules. If your company culture is careful and systematic rather than daring and entrepreneurial, you may not be able to function in an environment in which breakneck speed in decision making is going to be essential.

STEP 5: THINKING ABOUT PARTNERS

Having partners, defined as other formal sponsor-investors in the project, is a bit like having children: it is often rewarding but only occasionally a lot of fun. Usually, your partners are one of the first things you know. If you are partners in a petroleum field lease, for example, you knew your expected partners before the discovery well was drilled because you bid jointly on the lease. If the project involves working with a resource holder, such as a national company, you already know that the resource holder will be a critical partner in the venture. Before making even the most tentative decision about moving forward, some basic partner issues need to be addressed.

- What kind of partnership is this (probably) going to be? If you wish to be the lead or operating partner, do your partners accept you in that role? Do they get actively engaged in projects in which they are not the lead operator? Is this project big enough/ prominent enough that they will require direct involvement this time? It is generally preferable to have a lead partner in a venture because it simplifies decision making, at least a bit. The worst arrangement is to have three or more equal partners; then decisions tend to get made by committee slowly. A dual 50/50 partnership is workable as long as the companies are compatible in terms of project outlook.

- What does your partner want/need out of the project? Partners can want all sorts of things. If they are host government company partners, they may need a whole set of social objectives met by the project. How they will be met is likely to become an issue for the partnership. Private sector partners also have mixed objectives, by which I mean things other than just money. For example, they may want to understand/acquire/steal your technological expertise. Is that going to be acceptable to you? Partners do not have to derive value from the same aspects of a project, but they have to derive value from the same result for the project. If they do, the goals are complementary; if they get value from a different result only, a collision is inevitable.

- Does your partner have an (equity) interest in a competing project or in a venture that will be a supplier to your project? This is a recurring problem in petroleum production projects. Your partner may own a production platform adjacent to your planned project into which production might be tied. Or your partner may own interests in adjacent fields that are competing for customers, which is a particular problem for natural gas projects. Your partner may own or have an interest in an engineering and construction firm that they want employed on the project. Conflicts of interest can abound!

- Who is the champion of the project within the partner organization? How well positioned are they? Are there opponents to the project within the partner organization? (If you don't know, start devising a strategy for finding out.)

- What are your partner's capabilities to assist in the project? This can be critically important if your resources are thin. But it can also be a source of enormous risk for the project if you are relying on the partner's resources and they turn out not to actually have the capabilities they have promised. This is a very common problem with local partners who will "smooth the way with the host governments." When the relationship is just forming, it is easy for them to promise things that will be very difficult to deliver later on.

- What is your partner's approach to capital projects? Is it compatible with yours? For example, does your partner have an approach to front-end development and definition that is compatible with yours? Is your partner going to be willing to pay for the FEL work that you insist is necessary for a successful project? Does your partner want to contract everything on a whole project, fixed-price basis, whereas you prefer reimbursable?

- Is your partner's cash flow constrained? Is your partner going to be able to easily fund his or her portion, including overruns, or will financing be needed? Is your partner able to borrow from commercial banks?
- Is there balance and consistency between your role, your risks, and your potential returns and those of the partner?
- Finally, if your partner has a history in the country, how is the partner viewed by the host governments and, if relevant, by the will-be neighbors of your project? If the reputation is poor, you may want to look elsewhere for a partner or get your partner as far in the background as possible.

Partners are supposed to be a way of laying off some of the risk on a project, not the source of added risk. When you can choose, choose wisely.

At this point, you have as much information as you are likely going to get to devise your shaping strategy. You have a good grasp of the context for the project. If all goes reasonably well, you have an understanding of how much value the project could produce overall. More important, you have a clear understanding of why this project is the right one for your company. All of the stakeholders, who are claimants for some portion of your project's value, have been identified, and you have learned as much about their motives and goals as possible. And finally, you have thought about your partners who will be investing in the effort with you. Before moving on to fashion your strategy and execute the shaping process, there is just one more topic to consider: money.

Finance

Early in the shaping process the lead sponsor must address the issue of where all the money will come from. If the lead sponsor *or any partner* will need to seek bank financing, this introduces a new set of issues, and these issues need to be addressed earlier rather than later.

If all of the sponsors have strong balance sheets and one or more simply want to increase their gearing with the project, financing may be reasonably straightforward, although in my experience it will still be late. If one or more of the sponsors have weak balance sheets, the inability to finance the project may be a killer, at least to that sponsor.

When the banks' guarantee of the loan is the project itself without the ability of the banks to attach other corporate assets, that is, nonrecourse financing, then the banks will have a considerable say in how the project will be developed and executed. And that's the problem. In my experience, bankers know less about major capital projects than any other group of humans on the planet, including lawyers. Quite understandably, bankers seek to take on as little risk as possible when they lend money for a project. But their behavior often ultimately leads to much higher costs without any corresponding decrease in project risk. Bankers almost always seek to force EPC lump-sum contracting on the project, regardless of the contracting market situation, because they believe that a lump-sum contract imposes a ceiling on what the project will cost. Except in periods of very low demand for EPC services, attempted risk transfer on megaprojects via lump-sum contracting is expensive in terms of the bids received and ineffective in terms of actual risk transferred.

The banks do focus—as they should—on the cash flows that will be generated by the project. However, they need to focus on the core elements of risk to project execution when they fund. Those risk elements are discussed extensively in Part Three of this book when we discuss the Basic (technical) Data, project teams, and project preparation (front-end loading). We return to the issues of risk transfer via contracts in Chapter 11.

Finally, financing usually is a very slow process. It takes the banks time to syndicate the loan, and a good deal of negotiation about the details of the loan agreements may occur. An agreement in principle between the sponsor(s) and the banks should be in place before shaping closes. Once the project moves into FEL-3 the rate of spending will increase dramatically and the funding to actually execute the project needs to be ensured, even though the first tranche will not occur until a year or more later.

CHAPTER 5

DEVISING THE SHAPING STRATEGY

$\mathbf{A}$s I talk with business leaders of projects that have bogged down in the shaping process, I am often struck when they say things like, "We need to put together a game plan for getting this thing going." I think, but try not to say too often, how much easier it would have been if they had put that game plan together two years ago before the effort landed in this mess! The shaping strategy is your "game plan" for getting this idea turned into a project with a real scope and one that is ready to be authorized.

Now, imagine yourself as the lead project executive on a megaproject that is just getting put together by your company. It's a first-time assignment for you and a big opportunity. You finally persuaded your frugal (read "cheap") boss to spend some money on the country advance team, and they have given you a good reading on the project context. We have an idea of what this venture could be worth overall and a pretty clear idea of why we want to do it and what the business objectives will be. We have cast our net to understand who the players will be, and we have resigned ourselves to dealing with a difficult set of partners.

How do we lay out a process that will help us understand (1) where we are at any particular point in the development of the project; (2) what critical activities, decisions, commitments, or events have not happened; and (3) how all this should be synchronized with our usual project work process?

A good deal of what determines how clear the shaping process is going to be is the strength of the institutional environment for business in general and capital projects in particular. When the institutional context is very strong, for example, petroleum development in the Norwegian or UK North Sea, what needs to be done to negotiate the process is clear. That does *not* necessarily mean that the path will be easy. If your particular project poses extraordinary environmental risks, for example, the strong institutional environment may actually hurt your chances of getting the project approved. If your project falls outside permissible boundaries, the answer may well be a polite, but firm, no. When institutional environments are weak, everything is negotiable. Although that may appeal to the entrepreneur, it also poses real problems.

CONCEPTUALIZING SHAPING

The goals of shaping are to arrive at a point in time when the following have been accomplished:

- All of the stakeholders—claimants on project value—are either content with their allocation from the project or have been rendered unimportant; that is, they are no longer stakeholders.
- The project environment has been stabilized sufficiently so that you will not be fighting battles and skirmishes with disgruntled stakeholders while trying to execute the project.
- With these things accomplished, there is still sufficient value in the project for your firm that your board will ratify going forward without qualification.

There are several different ways of conceptualizing the process you will have to follow. In the simple case with a strong institutional environment, a straightforward partner situation (including no partners), and no nongovernmental organization (NGO) opposition, the shaping process can be viewed as a game against nature.[1] In a game against nature, there are no other players who are intent on either blocking you or taking some, or all, of your share of the spoils; rather, the problems you confront are random, not purposive. For example, if you carefully follow the prescribed rules, you will receive your permits in a timely and predictable fashion. When you play games against nature, you should fail only if you encounter very bad luck.

The most common megaprojects shaped in a game against nature are petroleum development projects in areas with very strong institutional environments. For example, for petroleum development projects in the U.S. Gulf of Mexico and in most of the North Sea, allocation of ownership rights among partners rarely arises as an issue. Ownership rights, and usually the issue of who can be the lead operator, have been decided as part of the bidding process for leased blocks. Although governments are the resource owners, they rarely exercise their ownership rights in the form of renegotiating the allocation of rewards and in most cases would find themselves blocked by the court systems if they attempted to make retroactive changes in provisions. Sadly, many megaprojects for which shaping was a game against nature did in fact fail. But they usually failed for reasons outside the shaping process.

In the more difficult (and interesting) cases, imagining oneself in a game against nature is a recipe for disaster. When a project has active opponents or partners vying for more and the allocation of project value is at stake, the sponsors find themselves engaged in a set of often complex negotiations, complete with threats, promises, feints, and posturing. Mostly, the game is a mixed conflict/cooperation game. Only occasionally will the game be zero-sum, which is one where every gain for me is an equal loss for others; it is a pure conflict game. In some cases, shaping is a zero-sum game against those who oppose the project under all circumstances. These may be unhappy neighbors opposing your project in their backyard. It may be environmental groups who cannot see how your project could be made acceptable in any way.

If you are in a zero-sum game with strong, well-resourced opponents, the usual course is to try to transform the game into one of cooperation by making changes to the project that seek to accommodate their concerns. If this is not possible and the opponents are strong, the size of the prize will have to be quite large for continuation of the effort to make sense. Sometimes you lose; it is best to do so gracefully.

The more common situation is one in which all of the stakeholders want the project to go forward under some circumstances, but the issue is what those circumstances should be.* When that is the case,

---

*There are certainly instances in which some of the stakeholders do not want the project to go forward under any circumstances. That renders the shaping game zero-sum vis-à-vis those stakeholders, and the goal may be to neutralize (defeat) them rather than placate.

you are playing a conflict-cooperation game. You are in a negotiating situation that may range from straightforward to very complex. In our experience, the key to success consists of creating an intellectual framework that is made up of milestones for commitments, kill criteria, closure criteria, and close coordination of project progress with the shaping framework milestones.

The various sponsors and other stakeholders must agree about what constitutes progress toward a deal. It may be, for example, a formula that governs pricing arrangements. Very often, the government approval process is used to provide milestones for sponsors. The environmental permitting process often provides the milestones for the NGOs. Agreement in principle by a bank for syndication of loans may be a milestone for sponsors. For some projects, liquefied natural gas (LNG), for example, sales agreements covering a certain portion of the output may signal a key milestone.

As the lead sponsor, you have to establish what needs to happen by when, as well as what the consequences will be if the date passes and nothing has happened. It is in this context that careful alignment between the project's development and shaping development is critical. The overall deal—that is, the allocation of value among all the stakeholders—must control the engineering scope of the project. If the scope development gets out in front of the shaping development, it is likely that the scope development work will turn out to be incorrect. As more and more project money is spent without a deal, the sponsors paying the bill will find themselves falling into the forward-going economics trap: we have invested so much in this thing that we can't turn back now.

A common ploy used by some resource holders to entice investor sponsors into development is to try to remove any decision points in the development process until the full-funds sanction point. At that point, 3 to 5 percent of eventual total cost may have been spent, and another 10 to 15 percent has been committed, some which would be lost if the venture is canceled. A large number of sponsor-investors' people have been working on the project for many months, and expectations may have been formed in the financial community that the project will go forward. Withdrawing from the project at this point will likely be a serious embarrassment to the sponsor-investor.

This tactic seeks to create a closure point for the shaping process that is later than most sponsor-investors would prefer. The tactic makes withdrawal from the project expensive. We have seen this tactic used a number of times, but we have yet to see it work from the resource holder's point of view. The sponsor-investor either insists that an interim closure point be established or ends up withdrawing after front-end engineering design (FEED), with all of the associated costs.

KILL CRITERIA

One of the questions I routinely ask business leaders and project directors during the shaping phase of a megaproject is what would cause them to pull the plug on the project. Even after years of receiving the answer, I am shocked when the response is, "Nothing. This project is going forward!" Of course, part of this response is just cheerleading and bravado, but it also tells me that the sponsor has not carefully thought through the minimum necessary conditions for the project.

It really isn't a question of whether there *are* kill criteria for the project; there always are points beyond which no potential sponsor will go. The real question is whether you have worked through what the killer issues are and whether you have shared those with all members of your negotiating team.* To convey to other stakeholders that you will proceed no matter what sends a message that you are willing to take whatever they decide to leave you.

ACHIEVING FINAL CLOSURE

Final closure occurs when the stakeholders are satisfied with the configuration of the deal and project and agree to proceed with final definition and execution. The closure may or may not be accompanied by a signature ceremony or some other ritual. Except where the institutional environment is strong, a ceremony closing the shaping phase is probably a good idea.

---

*The project professionals working on the development of the scope of the project must also be privy to this information. If you are communicating to all that the project will go forward "no matter what," that (lack of) position will leak to the other stakeholders.

In weak institutional environments, reaching an enforceable closure point is often difficult. This is one reason why weak institutional environments are inherently economically inefficient. The problem is not so much agreement—it is whether the agreement means anything. In some situations, as often happens in China, for example, a written agreement (a contract) is merely a document that defines the minimum that you will bring to the deal. The other side doesn't feel bound in the slightest, and because the institutional environment is weak, that piece of paper is enforceable against you only.

A deal is enforceable only if the other side believes that you will walk away if that agreement is not honored. In several cases among the projects in our database, this meant that the lead sponsor halted all work on the project and demobilized its team to send the message that the failure to reach closure is not acceptable or that the breach of the closure agreement will not pass. Some companies have developed enviable reputations for their willingness to immediately walk away at any attempt to breach the closure agreement. For example, ExxonMobil's decision not to agree to the Venezuelan government's demand that they renegotiate the ownership and financial terms of the Cerro Negro "association" joint venture and to take Venezuela to court sends the message to others considering similar action that a price will be paid. The more one develops a reputation for being willing to walk away, the less often situations will arise. Some companies have developed reputations of being vacillating and unsure, which means an attempt to get more at the last minute may well pay off. It is worth a lot to a company to develop a reputation of "saying what you mean and meaning what you say," both verbally and in the contracts that it executes.[2]

When dealing with government stakeholders in weak institutional frameworks, the most important enforcement mechanism for closure agreements is reputation. A reputation for not abiding by agreements increases the risk profile of investment in the country and makes future investors demand higher returns. When then Russian President Vladimir Putin used an environmental permit pretext for forcing Royal Dutch Shell to relinquish a large portion of its equity in the Sakhalin-2 Project to Gazprom, he reminded every global investor that the institutional environment in Russia remains weak. When Hugo Chavez expropriated the heavy oil ventures in Venezuela, he thereby increased the cost to Venezuela of future investment. Because reputation is valuable to governments as well as private firms, the smart sponsor may wish to be sure that the closure of a deal for a venture and its terms are well publicized. By doing so, the cost to the other side of reneging is increased.

REAL OPTIONS: ANOTHER WAY OF THINKING ABOUT SHAPING

Thinking about megaproject shaping as a mixed conflict-cooperation game and creating a framework and scenarios (moves) for playing the game is a strong and perhaps necessary way of thinking. There is, however, an alternative or additional method borrowed from the world of finance: real options and real options analysis (ROA). It is not my purpose here to attempt a discourse on ROA, but I will briefly describe it and the reader can pursue study *ad libitum*. Unlike Miller and Olleros,[3] I doubt that a rigorous application of ROA is feasible or even the right approach to shaping. I am suggesting that the core idea of real options captures some of the key elements in a successful shaping process.

A real option is a right to do something or decide something at a later point.* One has to pay for real options—nothing is free, and the point at which the option is to be exercised is defined—in our previous parlance, a milestone. ROA is an approach to valuation that explicitly treats and incorporates uncertainty and recognizes that uncertainty changes over time. Traditional valuation techniques, such as net present value (NPV) and discounted cash flow (DCF) rate of return, fix uncertainty for valuation purposes. ROA produces a tentative expected NPV but allows one to adjust one's view of project risk at each real option point.[4]

The appeal of this approach to making shaping decisions should be obvious. It demands that we establish decision points with the creation of options, and it acknowledges that circumstances change as

---

*The biggest difference between a real option and a financial option is that the latter can be traded, whereas the former cannot. This is important because when something is traded in markets, its value is thereby assigned. Valuing a real option, which by its nature cannot be traded, is much more difficult and subjective. That means you can "overpay" for a real option and you can undervalue and therefore be unwilling to pay a "fair" price as well. Tradable options cost what they cost.

we progress. A project that looked excellent when we started may look quite anemic when that first option (milestone) comes due and our chances of securing our mining permit (or whatever) look bleak. Even better, ROA is all about buying information. An option, after all, is a statement that "I am not yet ready to decide; I need more information." As outlined right at the outset of this section, shaping must be viewed in that context if it is to be successful. The key aspect of an option is its expiration date. The expiration date for a shaping option is what I call a "kill point" and ultimately (we hope) a successful closure point.

I was recently in Manhattan meeting with a couple of investment bankers who were considering supporting a very large new technology energy project. As we were discussing their decision-making process, I said, "It's like a real options exercise," to which one of them replied, "No, it *is* a real options exercise!" Even though ROA is not a common notion for most industrial company personnel, it is a very powerful way of conceptualizing the shaping process. It is worth the effort to learn it.

WHEN SHOULD SHAPING END?

The shaping process comes to final closure when all of the stakeholders—investor sponsors, regulators, NGOs, local organizations, and governments—agree to the project proceeding as planned and outlined. There is no single document or activity that defines the end of shaping in all cases. Sometimes it is a set of formal contracts. Sometimes it is a so-called memorandum of understanding (MOU). It could be a ceremonial handshake. What is critical for a successful closing of the shaping process is that all stakeholders have a common understanding of what the closure means.

Regardless of the activity that signals the end of shaping, things may come unstuck later; the end of shaping is not the end of risk, after all. However, usually the shaping closure agreements do not come unstuck unless the project as outlined is not the project that eventually takes form. For example, if 10 months after shaping is closed, the estimated cost of the project has risen 40 percent, the shaping agreement may well dissolve. If the schedule has slipped two years or the environmental footprint is very different, some of the stakeholders may feel cheated and seek redress. For example, the schedule slippage experienced by the massive Kashagan oil field development in Kazakhstan opened up the project's value allocation for renegotiation. This is why the last step of the shaping process—synchronization with the project process—is so important.

Linking Opportunity Shaping with Project Development

While the business leadership has been busy fashioning this opportunity into a stable deal, the technical teams have been busy as well. One team or set of teams may have been developing the needed Basic Technical Data from the earliest days of the shaping process. Another team has been working on developing the contours of the actual physical scope that will, if all goes well, constitute the project when it is complete. If the effort is being properly managed, all of these teams have been talking to each other very actively and sharing progress and difficulties at every step of the way.

The communication is necessary because the various processes at work affect each other. In complex partnership situations, it is common to withhold resources for the project side while bargaining for better value allocation on the shaping side. Surprises from the Basic Data development may change the understanding of the project's potential value, either up or down, by large amounts. Vitally important, the project work process requires input about the business parameters of the project at certain times or the project work may need to stop; otherwise, it will be working in the wrong direction. For example, if, as a result of the shaping activities, one of the partners sets a cap on the total cost of the project due to financial limitations or other commitments, failing to inform the project team of this is borderline criminal—and it happens all the time.*

---

*I believe the reader will see the appeal of the real options approach to thinking about the shaping process here. Uncertainties about the project are very dynamic during shaping with the expected value of the project changing up and down multiple times. A traditional DCF internal rate of return (IRR)/NPV approach, which is inherently static in each assessment, fails to capture this important part of the process.

Figure 5.1
The Typical Phase and Gated Project Work Process

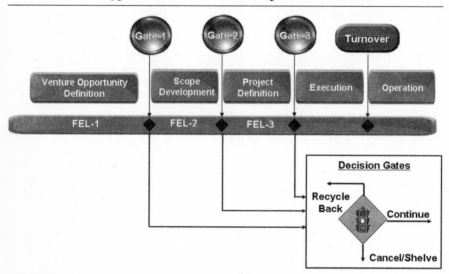

It is helpful when discussing the need to synchronize, and to some extent integrating the shaping and project work processes, to consider that virtually all modern project systems are organized using a work process that consists of a series of stages with a set of defined products ("deliverables" as they are awkwardly called) at the end of each stage. The most common form of this process is shown in Figure 5.1.

The phase prior to the first formal gate is spent trying to define the business opportunity and decide whether a capital project is the appropriate solution to the business need.

One should remember that projects are not the only way to acquire production and manufacturing capability. Merger and acquisition is an alternative; tolling of manufacturing is another alternative. Occasionally, there is even an operating change that can meet a need that would otherwise consume capital. Often, a capital project solution is chosen before nonproject solutions are fully explored.

In well-managed systems, FEL-1 results in a business case package that reflects an assessment of the extent to which a business opportunity actually exists and whether a capital project is the appropriate vehicle for realizing that opportunity. As a typical project passes through Gate 1, a technical team is formed to start the assembly of a project scope that will meet the business requirement as defined in the Gate 1 package. Some of the Phase 1 activities are very similar to the overall shaping process but at a much-reduced scale for most non-megaprojects.

Phase 2 is devoted to scope development. Provided that a business opportunity does in fact exist, Phase 2 is the most important stage in any project's development. If the scope development phase is working correctly, it will also make clear when a business opportunity does not in fact exist. At the end of scope development, conducted appropriately, it is possible to generate a reliable cost estimate and schedule for the project. By *reliable,* we do not mean "highly accurate." Rather, we mean an estimate with a *meaningful* range placed around that most likely value. (We will return to this subject later and attempt to sort out some of the endemic confusion about this topic.) If the project looks attractive economically at the high end of the range, it will likely be approved to enter the third phase of front-end loading: detailed definition and execution planning.

Although Phase 3 is formally part of FEL and full-funds authorization of the project will not be granted until the end of this phase, projects, including megaprojects, are actually approved from a business standpoint at the end of FEL-2. If there is significant real cost growth between the nominal end of FEL-2 and the end of FEL-3, it is almost always due to FEL-2 being inadequate such that significant amounts of scope had not been identified and estimated. In that event the FEL-2 phase has failed, along with the gatekeeping that was supposed to prevent projects that are not fully defined in terms of scope from passing through to FEL-3.

FEL-3 (FEED/feasibility) should take the completed scope and advance the design to a point that all piping and instrumentation diagrams (P&IDs) and electrical single lines are complete. It is during this phase that the execution plan, which was only sketched out at a high level during FEL-2, is brought to completion.

Every lead sponsor of every project examined in this study had a work process similar to the one just very briefly outlined. That is not to say that every project followed such a process, and relatively few followed the process in a way that IPA would describe as best practice. This just underscores the reality that no work process or business system creates advantage; only the disciplined execution of the work process creates advantage. We return to this subject in detail in Chapter 10.

The synchronization of the shaping process with the project work process should ideally proceed in the following way:

- The shaping framework, which the lead business executive for the project has developed with the advice and counsel of all participants, including the country team, the core technical teams, and the corporate management, establishes a set of decision points, milestones, or options points (as you prefer) as discussed earlier in this chapter.

- The business and project core team agree on how far the project work will be allowed to advance, considering each milestone. The usual problem is that the shaping progress lags the project progress, not vice versa. However, either one is a problem.

- The contours of the overall deal need to be available to the core project team when they start their work on Phase 2, scope development. Both financial and time constraints need to be articulated. Artificial time constraints are particularly important because they may render the project undoable or doom it to failure. We will come back to this issue shortly. The contours of the deal then should shape the scope development process.

- The closure of shaping should coincide with the completion of the scope development phase of the front-end loading. Until scope development is complete, shaping closure should not be attempted because the cost of the project is still unknown. Conversely, *until shaping closes, FEL-3 should not commence.* Beginning FEL-3 (FEED, feasibility, define) before shaping is closed will quickly start to affect the relative positions of those involved in the shaping process. For example, if an important government approval was supposed to be granted to close shaping and FEL-3 starts without it, the sponsor-investors are progressively disadvantaged in their negotiations with the government about that approval. They are progressively overcommitted.

- The closure of shaping must also mark the start of *no further changes of scope*. This is necessary for both the business and project sides. Significant changes coming from the project side jeopardize the finality of shaping closure. Significant changes from the business side will cause the work in FEL-3 (FEED) to be seriously disrupted and its quality to decline. If major changes must occur either for business or project reasons after the closing of shaping, the project is at risk, and unless it is materially slowed down at this point, it will surely fail.

The data clearly and strongly support the importance of bringing the business issues to closure in conjunction with the completion of FEL-2. More than 40 percent of our megaprojects had changes in business objective in FEL-3, which means that the shaping process had not closed. Only 22 percent of those projects ended up as successes at the end of the day.*

If thinking about shaping in a real options context, it is critically important to understand that all flexibility in decision making ends with shaping closure. Shaping closure is when the option period expires and a final and essentially irreversible decision to move forward must be made.

How Shaping Errors and Omissions Lead to Failure

Projects fail for reasons having nothing to do with shaping, but not very often. Shaping errors and omissions are the most common root cause of megaproject failure. These errors and omissions fall into five groups, with the fourth one being by far the most common:

1. Failure to achieve full stakeholder alignment
2. Ceding so much value to other stakeholders that the project has no value

---

*The difference in the rate of success is statistically significant at less than .0001 based on the Pearson chi-square.

3. Failure to develop coherent objectives
4. Impracticable cost, schedule, and quality trade-offs
5. Set overly conservative targets

We discuss each of these in turn.

Failure to Achieve Stakeholder Alignment

When the shaping process has not been properly articulated, projects can blow right through the appropriate closure point at the end of FEL-2 without alignment. Sometimes these projects die after FEL-3; sometimes, unfortunately, they are sanctioned. Lack of partner alignment on issues, such as owner staffing, completeness of FEL-3 (FEED), contracting strategy, financing strategy, and schedule, ultimately result in late cancellation of the project or project failure.

The failure to properly identify all of the stakeholders can result in late NGO intervention on environmental or other grounds. In some cases, the failure to identify a set of stakeholders can be tragic as, for example, serious illness for the local population, which was not identified and mitigated.* Sometimes there is a failure to identify the sponsors of "third-party projects" on which your project depends as stakeholders. In one recent example in the Middle East, a third-party project tied up a $5 billion investment for 18 months by being completed late. If the sponsors of the third-party project had been viewed as stakeholders in the larger effort, they would have either been fully incorporated into the project or the project would have been reconfigured to eliminate its dependence on the third-party project.

If there are disgruntled stakeholders in projects, government officials, either politicians or bureaucrats, are the most common. When political or bureaucratic stakeholders are not fully brought into the shaping of the project at the closure point, they have many ways to disrupt your progress. In a recent project in Central Asia, the government withheld a permit while wanting to renegotiate the allocation of value that had long been established and agreed upon with the sponsor-investors.

---

*A particularly sad example of this occurred in a hydroelectric project in Africa that accelerated the growth of a bacterium in the still water in the impoundment that caused widespread blindness in the local population. The sponsors missed the effect because they failed to consult local health officials who were aware of the potential problem. The local population was not viewed as a stakeholder in this regard until enormous damage had been inflicted.

The sponsor-investors finally shut down the entire project just prior to what would have been authorization and disbanded its team in order to bargain credibly with the reneging government. The government finally did relent, and the project went forward; however, the disruption caused by the shutdown, plus a late government change in the local content rules, generated massive overruns.

Ceding Too Much to Others

As discussed earlier, the shaping process has to balance the stability created in the project environment via value allocation with the value created to the sponsor-investors. If a stable project environment comes with too high a price, there is insufficient value left to the sponsor-investors to make a good investment. The analogy that I like to draw is that you are the host at a large dinner party. A beautiful roast of lamb is the centerpiece of the dinner, and you are very much looking forward to enjoying a nice portion of it yourself. Your guests, however, turn out to be a surprisingly hungry lot, and you find yourself cutting slice after slice, handing them along until it is, at last, your turn . . . and only the bone remains.

If running out of lamb were obvious, you could have tried cutting smaller portions. Or you might have simply said, "This isn't going to work." Often, however, the loss of value to you is insidious and will occur in ways you did not anticipate. Let me relate a classic example, which is also a case of local content run amok.

The owner project team had worked with an excellent contractor team to develop the scope of this technically difficult megaproject. The contractor had done an excellent job and brought a good deal of technology know-how to the project. Because the market was softening, the contractor offered an attractive lump-sum price to execute and start up the project. The host government, which was not an equity investor, but a royalty stakeholder, objected that it wanted a local contractor to have an opportunity to bid on the work. (They also made clear that the license extension and royalty relief the sponsor was looking for would depend on the local contractor winning. In other words, they rigged the contest.)

So the project was put out to tender, and two bids came back: one from the FEL contractor and another from the local contractor. The local contractor's tender offer was abysmal. To quote from our closeout report on the project, [the local contractor's] "tendered design was unacceptable for both HSE and operational reasons; it did not even comply with government regulations." And it was higher than the bid of the competent firm. Surprise! The local contractor received the award anyway and proceeded to completely foul up the project: 100 percent cost overrun, 18 months late to mechanical completion, and then it was an operations disaster. Now, you know this sort of thing does happen from time to time in the Third World. But . . . this particular example was in Scandinavia. The business executive who yielded on this critical issue had no idea that he had just given away more than the total value of the project.

Failure to Develop Coherent Objectives

Shaping is a process of successive approximations leading finally to a stable "platform" of stakeholders aligned around a set of understood and coherent objectives. Too often, the sponsor-investor's business leaders do not understand that the process of adjusting objectives must stop at some point. Again, the real options analysis conceptualization of the process is useful. At a *defined* point, the option must be exercised or dropped. That point for projects is the end of scope development (FEL-2). The problem is that all too often, objectives continue to be "improved." (This is one of many examples where business education and capital project effectiveness collide. "Dynamic adjustment of objectives to a changing business environment" sounds nice, but it isn't.) Large projects are by their nature clumsy. Once finally set in motion, they cannot respond rapidly to changes in direction, and attempts to make them do so result in chaos.

Changes in objectives after the end of FEL-2 take many forms, but they are almost always problematic. One project, for example, increased the capacity of an LNG complex by about 10 percent, just prior to sanction, to take advantage of a strong LNG sales market. The change, which was to be made without significant change in design, used up all the design margin in all the facilities. When some of that design margin was needed at startup, the facilities would not operate. The sponsor-investors bled money profusely because all of the output was forward sold on take-or-pay/provide-or-pay contracts. Of the projects that made changes to business objectives during FEL-3, a stunning 82 percent failed. They were significantly poorer in every outcome dimension.*

Impracticable Cost, Schedule, and Quality Trade-Offs

One key product of the shaping process is a constellation of expected results, among which are how much the project will cost, when it will be done, and how much product it will reliably produce over time. As everyone familiar with projects knows, these three outcomes—cost, schedule, and quality—can trade off against each other. The three actually constitute a fairly complex optimization problem, which is complicated by several factors. The three outcomes do not trade smoothly. There are some regions† in which outcomes can be improved without affecting any trade, provided that practices are appropriate. More vexing to the decision maker, the trade-off functions are uncertain, although far from entirely so. And finally, the trade-off functions are different for different projects and at different times. For example, the cost-schedule trade-off is clearly different as a function of market conditions for project inputs.

These targeted results are important because they together establish the expected direct economic value of the project. Obviously, the targets need to be established at points in which all three outcomes are, at least in principle, feasible and, taken together, will constitute a valuable outcome. Unfortunately, this is not always the case.

As discussed earlier in this chapter, DCF rate of return calculations are not particularly useful during the shaping process because it is a period in which uncertainty remains high and flexibility is essential. However, when we reach shaping closure, DCF is useful because maintaining flexibility in the form of making changes has a very high

---

*All differences were statistically significant at .01 or less.
†Regions in the sense of mathematical functions, not geography.

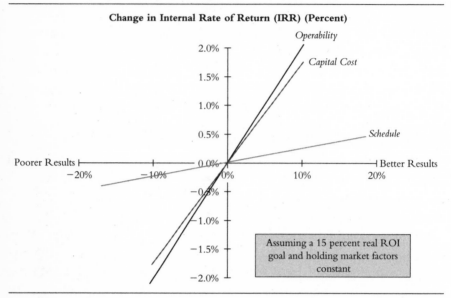

Figure 5.2
Operability and Capital Cost Driver Returns

Change in Internal Rate of Return (IRR) (Percent)

price in megaprojects.* In Figure 5.2, you see the results of a standard DCF model in showing the relative effects of changes in capital cost, schedule, and operability (production).

We selected an inflation-free rate of return of 15 percent because that is about the average long-term return on capital for the commodity industries that do the sorts of megaprojects we are examining. Most of these firms calculate their cost of capital on a risk-free basis from 9 percent for the very strongest to about 11 percent for the typical firm. If the return on investment realized falls below the cost of capital, shareholder wealth is being destroyed by the project. In other words, doing nothing would have been more beneficial than making the investment.

It is important to realize that most megaprojects are relatively low rate-of-return projects. By that I mean they typically aim to earn 4 to

---

*The cost of changes after closure is reached in megaprojects appears much larger than for small projects. Because megaprojects have so many interconnected pieces, changes are very difficult to implement in an efficient way. In megaprojects, we also have the added problem that the shaping agreement among the stakeholders can easily come apart if one of the stakeholder-investors wants to make a change.

8 percent more than the cost of capital. There are exceptions, such as oil projects in countries like the United States with low royalty and tax regimes. In general, smaller projects have more potential to be high-return projects. They are more flexible, they can be completed faster, and they can be reconfigured more easily. The great business purpose of megaprojects is to produce large cash flows. Even though the returns are relatively low, the NPV is large because of the size of the investment. Cash flow from megaprojects funds smaller higher-return projects.

Referring to Figure 5.2, you see that the most leveraging outcome is production. Production is actually even more leveraging than it appears here because we cannot easily parameterize the losses associated with higher maintenance and "fix-it" projects that are needed when operability is poor. It should not be surprising that operability is the most leveraging result. After all, a project that produces at half the intended rate has effectively doubled its capital cost per unit of product, and the operating costs may have gone up even more.

What may be more surprising to some readers, especially business professionals, is the modest effect of schedule—either acceleration or slip—on the rate of return. Capital cost is actually considerably more important to the rate of return than the amount of time needed to execute the project. What this does not show, of course, is that the value of schedule changes as the project progresses. When the project is approaching completion, schedule becomes quite important to the returns because almost all of the investment is in place and earning nothing. But the value of schedule in the early days is extremely modest because almost none of the investment has yet been made.

The elements of schedule value that cannot be shown on a chart like that in Figure 5.2 are the effect of commercial agreements. Schedule promises have some value when forward-selling product in competitive situations. Once product has been forward sold, the cost of being late can be quite substantial. That means that the downside of making delivery promises that cannot be met or cannot be met without substantially higher investment costs is very large.

Note also how leveraging capital cost is. A 10 percent increase in the capital cost of the project decreases the return from 15 to 13.25 percent. This means that with 30 percent cost growth, our investment returns less than 10 percent, which means that the NPV is likely negative.

Setting Overly Conservative Targets

Sometimes targets are set so conservatively that value of the project is hugely diminished from the outset. This occurs when sponsors are extremely risk averse with respect to cost and schedule overruns. These megaprojects are most common in the Middle East among national companies.* For cultural and historical reasons, poor outcomes vis-à-vis promises are viewed extremely negatively within the sponsoring companies. As a result, all risks associated with cost, schedule, and often even operability† are transferred to the engineering, procurement, and construction (EPC) contractors. During periods when project input markets are soft (buyers' markets), these projects are successful, even though they are generally 10 to 15 percent above industry average cost and 10 to 20 percent slower than average. In heated markets, the contractors require such large premiums to accept the transfer of risk that these projects end up as failures on our cost–competitiveness measures. We discuss the reasons that wholesale risk transfer to contractors is economically inefficient in Chapter 11.

MISGUIDED TRADE-OFFS

Cases like those described earlier in this chapter are relatively rare and mostly confined to a few locales. The much more common problem with the configuring of targeted outcomes is that one or more of the targets is set so aggressively that the project is more or less bound to end up being a major disappointment. There are four forms of these misconfigured projects:

1. Quality is sacrificed for low cost.
2. Cost is sacrificed for fast schedules.
3. Quality is sacrificed for fast schedules.
4. Safety is sacrificed for speed.

---

*The national companies may be using discount rates that are much lower than their commercial counterparts, in which case the projects remain NPV positive even while overspending by large amounts. That does not, however, in any way mitigate the loss of sponsor-investor value associated with the economically inefficient risk transfer.

†In the form of a "turnkey" contract in which the contractor is responsible for starting up the facilities and achieving the intended production rates.

Sacrifice Quality for Cost

Trading poor quality, which translates into poor production relative to plan, for lower capital cost is almost always unintentional. It is not, however, truly accidental. Trading quality for low cost is usually an unintended by-product of accepting a very low lump-sum bid. There are many examples of this kind of trade-off in the database, often involving government-owner situations in which taking the low bid is a legal necessity. This sort of trade-off is not supposed to happen if you do things properly: prequalify the bidders, allow only bidders who can actually handle the risk they are taking on, and so forth. But, in fact, winning in such situations is very problematic.

Let me cite an example—and I select this one because the project team did everything correctly, and the result was still poor. This was a joint venture project in the Middle East with a U.S. firm taking the leadership role. Four bids were received from four of the biggest and most competent EPC contractors in the world. The lowest bid was $175 million less than the other three bids, which were tightly grouped. There was no legal requirement to accept the low bid. The schedule from the lowest bidder was also four months faster than each of the other bids, the owners' schedule, and our benchmark. After selection but before award, the lead sponsor offered a longer schedule to the winning contractor, who demurred that it was not necessary. The sponsor set the onset of liquidated damages later than the contractor stipulated anyway because the project director and all of our benchmarks said the project could not be done on the contractor's schedule. The project director warned the business that the bid was too low to be real, but the business leadership overruled the project director's preference to take one of the other bidders.

A couple of months into execution, the contractor realized they had made a horrendous estimating error. The estimate was originally prepared based on their home office location and then would be translated to the Middle East setting. (This is normal-enough procedure.) The translation of the estimate to the Middle East in terms of hours required never occurred, although the wage rates were adjusted. The effect was that the estimate was 16 million field hours short. That single error explained the schedule difference, as well as the cost difference. So what ensued?

First, the contractor's project leader quit. He did not want his career sullied by a bad project. Second, knowing they were in a huge loss position, the contractor cut every corner imaginable. The owner's controls organization was excellent, but they had no hope of catching everything. Equipment and engineered bulk materials were sourced from incompetent, but low-cost, vendors. Engineering costs were reduced by farming out some of the utility work to other firms. Despite the fact that there were performance guarantees, startup took 20 months, and finally a major fix-it project was necessary to make the facility run adequately. It will never be a good-quality facility.

They "saved" the $175 million. They didn't pay the contractor anything more because they made no changes that would open up that opportunity. But at the end of the day, they lost several times that $175 million and didn't meet their customers' demands either. The project was mechanically complete right on the benchmark schedule, four months late.

One of my reviewers reminded me that he had a megaproject that looked very much like the preceding example, save for one critical difference: they put enough money in their authorization to make the contractor whole. They then allowed the contractor to increase costs to ensure that the right people were put on the job. It was completed slightly below their internal estimate (and our benchmark) with excellent quality and safety. They had also made a friend of the contractor for many years to come. Cost and value are not always the same thing.

Sacrifice Cost for Schedule

The most common misconfiguration is trading cost for schedule. Referring back to Figure 5.2, you can see that in the normal case, one would have to gain more than 5 percent schedule advantage for every 1 percent of added capital to be return on investment neutral. However, for many reasons, most of them bad, this is not how businesses tend to see the cost-schedule trade-off.

In the normal course of things, when a project experiences a large real cost overrun, it overruns its schedule substantially as well. The reason is that most large overruns are caused by the discovery of considerably more work to do than expected, which takes time. Those relatively few projects that collapsed in the field are normally associated with slips in schedule as well.

However, more than 20 percent of the failed projects combined large overruns (more than 25 percent in real terms) with very little schedule slippage. These projects averaged an overrun of 51 percent of their authorization estimates while slipping execution schedule by a mere 5 percent. Almost 90 percent of these projects were oil developments, far more than would be expected from a random draw. These projects threw heaps of money at the schedules.

There are several forces at work encouraging oil projects to behave this way. In a few cases there were weather windows that meant that slipping installation by more than a month or so would result in a slip of six to eight months because installation during the winter season is not possible. In another couple of cases, the scheduling of installation vessels was so difficult that, again, a very long delay would have resulted if the project missed its tow-out and installation date. Most of the cases, however, result from the strange, even perverse, structuring of many oil leases and concessions with national resource holders.

Two types of contracts distorted outcomes. One involves lease concessions that are too short to develop the petroleum resource in a way that would maximize the total value from the reservoirs. When a company is given a 15-year concession to develop a resource that would take 25 years to develop optimally, it wants to spend as little time as possible on the project development and execution and as much time as possible in production. The sponsor-investor is therefore willing to overspend substantially to get the production started if they believe it can be done faster with a higher spend. Ironically, for reasons described in the next trade-off area, the breakneck speed often results in very poor production rates relative to plan. We also strongly suspect that these arrangements sometimes result in attempts to produce oil so rapidly that the reservoirs are permanently damaged and the eventual total recovery is reduced.

The second type of distorting concession agreement involves repaying the sponsor-investors' capital immediately from the proceeds of production in a way that makes capital nearly free. This produces a tendency to overcapitalize in much the same way that public utilities that earn returns on their capital rate base are known to overcapitalize.[5]

The effect can be quite extreme, inducing companies to spend much more than necessary to develop the resource while effecting large wealth transfers from the resource holder to the developers.

These deals involve a shaping allocation that increases the value generated to sponsor-investors while reducing the amount of total value created. The residents of the resource-holding countries lose a great deal in these sorts of arrangements. These arrangements could make economic sense only if the social discount rates of the resource holders were much higher than those of the sponsor-investors. However, quite the opposite should be true.* Generally, private sector investors need a higher return than governments do to be willing to make investments. Public sector investors have objectives, such as jobs creation or security enhancement, that have no value for private sponsors.

Sacrifice Quality for Schedule

Like sacrificing quality for cost, this result is almost always unintended because it degrades the asset value substantially. It is, however, very common. The desired schedule outcome is one of the products of the shaping process. The schedule strategy is generally among the first outcome "fixed" in the shaping process, generally in the form of "production will commence the first of December _____ (year)." In other words, they will decide when they will start producing before they have figured out what "it" is! Schedules developed in this way have only one thing in common: They are almost always too short to get all of the needed work completed.

Under these circumstances, there are several paths to quality degradation. One is that the front-end loading schedule is so rushed that the scope is not appropriate and the project suffers operability problems. Sometimes execution is so rushed that corners are cut to meet a first-production date target. But the most common problem is that some of the background technical data, which are essential to correct design, are never fully developed. As we discuss in Chapter 7, incorrect Basic Data create problems from which it is usually impossible to recover.

---

*Of course, the discount rates of government officials making the deals may well be extremely high.

Speed Kills Projects

The drive for unattainable speed in megaproject development and execution is a symptom of serious pathology in the modern industrial firm. It has been responsible for the sheer vaporization of hundreds of billions of dollars of shareholder wealth. That speed destroys megaprojects has been widely known within the IPA customer community for many years. And yet the push to develop and execute these projects too quickly has seen no relief. If many industrial firms aspire to be learning organizations, there is precious little evidence of it here.

There are a number of compelling reasons that megaprojects cannot be effectively speeded up, which we discuss in detail in later chapters of this book. What I want to discuss here is why the drive for speed continues despite the overwhelming evidence that it destroys project outcomes.

One reason surely is ignorance on the part of the business decision makers who control the shaping process for megaprojects. They simply do not understand why these projects are fragile and why speed kills the projects because they lack enough knowledge of how these projects work that they are unable to "connect the dots." This reason, of course, simply begs the question of why those who are ignorant of the process are in charge or why they fail to listen to those who do understand how the projects work. I believe that in order to explain the ignorance, one has to look at the dramatic weakening of technical expertise and influence within industrial firms in the past 30 years.

Starting in the early 1980s, we saw a systematic dismantling of technical organizations inside industrial firms, first in the United States and later throughout the Organization for Economic Cooperation and Development (OECD). There is no doubt in my mind that the technical functions needed reformation. Rather than being reformed, however, they were largely dismantled. Outsourcing of technical expertise was sold by consultants, business schools, and contractors as a modern and necessary approach to making the industrial firm leaner and less subject to cyclical swings.

The 1990s made outsourcing seem viable. This was a decade of very low spending on capital projects. The oil industry was depressed by very low petroleum prices. A huge capacity overhang depressed minerals spending, and the chemical industry continued to be highly cyclical with prices overall trending down. The result was a period of overcapacity in engineering and construction management services throughout the OECD area. The companies were also left with a residuum of very talented and experienced baby boomers. The result is that projects, even large projects, did not suffer too much during this period. But there was in most companies almost no renewal of technical personnel with young people. When there were demands for unachievable speed in large projects, the technical organizations used to be strong enough to say no. Now you do so at your peril.

Ultimately, the problem comes down to a simple matter of a lack of accountability. Business executives who set in motion a process that will destroy huge amounts of shareholder wealth are rarely held accountable for their errors and omissions. In the usual case, not the extraordinary one, the executive that championed a bad project at the outset has been promoted out of any line of responsibility and accountability for the poor result long before the depth of the problems becomes known. This same lack of accountability for long-term results is the curse of the modern corporation. It goes to the heart of corporate governance. The relationship between governance and megaprojects is the subject of the next section.

Sacrificing Safety for Speed: Speed Kills People Too   Not one of the 150 industrial firms for which IPA works would admit to sacrificing anything for safety, often not even to themselves. Yet many of them do actually sacrifice safety quite regularly, and it is almost always for speed, not for cost. Almost all of our customers are willing to pay to improve safety, and most consider the costs a good investment. But it is actually the drive for speed that causes most accidents and injuries both directly and indirectly. Speed causes accidents directly by making the construction workforce less sensitive to safety protocol and hazards. Speed increases the amount of construction rework, and rework is known to be much less safe on average than primary tasks because it is often unplanned work. The drive for speed is associated with long work hours, and fatigue is a primary precursor to accidents.

When speed is of prime concern, the underlying foundation of a safe project is put at risk because project preparation suffers. Statistically, the largest driver of accidents is poor front-end loading, which means poor preparation to execute the project. It means more undisciplined and chaotic work sites. It means more people will be injured or killed to create the company's capital assets.

AN EXAMPLE OF SUCCESSFUL OPPORTUNITY SHAPING

The project consisted of three large pieces: a new metals processing complex, a new port, and the utilities infrastructure. The third part of the scope was a government-sponsored third-party project. Total investment was about $3.6 billion.

The Challenges

The project had been kicking around for more than 20 years in the country because the availability of the resource was well established. However, the project would disturb a large area (>1,000 sq km) of pristine wilderness, and in this environmentally concerned nation, that made the project highly controversial. Environmental NGOs from around the world were aware of the project and mostly opposed.

The company that ultimately sponsored the development had considered attempting to get the project going several times before but felt that the opposition to the project made it too risky to pursue. On the other hand, the resource situation promised the holy grail of manufacturing: an enduring low-cost producer status. While the sponsor watched, competitors had tried twice to get approval for the development, but they were either denied outright or found the opposition too daunting. The government was also the resource owner and had been holding out for a resource price that would have eroded the economics significantly.

The project geography was remote but with harbor and port development could be accessed from the ocean.

The Strategy

The first and most important element of the sponsor's shaping strategy was old-fashioned patience. They understood that unless or until there were the makings of a constituency for the project, it would never fly. The project would require passage of legislation, enabling use of the resource and access. An economic downturn and a change of government that had promised job development was the tipping point in the project's favor. When the political change came, the company was ready to respond to the opportunity. They had been researching the issues in-country for several years.

The second element of the strategy was to be all over the environmental aspects of the project. The sponsor had in-country teams on air quality, water use and quality, land disturbance, and community relations and development. The in-country teams very actively engaged the environmentalists and made a number of changes that the environmentalists wanted. It didn't eliminate the issue, but it blunted it substantially, as some groups dropped their opposition.

The third element was interesting and clever: the actual resource development, rather than the processing facilities, carried the highest environmental risk and opposition. So the sponsor strongly supported the government developing the resource, which it owned after all, and sold the feedstock to the company on a long-term take-or-pay contract.

This was an admittedly risky approach, but it had some advantages. The downside risk was that the government would not get the resource developed in a timely way. The upside was that the cost of capital was lower to the government, and the company's contract made the terms available to the government to borrow the money very attractive. Furthermore, the government could take the credit for jobs creation and take the heat for the environmental opposition. It was also very important to the sponsor's risk profile that the government is solidly and actively in favor of the development.

This last point turned out to be extraordinarily important because a politician seeking to reinvigorate a fading career launched a legal challenge to the permit on procedural grounds. (Interestingly, the NGOs did not join the suit.) The suit was ultimately successful, but because the political support was strong, the relevant ministry allowed work to continue while the environmental impact statement was reworked to meet the court's decision. Bureaucrats will not normally subject themselves to such criticism without very strong political support.

One other element of the shaping strategy needs mentioning. Because there was substantial unemployment in the area in which the processing facilities were constructed, local politicians demanded that local labor be used for construction and that a quota be set. Normally, a businessperson would agree to such a demand without much thought, but in this case he did the right thing: he checked with the project director. The project director explained that given the nature of the construction, the local workforce completely lacked the needed skills and experience. It would also create a mixed culture in the camp, which is a complicating factor. Instead, promise the permanent jobs and denigrate the advantages of construction jobs. Furthermore, emphasize that the local service industry would provision the labor camp. Although there was grumbling throughout the project about no local construction jobs, the project director believed the execution would have been a nightmare with them. As it was, modules were used wherever possible, and a highly skilled labor force was imported without incident.

Project Results

The project had a 5 percent cost overrun, slipped its schedule by four months, and had a flawless startup. The government was indeed late getting its project completed by six months, but a work-around strategy had already been developed that enabled the time to be used for commissioning and startup without difficulty. It was a successful megaproject.

Why Were They Successful?

The venture was fully aligned at the top of the company. It fit with the company's strategy and was a potentially attractive development, but not at any price. The company worked out internally what its requirements were and then was willing to wait. No one was allowed to attempt to force the project, which would have surely failed. The sponsor worked through conceptually what the shaping process was supposed to look like and was therefore in a position to respond flexibly when necessary. The front-end development of the project was not rushed. FEL took two and a half years, and no authorization was going to be made until the political commitment to the project was made by the government and the legislature. There were no cowboys on the project.

AN EXAMPLE OF UNSUCCESSFUL OPPORTUNITY SHAPING

If the preceding project explains how to approach shaping an opportunity in an environmentally sensitive area appropriately, this example shows how to do it exactly wrong. This is an oil production project in an environmentally sensitive area. The project was to develop a reservoir of moderate size, estimated at fewer than 200 million recoverable barrels. The reserves estimate was based on high recovery rates, so there was very little upside potential to the reservoir. The project has both onshore and close-in offshore components. The project was expected to cost $900 million for both facilities and drilling. Two partners were making the investment. The lead sponsor was an international oil company with lots of experience developing and executing megaprojects around the world. The other partner, also an oil company, was almost entirely silent in all aspects of the project, except to provide additional money when it was required.

The Challenges

The project location is remote and environmentally sensitive. The area has very active and savvy NGOs and other citizens groups who oppose selected developments. Because this project posed some particular environmental risks to marine life, environmental groups staked out a position of opposition early on. The institutional framework for petroleum development is at best moderately strong. Court decisions are respected but are often circumvented by officials. Projects are intensely political, and both central and local political authorities can derail a project if they wish. Projects are routinely used for political advantage and have been known to generate cash above and below the table for politicians who offer support.

The project posed no great technological challenges outside the need to minimize environmental disruption in a fragile area.

The Strategy

There really doesn't seem to have been a coherent shaping strategy for the project, which is surprising given that the sponsor had worked in the area before and expected to do so again. The sponsor knew the project to be contentious. Soon after permit applications were filed, a citizen's group filed a lawsuit, not on environmental grounds, but claiming that the local residents should get a bigger share of the proceeds. This suit stopped the project dead for 18 months and should have been the best thing that could have happened for the sponsor.

In the hiatus, the project team continued to work on the definition of the project, which was decidedly poor when the $900 million authorization estimate was made. When the problem regarding the citizen suit had been settled, a new cost estimate was available, which now showed the cost to have risen to $1.65 billion in constant dollar terms! Recoverable reserves had also been revised downward and operating costs had been revised upward. The project economics, which had never been very robust, now looked very poor. So the obvious route would be to abandon the project.

Not so fast! During the hiatus period, the company had aligned itself with the political groups seeking to crush the influence of the NGOs. Indeed, one of the stated business objectives of the project was now to "crush the environmentalists." Having expended a great deal of political capital to "align" the needed politicians, the lead sponsor would look weak and foolish if it abandoned the project. So the sponsor now found itself in a very difficult position: the project cost too much but was now too high profile to abandon. Because the project was now marginal economically, a couple of truly stupid steps were taken to keep costs down. First, the owner project team size was kept small, and second, a very complex incentivized contractual form was employed with a very large number of contractors, some whom were qualified and some of whom were not. So the project soldiered on under very difficult circumstances.

Project Results

The project was finally completed at a cost exceeding $1.8 billion, more than double the original estimate. The project produced as planned but was a negative NPV development that destroyed a good deal of shareholder wealth.

Why Did They Fail?

There were several flaws in the lead sponsor's approach to the project. First, the sponsor never created an overarching framework for the shaping process. It was, therefore, always in a reactive mode. The various stakeholders were never aligned or mollified because there wasn't a plan for doing so. Because the project was very poorly defined when the sponsors decided to proceed, cost growth was almost inevitable. The cost growth occurred while the sponsor's business folks were busy getting the company overcommitted to what was at the same time becoming a poor venture. Because shaping was not planned, there was no closure point where the project scope and the shaping process would come together to yield the information needed for a rational decision.

The nonoperating sponsor of the project completely abdicated any role that it might have played in preventing this mess. If the second player had exercised even basic due diligence, it would have required that the project development and execution be properly synchronized with the open shaping issues.

Finally, the subplot of teaching the NGOs a lesson was absurd and moronic. The businesspeople had "gone native" and aligned themselves with one of the many political factions in the area. Furthermore, the goal of damaging the NGOs was directly contrary to company policy. The business decision makers responsible needed to be called home and reassigned to more menial work.

In case you were wondering, the project was in an OECD country, not the developing world!

CHAPTER 6

MEGAPROJECTS AND CORPORATE GOVERNANCE

The first decade of the twenty-first century was not a good one for corporate governance. The decade started with the collapse of a fraudulent empire called Enron and ended with the worst environmental disaster in the history of the oil industry. Sandwiched between was the worst global recession since the Great Depression, which was largely created by the "financial community" in the United States. Something is clearly wrong with the modern joint-stock company. What does this have to do with megaprojects? Actually, quite a lot. Much of the pathology we see in megaprojects reflects the nature and problems of the modern industrial firm and the way in which it is governed.

What Is Governance?

Issues of corporate governance have been prominent in the past decade as the realization that something is clearly amiss has sunk into the public consciousness. Above all else, governance is about accountability of management for the health and performance of the corporation.* Good governance also requires that incentives for decision makers are aligned with the long-term health of the corporation. And finally, good governance requires that the corporation is responsible for securing the resources to ensure that work is done safely and correctly.

In 2010, the process industries—oil, chemicals, and minerals—spent about $1 trillion in capital, mostly on projects.[1] An increasing

---

*The real issue, it seems to me, is whether management is responsible for the short-term enrichment of shareholders (and themselves) or the long-term enrichment of shareholders and society.

share of that is spent on very large projects and, as we have seen, those projects are not doing well. Just the failed megaprojects in our database squandered hundreds of billions of dollars of private and public capital. Many of the failures in large capital projects are the direct consequence of corporate decisions to reduce the depth and breadth of technical expertise in their firms. The evidence for this last statement is overwhelming and can be found in the next two chapters that discuss errors in basic technical data and the effects of lean owner staffing on megaprojects.

From about 1980 to 2000, heavy industrial firms in the OECD radically transformed the relationship between the firm and its technical functions. The technical functions include research and development (R&D), specialists in particular technologies, the resource explorers and resource appraisers, engineering, technical support to operations, and project management.

In 1980, most major industrial firms performed technical work with in-house organizations. In too many cases, those technical organizations were powers unto themselves. They were often unresponsive to business direction or business needs. They were in need of reform and rationalization. What actually happened was change but not reform. Instead, many of the technical organizations were simply gutted, leaving them marginally competent at best. By the turn of the century, this was the situation in most (although not all) of American, European, and Australian heavy industrial firms:

- Outsourced and greatly diminished technical expertise
- Poor internal communication, especially between business and the technical functions
- Lack of basic accountability for capital results

The Outsourcing of Technical Expertise

The outsourcing trend started soon after oil prices collapsed in 1984. During the same period, chemical prices were stubbornly low and the minerals industry was suffering a huge capacity overhang that would take almost a generation to work off. This set off a relative lull in capital project activity that would last until 2003. By 1985, engineers and technical specialists, who had been in short supply, were in serious overcapacity in the OECD countries. Market signals got to the university students in a hurry: 1985 was the largest class of engineers ever graduated in the United States and other OECD countries. That was because the kids who were in their third year when the market crashed in 1984 were too late to change their programs. Those a year behind them weren't.

At the same time, there was a strain in business education that was pushing the notion that all businesses were essentially the same. To me, the most telling quote was along the lines of: "Running an oil company is not fundamentally different than running your local McDonald's." A set of consultants, mostly drawn from America's best business schools, started selling a radically revised version of the modern industrial firm. And, at the same time, nontechnically trained executives, often drawn from finance, were for the first time becoming the chief executives at many industrial firms, especially in the United States.

The outsourcing craze hit almost everybody, starting in the United States. Even firms with highly effective engineering organizations, such as DuPont and Exxon, followed along to some degree. The only major U.S. process industry firm that did not was the Dow Chemical Company. Australian and European firms followed suit. Asian firms did not. The outsourcing of technical expertise was a fateful decision, and it appeared to (sort of) work.

The theory being sold by the consultants (and not surprisingly, the contractors) was that markets would supply all the technical and engineering expertise needed. That mostly meant that engineering contractors would fill the need. For a while, it appeared to work reasonably well. Engineering contractors, often with a strong push from owners, were picking up many of the highly qualified people the owners were laying off. (That was often used as a way of salving the consciences of owner executives who were firing employees that had implicitly been promised lifetime employment.) The other factor making the process appear plausible was that the project workload was quite low. This meant that the contractors, who were suffering with surplus people, could bring reinforcements to struggling projects during the 1990s without much difficulty. In fact, even some megaprojects in which the owners did a great deal wrong managed to succeed during this period due to the capabilities of the EPC industry. Also, the people that the outsourcing owner firms had left were often the very best of their organizations. They were highly experienced and were most likely to succeed even in an environment with thinned-out skills around them.

However, there were at least three flaws in the consultants' view of the world, any one of which would sooner or later turn out to be fatal.

1. **Contractors cannot do owners' work.**

   An implicit assumption in the outsourcing initiative was that contractors would be able to do almost all project-related work. This turned out to be quite wrong, but this is an easy mistake to make if not deeply versed in what makes projects successful. After all, owner and contractor engineers have the same formal education, they carry the same titles, and they would seem to be entirely interchangeable.

   Formal education plays an important role in preparing people to engage in the practice of engineering. It plays a much smaller role in preparing people to work in project roles. Early in their careers, contractor and owner personnel are in fact largely interchangeable. Within five years, however, these roles have become very different.

   The contractor's job is to deliver a project as specified, on time and on budget. The owner's job is to specify the right project and then deliver an asset to the business's operations organization. Although the two roles are in constant relationship to one another, they are very different in almost every respect.

   I characterize the owner project management cadre as the glue that binds all of the owner functions together to create an asset. The owner project management cadre must be able to cajole the business into articulating more fully what the project must deliver when the objectives are unclear. The input from the highly skilled technical functions, such as R&D or the geoscientists in the case of petroleum and minerals, must be integrated into the front-end development of the asset. Operations input must be integrated, again at the right time, in the right way. Learning how to bind a company together in a way that will realize an effective asset is altogether on-the-job learning, and it takes quite a lot of time.

The proof of this argument is seen when contractor personnel are hired mid-career or later by owners. They find the transition to productive owner leadership roles very difficult. They sometimes manage, but only if they are "quick studies." A number of firms in petroleum, chemicals, and minerals have hired contractor senior executives to lead their owner project management organizations. This is done by senior business leaders who do not understand the difference between owner and contractor roles. The results have been disappointing in terms of project quality.

Upon reflection, I am not surprised that many owner businesspeople believe that contractors can do their project work and that owner people are unnecessary. Businesspeople who lack project understanding are often in conflict with their project organizations. They are constantly disappointed that their projects are not faster, cheaper, and better. Being human, they sincerely doubt that any of the blame for that could rest with themselves. Whispering in their ear are contractors saying, "We can do the job just right without all the arguing, Boss!"

The transition in the other direction—from owner to contractor at mid-career—is even more problematic. Owners and contractors view projects from such different perspectives that it is sometimes hard to believe they are looking at the same phenomena. Most long-time owner personnel leave contractors soon after hire.

2. **Contractors cannot hold specialty resources.**

EPC contractors are variable-cost firms. They earn primarily by selling the services of people, and people make up the largest component of their cost by far. This really hit home when the chief executive officer of one of the big contractors said to me, "You know why we are called contractors, don't you? Because we are so good at contracting," as he brought his hands together making something small. When business turns down, EPCs must shed people rapidly because it is their only mechanism to reduce costs. Especially problematic for them are highly paid staff who are not in sales. These would be the technical experts that the consultants thought the engineering contractors would hold as they were shed by owners. Not only does the contractor business model make holding these resources difficult, it also precludes renewing such resources.

3. **Owners could not renew.**

The final problem with the outsourced model of project management competencies is that as owners outsourced, they naturally stopped hiring. This meant inevitably that the demographics of the owner project management cadre became progressively top heavy, and when the baby boomers making up the bulge at the top started to retire, there was very little behind them.

Throughout the 1990s and into the first decade of this century, I heard owner executives bemoan the lack of interest in engineering and other technical careers by young people in the United States, Europe, and other OECD countries. They complained that the kids didn't see the energy, chemical, and minerals industries as "sexy," like information technology (IT) or law. But these are the same kids who watched as their fathers and uncles and the occasional mother and aunt were laid off in the prime of their careers by much of the same people doing the whining. When exactly did we come to believe that unemployment should be seen as sexy?

THE IMPLICATIONS OF THE LOSS OF OWNER EXPERTISE FOR MEGAPROJECTS

The outsourcing of technical expertise has made all projects, large and small, more difficult. But it has been especially damaging to megaprojects. As we discuss at some length in Chapter 8, megaproject success depends greatly on robust owner staffing. When the owner cadre is too small, contractors are not provided with enough direction and not nearly enough oversight. Even worse, when the owner staff is too thin, businesspeople often start dealing directly with the contractors. Neither the business executives nor the contractors are equipped to navigate that relationship successfully.

When the owner project management function is weakened, the owner organization becomes incoherent both internally and with respect to other firms, such as the contractors. Sometimes the degree of incoherence is amazing. In times past, it was normal for owners to keep careful scorecards of the performance of prime contractors on their projects. Contractors that performed poorly would move down the priority list, and those that performed well would move up. Today, most owner project teams have no idea of how well or how poorly the contractors they are considering have performed on recent projects for the company. I will never forget having to inform a project team about to sign up for an EPC megaproject that the same contractor was suing the company for a $300 million claim on another project after the EPC had clearly messed the project up. They were dumbfounded; nobody had told them.

The most important problem created by weakness in the owner project cadre is internal incoherence. As I suggested previously, the owner project teams glue the owner functions together to make a coherent project. Without some group to perform that essential function, the high level of internal cooperation necessary to generate a successful megaproject cannot be mustered. Most companies cannot even get feedback from operations to engineering about what aspects of the design were poor because operations doesn't have the time to be bothered, and no one cares anymore about the long-term health of the company and its assets. I once asked the top technology officer at one of the supermajor oil companies if he knew how many project personnel of any description he had in the company. After a thoughtful pause, his answer was, "It is not just that I have no idea. I am utterly certain no one else does either!" This isn't the odd company here and there. Again, most companies even with a senior management push cannot get basic cooperation between functions. This is the legacy of the short-term focus of most senior managements in OECD industrial firms in the early twenty-first century.

Lack of Accountability for Capital

Although there were a number of drawbacks to the traditional "monolithic engineering department" model, one of its strengths was accountability. Project results were owned by engineering, and poor project results in terms of safety, cost, schedule, or operability would result in career repercussions for those responsible. When the technical organizations were weakened, they were left with responsibility but not authority. One of the most profound changes that occurred with the transformation of the technical functions is they lost the ability to say, "No!" to the businesses around issues that are fundamentally technical in nature. For many of the major industrial corporations in the world, including many with megaprojects in this study, there is no one in the technology or engineering functions who can stop a train wreck in the making. The businesses have been empowered to make all decisions but largely lack accountability for even catastrophic results because no accountability mechanisms have been established to replace technical functional accountability. Meanwhile, technical function accountability is a sham because the functions are without genuine authority.

Megaprojects create and destroy careers. Unfortunately, however, there is a very large random element in who wins and who loses. Most megaprojects that fail do so because the opportunity was not shaped in a way that yielded a practicable project. Of the projects that fail for technology- and project management—related reasons, the technical functions responsible simply lack the depth necessary to do the project correctly and thereby find themselves very heavily dependent on others, that is, the contractors.

Incentive Problems within the Sponsor Organization

Other things being equal, everybody within a sponsor organization wants every project to be successful. To want otherwise is to be bloody-minded. However, in many organizations, individuals are also heavily incentivized to behave in ways that damage projects. Business leaders often focus much more on making a deal than making a deal that can result in a successful project because they are incentivized around making a deal rather than making money. The head of exploration and production for one of the major oil companies once responded to a question about the need to follow good project process with, "Process, schmacess. Let's make a deal, and pump some oil!" He was responsible for shaping many a train wreck.

Rising stars within the business group sometimes see generating a big project as a stepping stone in their careers. They too often count on being promoted before they can be held accountable for any poor results. And far too often, that calculation is correct. Many times, business errors are interpreted as project management mistakes. Or as my friend Jacques Cheylan used to say in his heavy French accent, "In the projects, we have the expression: first we hire the scape-a-goats!"

The Effect of Outsourcing on the EPC Marketplace

Those encouraging the outsourcing of industrial firms' technical expertise must certainly have believed that the effect on the relationship between owners and contractors would be positive or at least neutral. In fact, however, the loss of owner technical competence has created a fundamentally dysfunctional buyer–seller relationship for the industry.

Almost all business contracts are self-enforcing. Buyers and sellers do their best to honor the agreements they have made, not because a court would require it, but because being able to continue the business relationship requires it. If agreements were not largely self-enforcing, capitalism would be impossible because there would be so much friction in the marketplace that benefits would be ground up in transactions costs.

The relationships between professional service providers and their clients have always been among the most consistently self-enforcing. In general, good reputation and repeat business are necessary conditions of a successful professional services firm. Doing good work and meeting commitments has value far beyond the particular engagement.

Prior to the downsizing of owner engineering organizations, relationships between owners and engineering and construction firms were almost completely self-enforcing, just as with any other professional services firm situation. Owners very carefully kept track of the performance of contractors on every project and maintained a central database that was used to help select the contractors for the next project that had performed best. Before downsizing, the relationship between owners and contractors was almost always managed by the owner engineering organization and rarely, if ever, by the businesses or any other function. Long-term relationships were the norm, even though most of the long-term relationships were entirely informal. This is not to say that the relationships were somehow idyllic; they weren't. But they *were* normal professional relationships.

The radical downsizing of owner engineering organizations largely ended the self-enforcing nature of owner-contractor relationships. The coherence on the owner side disappeared. Contractors found they could court businesspeople directly and bypass the weakened engineering organizations. Owner business executives are largely ill-equipped by experience or temperament to deal with these relationships.

Owner businesspeople started referring to engineering as "just another commodity" and in many cases turned the relationship management over to purchasing organizations to be procured along with office supplies.* Owners tried purchasing innovations for EPC services such as reverse auctions. And contractors discovered that how they performed on the immediate project had less and less effect on whether the next project would be awarded to them or to someone who promised a few pennies less per hour. They also found that they could engage in disputes with many owners, especially in larger firms, with complete impunity because the owner organizations were totally incoherent.

This change in the marketplace was articulated in the starkest and most eloquent way when the chairman and founder of one large EPC firm got up in front of a large industry audience and said, "To my contractor colleagues, I have only one thing to say: we are a bunch of whores; and to my friends on the owner side, you are the pimps!" Contractors that value long-term relationships with owners based on a self-enforcing basis have been systematically disadvantaged by this change in the marketplace. They have survived, but they have largely done so by avoiding very large projects.

Nowhere has the tendency to "one-night stands" been more apparent than in megaprojects. As discussed further in Chapter 11, the megaprojects' EPC market starts out constrained by a small number of

---

*Calling the work of EPCs a commodity is shockingly ignorant. A commodity is something that is purchased almost solely on the basis of price because there is very little variation in quality. No thoughtful observer would suggest that there is little variation in the quality of EPC services.

qualified firms. This lack of choice on the part of owners decreases the credibility of any threats not to use a contractor in the future for poor performance on any particular job. Even worse, the issue of who was responsible for what in megaprojects is often so clouded by hot market issues that most of the "blame game" is just that—a game.

The advent and rapid expansion of incentive contracting in the 1990s was a tacit acknowledgment by owners that the self-enforcing character of project contracting had broken down badly.* However nicely they are dressed up, incentives are, in effect, owners bribing contractors to get them to do their best. In a healthy market, that would never be necessary. As we discuss in Chapter 11, incentive contracts also have unintended consequences that vitiate their value to owners.

MEGAPROJECTS AND GOVERNANCE

When I started the research that ultimately resulted in this book, it was not my intention to critique the ways in which the modern industrial firm functions. In retrospect, I realize that was the inevitable result. Major capital projects always reflect the firms that sponsor them.

The pathologies that afflict major capital projects are merely another manifestation of the core pathologies that afflict the modern joint-stock company world:

- Poor managerial accountability for the fundamental health of the corporation.
- An intense focus on the short run at the expense of the long term.
- Deep contempt for the technically trained and oriented versus those trained in "business technique." Even in industries such as petroleum exploration and production, in which technological prowess and large capital projects are known to be essential to the health of the companies, there has been a wholesale downsizing and outsourcing of technical expertise.

*Incentive contracting involves sharing cost underruns between owners and contractors. Sometimes, bonuses are also paid for early schedule completion and only very occasionally for good operability of facilities. Often, sharing cost overruns is also called for by the contracts but is very difficult to actually enforce fairly.

Megaprojects are much more severely affected by these pathologies than smaller projects because they always require active business
involvement to achieve success, and they require more technical, engineering, and project management expertise than smaller projects. The
more intimately businesses are involved in the decision making around
these projects, the more likely the decisions will be unsound from the
viewpoint of effective project management. Put bluntly, too many
senior businesspeople involved in major capital projects do not know
what they are doing. The deeply intelligent ones know they don't
know and listen carefully to those who do. Unfortunately, intelligence
is normally distributed among businesspeople, just as it is in any other
class, and deep intelligence—by which I mean common sense—is
rare everywhere.

PART THREE

MAKING THE RIGHT PROJECT DECISIONS

CHAPTER 7

BASIC DATA ARE BASIC
GET THEM RIGHT BEFORE YOU START TO DESIGN

Behind the design of any engineered project is a set of parameters that govern the design.* These parameters express the science underlying the engineering design of the facilities that will be built. We, like many in the industry, call these parameters, taken together, the Basic Data. The Basic Data sit behind and govern the design. They tell the engineer what materials to use, how to size things, how to sequence things, and what things are dangerous. Because different functional groups are often responsible for the development, those developing the design may be only dimly aware of how the Basic Data were generated and may be completely unaware of the quality.

Erroneous and incomplete Basic Data are a proximate cause of many megaproject failures. Basic data mistakes are quite common and, as we will see, quite devastating to the projects. In this chapter we address the following questions about the Basic Data:

- When should the complete Basic Data be available to the project team?
- When Basic Data are incorrect, what are the consequences?
- Under what circumstances are Basic Data most likely to be problematic?
- What are the *root causes* of most Basic Data mistakes?

---

*An important characteristic of the megaprojects that we are examining here is that they are all engineering intensive. Most of them require a high level of precision in the design, and they are very unforgiving of engineering errors. In many cases, engineering errors and omissions render the facilities highly unsafe as many of them handle and process large quantities of explosive, flammable, or toxic substances.

Before addressing these questions, I would like to describe the Basic Data for different kinds of projects so that the reader appreciates the breadth and complexity of the issues involved. It is not my purpose to present anything like a complete set of Basic Data requirements. A complete Basic Data for a single megaproject could easily require as many pages as this book.

Processing Facilities Basic Data

Following are some examples of Basic Data for a chemical or physical process, relating only to the heart of the process:*

- Detailed product characteristics and specifications
- Reaction temperature and pressure ranges and tolerances
- Reaction yield data (including waste quantities and waste composition)
- Reaction products, especially side reaction products
- Production of impurities, recycle buildup potential
- Separation efficiency/completeness and problematic characteristics
- Particle behavior in processing (diminution, agglomeration, etc.)
- Heat (energy) and material (mass) balances for every step
- Vapor liquid equilibria (VLE) data for column design
- Set, control, and alarm points
- Hydraulic requirements for pumps
- Materials of construction test results
- Raw material composition and variability
- Scale-up effects as applicable

All of these need to be understood not just for normal operating conditions but for startup, shut down, and upset conditions as well.

If the process is commercially established, the Basic Data may be known and codified. If the technology is to be procured from a licensor, all of the Basic Data around the heart of the process should be

---

*Almost all industrial megaprojects entail chemical or physical processing, even if the project's technology is not normally considered a "chemical process." For example, crude oil production involves the separation of water and gas from the oil, which in some cases is actually quite difficult and complex. Liquefied natural gas (LNG) involves primarily physical processing, with chemical processing required for the removal and disposal of sulfur and other impurities.

provided or incorporated into the package that the licensor is selling. If the process is new, all of the aforementioned data and more will have to be developed by research and development (R&D). Because the process has not been commercialized previously, the data will remain somewhat uncertain until after a successful startup and initial operation. There may be 4 to 12 separate chemical processes in a megaproject; the most complex we have seen has more than 30. All of the aforementioned data will have to be provided or developed for every process. But that is merely the beginning of the Basic Data development!

Megaprojects often require substantial amounts of infrastructure development: ports, pipelines, roads and bridges, power plants, and so forth. Each one of these has its own Basic Data requirements, some of which may be very complex.

Let me give you an example that illustrates just how difficult the Basic Data requirements can be for an ancillary facility, a seawater cooling system. Many processes require large amounts of heat removal at various stages. If large amounts of freshwater are not available or its use is not permitted, seawater may be required as the heat sink for the facilities. Here are some of the data requirements for a seawater cooling system, with no pretense that the list is complete:

- Maximum total cooling load that will be carried by seawater system at any time
- Seawater hardness and variability of hardness (driver of scaling)
- Chloride content (a driver of corrosion and therefore materials requirements)
- Seawater withdrawal that will be permissible
- Seawater temperature:
  — By season
  — With year-to-year variation
  — By water depth at potential intake points
- Organisms present in the potential intake water:
  — Microorganisms will determine biofouling properties
  — And therefore biocide selection and effectiveness
  — Macroorganisms (shellfish, etc.) and potential for macrofouling and plugging
- Biocide types and levels in effluent water that will be permissible

- By-product formation from interaction of biocide (e.g., chlorine) with natural organic compounds
- Sea life kill that will likely occur and what will be permissible and socially acceptable
- Discharge water temperature:
  — By season
  — By facility loadings
- Discharge water temperature maximum that will occur and be permissible
- Water intake and effluent locations that will be permissible
- Other seawater cooling systems or other marine facilities being installed in the same area and their effect on all of the preceding

Behind many of these items, there is a host of required science. Figure 7.1 shows the integration needed for industrial seawater cooling systems.[1] The chart is instructive because it shows how much has to be considered just to decide what kind of biocides should be used and in what quantities. If the science or the data are incorrect, the system will not work as intended and may not even work at all. This example is of an ancillary part of a development that may well be considered quite mundane but turns out to be quite complex. Even worse than complexity, however, is the time that may be required to produce accurate data. Unless someone has been collecting seawater information in the exact places that you require, you may need at least a year to collect the data to design the right seawater cooling system. For example, seasonal variation in thermal layer boundaries is quite common. If the intake turns out to be in the wrong water depth for part of the year, the fix may involve moving the intake many kilometers and getting permits to do so. Three megaprojects had seawater cooling systems that were so badly misdesigned that cooling could not be provided.

PETROLEUM PRODUCTION PROJECTS BASIC DATA

Whenever a project involves the development of a new petroleum reservoir, we open a new arena of essential Basic Data. What and how much are down there, how is it deposited, and what is around it?

Figure 7.1
Seawater Cooling Basic Data Are Complex

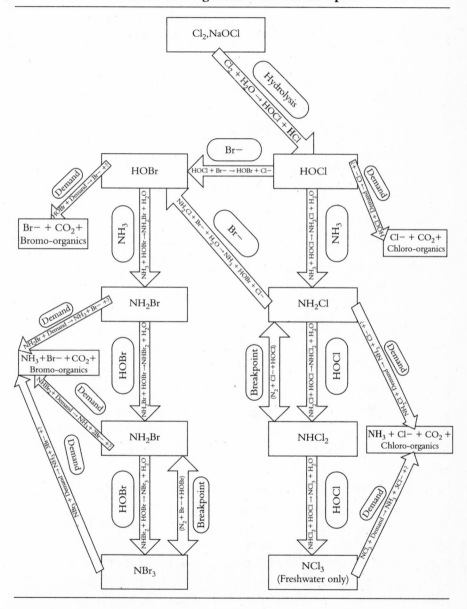

The biggest problem with reservoir information is inaccessibility. The only way to directly inspect a reservoir is by drilling into it. The more wells that are drilled, the better the reservoir can be characterized. However, the number of holes we can drill is limited by economics.

Examples of the things we are trying to ascertain about a reservoir include:
- Reservoir size (aerial extent and thickness)
- Reservoir properties (porosity, permeability, net-to-gross, compressibility)
- Fluids composition (gas/oil ratio, impurities, viscosity, gravity, etc.)
- Fluids composition variability across the reservoir
- Gas/oil/water contact points
- Reservoir temperature
- Reservoir pressure
- Drive mechanism, reservoir energy, or lack thereof
- Presence of faults, fault density
- Complexity, compartmentalization
- Channeling, water production

Development of the Basic Data around a petroleum reservoir is the product of what is called the appraisal process. Appraisal is the next technical step after discovery. The data collection process involves seismic imaging, obtaining cores from wells, fluid samples, and pressure and reservoir limits information from well tests. The data are then interpreted and synthesized into a Basic Data for the particular reservoir being developed.

Reservoir appraisal can be time-consuming and expensive. But there is tremendous latitude around the amount of reservoir appraisal actually done. Generally, the extent of the appraisal process is a function of the expected size of the project that will be required to develop the reservoir; the larger the project will be, the more appraisal is justified to bring the project risk under control. But this rule of thumb is just that. We had one megaproject off West Africa in which the appraisal was limited to simple seismic imaging and the core from the discovery well. When this project was put into production, it produced for all of two weeks before going dry. It was a high-pressure pocket.

One of the most common sources of insufficient appraisal is a technical team's misplaced confidence that they understand a reservoir based on nearby producing fields. This has even occurred in oil sands development in which the reservoir is mined rather than pumped. One very large project assumed that all oil from Alberta oil sands would be the same, only to find that nature had failed to cooperate with their assumption. Significant operability problems followed.

Basic Data Requirements for Minerals Developments

The Basic Data requirements for minerals developments are analogous to petroleum. Because exploitable minerals are usually closer to the surface and on land, the costs of the "appraisal" are usually much less than for petroleum. Nonetheless, there is a good deal of variability in how much is done. Depending on the project scope, it will typically involve Basic Data collection aimed at defining the mining method (open-cut versus various underground methods), as well as the required metallurgical inputs to adequately process the ore.

Here are some of the data that should be acquired to classify the ore body and the overburden in terms of both physical properties for mine development and metallurgical data for associated processing facilities:

- Lithology and stratigraphy
- Physical properties and structures
- Wedge and slab formation
- Cavities
- In situ rock temperatures
- Metals content and metallization process
- Types of impurities
- Waste characteristics and volumes
- Particle sizing characteristics
- Heterogeneity
- Size, shape, and attitude
- Overburden features, properties, angle of repose
- Topsoil depth
- Weathered materials
- Groundwater location, sources, and character

To be complete, many thousands of individual items may need to be filled in for the Basic Data that will underpin the mine and the processing. Especially important are data around the variability of the ore body as that will define the design envelope for the processing facilities.

Basic Data Requirements for Expansion and Modernization Projects

When I was a young man, I made the sort of mistake that only a young man would make: I agreed to fix a leaky pipe in the upstairs bath of a lady friend who owned a very old house. Four anxious days and 14 pipes later, I found myself completing the job in the basement. My lady friend was much more impressed by my sheer incompetence at having broken so many pipes than my devotion to her or attention to task.

Modifying and modernizing an existing facility is one of the most taxing endeavors with respect to Basic Data development. For a greenfield development, those developing the scope have greater control and are more likely to know what they don't know. When modifying old facilities, you are heavily constrained by what is already there. The great challenge is to figure out what that really is.

The critical Basic Data problem for modernizations is trying to figure out exactly what is currently in place, its condition, and its performance. The Basic Data development often requires finding old plant records and documents that provide critical insights into what may lie underground. Maintenance records may (or may not) provide the condition of existing equipment. I once sat in on a peer review panel trying to understand why a petroleum refinery modernization was overrunning so badly. The chief culprit turned out to be the number of pieces of pipe that had to be replaced while making 9,000 tie-ins of new equipment to old. I was reminded of that leaky bathroom pipe from hell.

Even with the new tools available, such as lasergrammetry, the amount of work needed to understand the existing plant may equal or even exceed the engineering work required for the new units. This is in substantial part a legacy of the industry's unwillingness to maintain true as-built drawings and design while making the inevitable thousands of changes to facilities over the years. It is also one of the key reasons why so many major plant modernization megaprojects fail.

WHAT ARE THE CONSEQUENCES OF BASIC DATA ERRORS?

Just more than 20 percent of our sample suffered Basic Data errors or corrections to the data so late they could not be incorporated into the design. The differences in outcomes between projects with and without Basic Data problems are shown in Table 7.1. The differences are quite stark. Projects with Basic Data mistakes averaged 38 percent of planned production in months 7 through 12 after startup, versus 87 percent of plan for those projects without such problems. Equally disheartening is the time required to startup. Projects without Basic Data problems came to steady state, going in an average of 7 months versus the 5 months they had planned in their economic forecast. Projects with Basic Data problems averaged 22 months versus 9 months in their economic plans.

Table 7.1

Basic Data Errors Destroy Projects

Outcome Variable	Projects without Basic Data Errors	Projects with Basic Data Errors	Statistical Significance of Difference
Average production months 7–12 versus plan (%)	87	38	.0001
Time required for startup (months)	7	22	.0001
Forecast time for startup (months)	5	9	.008
Cost growth from authorization (% real)	18	34	.06
Slip in execution schedule[1] in percent	16	30	.06
Percent of projects that were successful	44	0	.0001

[1]Measured as actual time from authorization to mechanical completion divided by time estimated at authorization.

The fact that the planned times are longer suggests that the project teams sometimes knew that the data were shaky and tried to plan accordingly. Their plans rarely accounted for nearly enough slip in startup, and if they had, some of the projects would have been canceled. There are also substantial differences in cost overruns and execution schedule slippage, although those differences are not nearly as systematic as the measure related to operability. None of the projects with Basic Data errors were deemed to have been successful projects. Note, however, that being free of such problems does not even remotely guarantee success; 56 percent of the projects without Basic Data errors also failed.

WHEN SHOULD THE BASIC DATA BE COMPLETE AND AVAILABLE?

In a perfect world, the Basic Data would be available prior to the start of scope development, which we call FEL-2 or the select phase. The Basic Data constitute the foundation of the scope development team's effort. Realistically, if the Basic Data require much development, the middle of FEL-2 is about the best we are likely to achieve.* When significant changes to the Basic Data occur after the middle of FEL-2, there must be project consequences. What those consequences will be depends on how important the Basic Data changes are and how late they occur. Figure 7.2 illustrates what happens. If the Basic Data arrive early enough in select phase that the design can fully reflect them, all is well.

Basic Data that arrive during the define phase disrupt the engineering work that is trying to put piping and instrumentation diagrams (P&IDs) in place and becomes a major distraction for the project team. Recall also from the discussion in Chapter 5 that the shaping phase should have come to closure at the end of the select phase (or put differently, the beginning of the define phase should await shaping closure.) If Basic Data arrive after the middle of the select phase, they

---

*One of my colleagues who specializes in oil field development made an interesting comment here: all oil company work process maps look like Figure 7.2; appraisal is supposed to precede selecting the technology concept that will be used to develop the reservoir. In practice, however, appraisal almost always overlaps the select phase and often continues into the define and execute phases.

Figure 7.2
Timing of Basic Data Delivery Shapes the Outcome

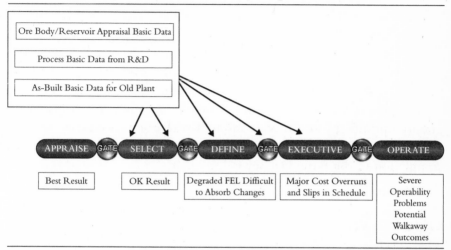

will likely delay the completion of the scope. If they arrive during the define phase, there is likely to be significant project cost growth. At best, that cost growth will occur prior to authorization, but it may continue after authorization as well. If the changes are significant enough, the shaping phase agreements may come unstuck and the project is now in serious trouble.

If the changes to Basic Data arrive after authorization, the project will very likely fail. The failure mode—cost, schedule, operability, or some combination—will depend on the particular situation. For example, in petroleum E&P, late data can sometimes be accommodated through a major change to the wells construction program. For example, the location of the targets in the reservoir may have to change substantially due to new information about the reservoir. This may force the wells to be drilled at a higher angle and may complicate the completion of the wells. The cost of the wells may go up substantially, but the change is accommodated. In mine development, the analog may be a more expensive mining scheme or a major change to the ore preparation prior to processing.

Sometimes, unfortunately, the Basic Data surprise simply cannot be accommodated, and we find ourselves building the wrong project altogether. What then can result is a complete loss of the asset, which we call a *walkaway*. From 2 to 3 percent of industrial megaprojects fall into this sorry class. Basic Data errors are at the root of all of them. And walkaways destroy businesses.

The timing of when the Basic Data is completed can also affect the business decisions and the shaping process for the project. When the Basic Data are incomplete, items are usually missing from the essential scope, which causes the cost and schedule estimates to be unduly optimistic. The rosy economics may even become a "reason" to fast-track the project, which makes the successful and timely completion of the Basic Data even less likely.

UNDER WHAT CIRCUMSTANCES ARE THE BASIC DATA MOST LIKELY TO BE INCORRECT?

There are a few situations that pose substantial risks of the Basic Data containing major errors:

- The use of new technology
- Situations in which the Basic Data are very expensive and difficult to obtain
- Inexperienced or relatively uninvolved lead sponsors

These situations should not be viewed as excuses for poor Basic Data. They are simply the situations in which errors are more likely to occur. Likewise, these situations are not the root causes. We discuss the most common root causes later.

New Technology

There is an old expression that certainly applies to incorporating new technology into megaprojects: "Try to make your mistakes on a small scale and to make your money on a large scale." New technology in a megaproject threatens to do the exact opposite. Any way you measure it, new technology increases project risks.[2] The mechanism by which risks increase is uncertainty, error, or tardiness in the Basic Data.

For this analysis, I have selected the following scale as our measure of new technology:*

- Conventional, "off-the-shelf" technology; widely deployed previously
- First-time integrations of conventional technology
- Minor modifications to existing technology; unchanged core technology but with improvements
- Major modifications to existing technology; modified core technology
- Substantially new core technology

A technology is considered core if it is central to the application. For example, a very innovative gas dehydration technology might be incorporated into the topsides of an otherwise conventional petroleum production platform. The dehydration technology would not be considered core because it is one of a number of steps in the overall process of separating impurities from gas, and other technologies could easily be substituted in the event of an unfixable problem with the new step. By contrast, an innovative mooring system for a floating platform would be considered core technology as would a new chemical conversion process or the use of a new ore in minerals.

How New Technology Affects Megaproject Results

New technology affects the results of megaprojects differently than it would those of smaller projects. In smaller projects, new technology use is associated with much more cost growth and poorer operability.† For megaprojects, new technology degrades cost very little while destroying operability. This difference occurs because in smaller projects, when new technology generates late information, the team changes the design during execution. In megaprojects, wholesale

---

*More precise measures are available for various technology subclasses of megaprojects, such as process plants, offshore fixed or floating platforms, and so forth. I chose this particular measure because it is available for all of the projects, regardless of the technology used.
†When the Basic Data errors were not associated with new technology, the association with cost growth and schedule slippage was very strong. Practices account for the difference.

Figure 7.3
Cutting-Edge Technology Increases Startup Time

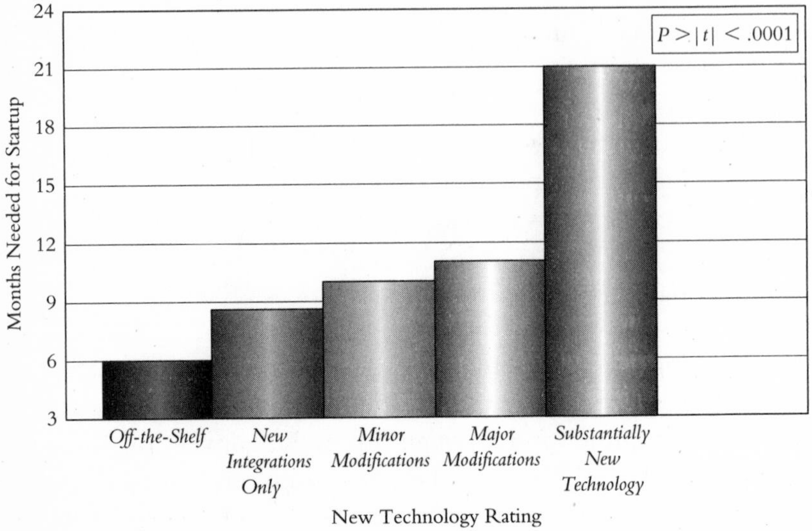

changes in design during execution are usually impossible. If the team does not act on the information, no cost growth is generated, but operability is affected, often in devastating ways. Figure 7.3 shows the relationship between new technology and the difficulty of getting production started up.* Note the very sharp break as the technology becomes substantially new.

New technology that simply does not work as expected is not a surprising result. Often, however, the technology ended up working well, but other parts of the facilities failed. This happens when the new technology changes the Basic Data for the rest of the plant in ways that were not obvious. Even more commonly, what happens is that so much emphasis is placed on the new technology that other things are neglected. For example, one quite innovative minerals processing facility got the new technology heart of the process right, but it

---

*Startup is defined as the period between mechanical completion of facilities (readiness to operate in principle) to steady-state going, even if intended production rates have not been achieved. Walkaway projects were capped at 36 months.

Figure 7.4
Cutting-Edge Technology Increases Risk of Operational Failure

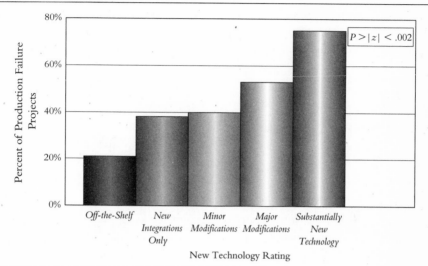

got the ore characteristics essential to the design of the front end of the process so completely wrong that the plant would not operate. That was the simple bit; the hard stuff they got right. The result was a walkaway nonetheless.

Figure 7.4 shows how increasing amounts of new technology are associated with increases in the frequency of projects that we label operational failures. Major modifications and substantially new technology are associated with operational failures more than half the time. Almost all of these failures were generated by serious gaps in the Basic Data.

This raises an obvious question: What would induce any sane sponsor to incorporate significant amounts of new technology into its megaproject? Most of the time, the use of new technology is necessary for project completion. For example, new technology to exploit petroleum reservoirs in deeper ocean waters is inherent to deepwater projects. In such cases, the technology risks are real, but the risks are often well understood going in.

More problematic are cases in which the use of a new technology is expected to make an otherwise economically marginal project viable. Such situations are problematic because the economics are likely still not very robust, and new technology project results have to be substantially discounted for the risks. There are very few miracles.

Other problematic situations exist as well. In some cases, the business leadership is unaware of the amount of technology risk that is being taken by the project team. Several of the walkaways had project teams that deliberately and carefully misled the businesses about the technology risk, claiming things had been demonstrated and proved when they had not.

One case was particularly instructive. This was a metal mining and processing complex exploiting an ore that was unusual from a chemistry standpoint. A technology team at the site had been working on the technology for many years, and the commercialization of the technology was the only way to keep the site open. As a single-owner project, there were no troublesome joint venture partners looking over their shoulders. The team carefully controlled and managed all information about the technology and the project. All reviews were carefully staged, and dissenting views about technology readiness were never aired with anyone outside the team. (I doubt they were raised inside the team either, but we do know that a report by a consulting engineer that was very critical of the technology's readiness was made to disappear after it surfaced during the postmortem.) The only red flag that appeared on the front end of the project was that the team leader was also the primary process developer. This is a conflict of interest situation, because process developers are often deeply enamored with their technology "babies." The result was ugly: The project cost more than doubled after the full-funds authorization; the process did not work when the project was ultimately completed (by a completely new project team); and the company closed the site permanently less than a year after the project was completed. There were two other cases that look almost identical to this one.

There were also instances in which no one involved on the project—business, project team, or technology developers—really understood the amount of step-out in technology that was being undertaken. This is easier than it may seem. Sometimes when making a number of incremental changes in technology, those changes interact to produce significant Basic Data surprises. Referring back to Figure 7.4, this is why integrating known technologies in new ways can generate failures. Almost 20 percent of the projects that had only new integrations generated serious Basic Data errors.

No megaproject should ever undertake new technology unless that technology is necessary to the mission of the project. Discretionary use of new technology is admirable in small projects, but it begs for trouble in megaprojects.

In some cases, technologies may be acquired via license from technology development firms. These licensors sell packages that usually include the preliminary design for the technology. Generally, licensed packages have reliable Basic Data, but not always. Prudent sponsors will want to see the licensed technology in operation elsewhere and talk to those who have licensed before about how complete and accurate the data provided by the licensor were. Check for the number of prior licenses that have been taken out. Being number one or two is not safe ground for a megaproject. The most problematic aspects of licensed packages are often the data around the supporting utility requirements for the technology. The use of licensors also adds interfaces that have to be managed and creates opportunities for schedule disruption when the licensors' data are late. The use of licensed packages also increases the number of required engineering hours significantly.

Expensive and Difficult-to-Obtain Data

Sometimes the Basic Data are simply very difficult to obtain and are always subject to uncertainty. For example, the characteristics of a petroleum reservoir constitute the most important part of the Basic Data for an oil and gas project. But because the reservoir is by its nature inaccessible, the data must be inferred and interpreted from measurements from seismic survey, appraisal wells, and extended well tests. The usual situation is that we have to make a trade-off between the cost and time associated with gathering information and the certainty and completeness of the information. Judging that trade-off correctly is one of the hallmarks of successful petroleum production companies.

Skimping on the Basic Data development when the reservoir is small and the project to develop it will also be small makes good sense. An extensive appraisal program for a small reservoir that is going to be developed with one or two subsea wells tied back to an existing host makes no economic sense. By contrast, skimping on the Basic Data development for a large reservoir that will require a multibillion-dollar project to develop is foolhardy unless some extreme constraints are in play.

In chemical and minerals processing, the most common source of Basic Data errors derives from a decision not to pilot a new process or not to pilot an old process for a new chemical feedstock or ore. Prior IPA research has shown that fully integrated pilot plants are essential whenever the process is complex or heterogeneous solids are being processed.[3] But a fully integrated pilot plant—that is, a pilot plant that includes all processing steps in the same fashion as the commercial design—is expensive. In some cases, it amounts to 25 percent of the eventual cost of the commercial scale facilities. The businesses considering the pilot plant decision sometimes tell me that the cost of the pilot plant will kill the economics of the venture, which actually means the venture is uneconomic.

Inexperienced (and Oblivious) Owners

Sometimes teams and their business leadership are simply oblivious to the risks they are running vis-à-vis Basic Data development. This occurs most often when the lead sponsor is either inexperienced with the type of project or in cases where the sponsor has turned leadership of the project over to a contractor. Of course, these situations are not mutually exclusive. Some examples should clarify what I mean.

In one case, a chemical company was sponsoring a multibillion-dollar grassroots complex using entirely conventional technology. Their chosen contracting strategy was EPC lump-sum turnkey with penalties for late completion and a penalty for failure to operate, the latter of which was a few percent of total cost—quite a sizeable penalty. Their experience with the core technologies was deep, and everything was carefully defined in a performance specification. But this project required a seawater cooling system, which was entirely outside of their expertise. The complex was built on time and on budget without difficulty and then took more than two years to start up because the seawater cooling system did not operate properly. First, the seawater temperature had been misspecified by the sponsor. (They had used old records of seawater temperatures in the area.) Second, biofouling was severe. Third, the system was subject to repeated breakdowns of uncertain origin. Ultimately, the system had to be redesigned and rebuilt from scratch by another contractor. Four years later, the complex was up and operating as intended. Because the sponsor provided the seawater temperature data, adjudicating who was accountable for what was very difficult and the contractor was hit with almost no penalty. The complex, which would have turned a nice profit, ended up with a negative net present value (NPV) because of the delay in production.

Here is another example that would almost be amusing if it had not been so expensive. A joint venture was building a grassroots LNG complex that required extensive air cooling. (LNG, of course, requires extensive heat transfer.) They secured the Basic Data for the ambient air temperatures and wind directions from the local weatherman. Guess what. In this case, even the weather person didn't know which way the wind was blowing! The wind direction combined with inaccurate air temperatures rendered the heat exchange inadequate to produce LNG anywhere close to capacity. Because of the plant layout, increasing the air cooler capacity is almost impossible, so the complex's output is limited permanently. Unfortunately in this case, 100 percent of capacity was forward sold with take-or-pay guarantees that obligated the sponsors to buy LNG on the merchant market to fulfill their obligations, even if they were unable to produce it. This was one very expensive Basic Data error. How could such a mistake occur? The company laid off almost all of its LNG-knowledgeable people after they had completed a prior project. There was nobody on the team who could signal the risk they were running by not verifying information acquired from a local source.

ROOT CAUSES OF BASIC DATA ERRORS

The most important cause of Basic Data errors is the drive for speed. I hope this surprises no one who has read Part Two of this book. To adapt the Iron Law of Oligarchy:*

Speed tends to kill and absolute speed kills absolutely!

---

*For those interested in trivia, the Iron Law of Oligarchy—power tends to corrupt and absolute power corrupts absolutely—was coined by obscure Swiss sociologist Robert Michels and is found in his book *Political Parties*. The Iron Law is often misattributed to Niccolo Machiavelli.

When pressure is applied to complete a project in less time than the normal gestation of the project, corners get cut. Project directors tend to cut the front end of the project because only by doing so can they even imagine completing the project on the schedule that the business leadership wants. It is extraordinarily difficult to accelerate Basic Data development successfully. A good deal of Basic Data development is necessarily sequential and cumulative. Errors or faulty assumptions will tend to cascade through the basis of design. When there were Basic Data errors in a project, the time spent on front-end loading phases two and three (select and define) was a third less, even after controlling for project size and technology.* On average, the seven to eight months "saved" in front-end loading was given back roughly four times over: twice in execution and another two times in startup. It behooves project directors to show these results to their business leaders who want megaprojects accelerated.

The second most common source of Basic Data errors is miscommunication or noncommunication between functions. Sometimes what I thought I said is not what you thought you heard. If you and I speak different professional languages, it is all too easy for us to miscommunicate. I will never forget listening to an angry exchange between a reservoir engineer and a facilities project manager during a postmortem of a problematic petroleum production project. At issue was the rapid buildup of wax in the wells of a gas and condensate reservoir. The reservoir engineer said, "I told you it was a high-pressure–high-temperature reservoir! Why didn't you listen?" The project manager said, "You never said anything about wax—not a word!" At which the reservoir engineer simply repeated what he had said before, only more vehemently; in his world, the word *wax* is assumed if the reservoir is high-pressure–high-temperature condensate.

Miscommunication across functions is common in all projects, but it is especially common in megaprojects. There tend to be more functions involved in these projects. It is much more likely that the Basic Data require development, which in turn requires more cross-functional communication. The businesses tend to be much more

*Result is significant $P |t| < .03$.

involved in megaprojects, and many businesspeople speak no project and many project people speak no business. As we discuss in the next chapters, project organizations and teams are rarely set up in ways that make cross-functional communication easy.

Finally, sometimes Basic Data errors occur because something was simply overlooked. This tends to be more common when the lead sponsor's personnel are not deeply familiar with all aspects of a project's technology. But that is the usual case with megaprojects. The volume, breadth, and depth of data that must be produced for a successful complex megaproject are breathtaking. Some things are inevitably missed, but most of those can be rectified later. Missing something critical can and does happen. When the Basic Data needs of a project are not understood at the beginning of project planning back in FEL-1, when the opportunity-shaping process is just getting started, it sometimes turns out to be too late to get good quality data when the need is recognized.

THE BASIC DATA PROTOCOL AS AN ANTIDOTE TO FAILURE

I believe that most, although probably not all, Basic Data failures are preventable. Surely those caused by excessive speed can be prevented if the right people can be persuaded that excessive speed is self-defeating. Nobody *wants* to fail.

The best way to prevent Basic Data failures caused by oversights is with a Basic Data protocol that covers *all* aspects of a project's technology. Many companies maintain protocols or checklists for all of the primary technologies they use. A Basic Data protocol goes a bit further than the standard basis of design document. First, it covers all aspects of a project, including parts that are not standard for the sponsor. That means that protocol development work is needed whenever a project's technology includes elements that have not been subjected to a Basic Data protocol before. Second, it is not enough to simply list an item and check it off later. There must be standards of quality, and there must be accountability for data accuracy and integrity. There must be a change procedure that notifies those whose design may be affected by the change.

Finally, every company needs to educate those who make the important decisions in their megaprojects (i.e., the businesses) that getting the Basic Data right is essential to success. I will always remember the answer given to an executive's question about why we don't just design conservatively if the Basic Data are uncertain: "Because then we would have a *conservatively designed,* but still very dead, white elephant."

CHAPTER 8

MEGAPROJECT TEAMS
PEOPLE DO PROJECTS

A great deal has been written about teams and how teams can perform much better than individuals. There are books about team leadership, how to produce "high performance teams," and how to motivate teams. I am sure that these books are right about lots of things (for example, they mostly agree that good teams need good leaders), but I don't find much of what the literature has to say very helpful in understanding project teams generally and megaproject teams in particular.

Unlike most other areas of business activity, functioning as part of a team is normal for project professionals. Virtually all of those in megaproject team leadership positions have a great deal of project experience, although often not on projects of the size and complexity of their current project. Personnel on megaprojects usually already understand what it means to be a team player: Someone who freely takes on tasks in your area of functional expertise and then delivers those tasks on time with quality.

I see lots of problems on megaproject teams, but they rarely have their genesis in things like "bad team chemistry" or "lack of teamwork." You don't have to like the person sitting next to you, but you do have to talk to him or her. I find that the roots of problematic teams are almost always found in some of the fundamentals of the project itself and how it was shaped.

I start the discussion of teams by discussing a few conditions that are necessary for effective megaproject teams. I then go through a number of key issues:

- Timing of team formation
- Size of the team

159

- Recruitment, absorption of new members, and shedding of members
- Importance of continuity
- Team leadership
- Development of "robust" megaproject teams

I conclude this chapter with a discussion of some team problems that are unique to megaprojects or particularly acute for megaprojects:

- Geographic dispersion
- Integrating joint venture partner personnel
- Interface management

These issues transition nicely to the next chapter, which focuses on different models of how to organize megaproject teams.

Team Precursors

Let's start our discussion of teams with the conditions that are prerequisite to building an effective project team:

- Understanding of the owner team's role
- Coherent project objectives
- Project work process

Owner Team Role

The first critical point in understanding megaproject teams is to agree on the role of the sponsor (owner) team. What does an owner team do that a contractor team cannot do? Why do we need all of these people? As I think back on many megaprojects, I am sure that the business organizations did not understand the role of the owner team and I am not even confident that all of the owner teams themselves knew why they were there.

The role of the owner team is to generate comparative advantage for the sponsors. The team is where all of the owner functions come together to take the business opportunity and generate a project that is fashioned to the particular strengths and talents of the sponsor organization(s).

With very few exceptions, megaprojects are substantially unique endeavors. Each project tends to have a scope that is not duplicated anywhere else, even if the individual pieces of the technology are quite conventional. Similarly, every sponsoring company that will operate a megaproject is unique in a number of ways that are important to how a megaproject is configured. Different manufacturing/operating organizations have different preferences in terms of technology, control systems, sparing philosophy, maintenance approaches, product mixes, and operating philosophy. These differences have evolved over many years to be harmonized with the business organizations that run the company.

The development of the scope and preparation for execution of a megaproject requires the involvement and active cooperation of many organizations, both inside and outside of the lead sponsor firm. It would be easy to assume that gaining cooperation from outside organizations is the more daunting problem, but often it is the inside organizations that are far more problematic. One of the facts of life in the modern industrial firm is that various parts of the company often fail to cooperate with other parts. Research and development (R&D) or exploration sees little benefit in cooperating with engineering, manufacturing or operations sees the businesses as the cost-cutting gnomes, and so on. So when project leadership calls on the various functions to place people on a project team or to work differently than their norm to meet project timing requirements, the result is often refusal or being ignored.

This problem has always been present in large companies to some extent. Different parts of the companies, which we call functions, have different reporting lines, different measures of success, and different concerns. But in the course of my career spanning the past 30 years, the problems of functional cooperation appear to have greatly worsened. For example, it used to be that getting operations to provide feedback on the performance of a new project was easy. They were happy to provide the needed information, especially as it provided an opportunity to complain about what the engineers denied them. Today, getting that sort of simple cooperation may require going all the way to the top of the company and forcing the issue downward. Even then, simply ignoring a dictate from above is not unusual.

I believe the reason for the change in the level of functional cooperation is simple: relentless pressure on head count has rendered most functional organizations unwilling to cooperate with others. This is especially true when another function is asking for high-quality personnel to be loaned, even if they are paying for 100 percent of the time. When companies do not cooperate internally, they become incoherent and they become easy prey for opportunistic outsiders. Many, perhaps most, of my client organizations—who are the "Who's Who" of the industrial world—are perched right on the precipice of incoherence. We see this at work when we discuss contracting later on, but we see it all the time in assembling megaproject teams.

The owner project team has to knit together a host of functions to create a project that meets the needs of the company. This work cannot be performed by contractors for a number of reasons. Contractors, with very few exceptions, have almost no knowledge of operations. It simply isn't what they do for a living. Contractors do not understand the businesses of the companies they serve and have no need to do so. Finally, contractors do work for shareholders, but they work for *their* shareholders, not for owner shareholders. Only the hopelessly naïve believe that is not the case. The contractors are indispensable for the execution of megaprojects. Even the few owners that do essentially all of their project work in-house have to rely on contractors to execute their megaprojects. But contractors cannot substitute for owner teams.

Objectives Make Teams

As we discussed in Chapter 4, the clarity of the business objectives to the project team correlates with key measures of project results: cost competitiveness ($P > |r|$ .005), cost overruns (.03),* execution schedule competitiveness (.02), schedule slippage (.003), operability (.008), and, of course, success ($P > |z|$ .002). Also, as the clarity of objectives

---

*After controlling for Corruption Perceptions Index (see Chapter 4).

as perceived by the project team declined, the number of dimensions in which the projects tended to fail increased $(P > |t| .0001)$.

The key to the formation and development of effective teams is developing project objectives. What are the key characteristics of these objectives?

- The objectives need to be worthy.

    By *worthy objectives* I simply mean objectives that a project professional would be proud to pursue. I mentioned in previous chapters examples where the objectives were deemed unworthy. Examples include putting the business's flagship technology in a position to be misappropriated or having the objective be to "crush" the nongovernmental organization (NGO). Another example involved the wholesale abuse of the terms of a production sharing agreement between a national resource holder and an international oil company. The terms repaid the sponsor's capital first and then benefits of production were shared. The details of the arrangement made capital virtually free to the international company. The business director ordered that a design from a much larger project be copied because it would save time, even though it would cost much more than the appropriate technology would have. The project team believed (correctly) that they were exploiting the host country. They reported, "It was so obvious what we were doing we had trouble looking our partners in the eye." The team effectively sabotaged the project until the business director was removed from the project and ultimately from the company.

- The objectives need to describe what will make the project a success from the viewpoint of all stakeholders, not just the lead sponsor(s).

    For example, if a specific number (or range) of direct jobs that will be created by the project was promised to the host government, that must be included in the objectives. Any agreements with NGOs around environmental or human rights compliance must be included. And any local content promised to the host government must be included. All of the key attributes that constitute success must be included.

- To the greatest possible extent, the objectives to the team need to provide insight into priorities among objectives, particularly the value of achieving a particular schedule.
- The objectives must be (seen as) *achievable* in principle by human beings with the time, money, and people available.

To absolutely guarantee poor team morale and quality, set objectives that are impossible to achieve. When the objectives are viewed as unachievable, recruiting and retention of high-quality team members is understandably difficult. Some companies have adopted a strategy of setting "stretch target" objectives for projects. Although that practice may have merit for smaller projects, it is a nonstarter for megaprojects. Megaprojects simply lack the flexibility necessary to achieve very fast schedules or very low cost targets.

Teams and Project Work Process

The third and final prerequisite to megaproject team effectiveness is the use of a systematic project work process. One of my colleagues has developed a "team functionality index" that measures the alignment of the team on a set of 27 measures. What he finds is that project team effectiveness occurs only when a strong and systematic work process is in play. This result should be expected.[1]

Work process tells members of the teams—most megaprojects have multiple teams—what work will be done, when, and in what order. The work process also is used by most teams as their key indicator of whether they are making progress. It provides a common vocabulary for team members and therefore facilitates communication.* Having an established work process is so important to megaproject success that I would actively discourage a company from attempting to take a

---

*Unfortunately, in many companies, different functions use different project work processes with different vocabularies. R&D, for example, may have a work process for bringing a development from a lab scale to ready-for-commercial-application that is structurally quite similar to the project organization's, but because the vocabulary is different, communication is hindered. This problem is perhaps most severe in petroleum project development, where the reservoir appraisal team, the facilities design team, and the wells teams are all working concurrently but with work processes that do not communicate or even worse, with work processes that only *appear* to communicate (i.e., they use the same words with different meanings).

leadership role in a megaproject if they had not already developed and trained on a project work process.

KEY TEAM TOPICS

Timing of Team Formation

The core project team needs to be formed as soon as there is a reasonable chance that a project will develop. There is an understandable desire to wait until "we are sure we have a project" to put the team together to save money. But early formation of the team ensures that there will be technical input available to business decision makers from the earliest points forward. That technical input is very important early on because in the process of starting the business deal, agreements may be made that greatly affect the ultimate viability of the project. Typically, early agreements that need technical input include:

- Site selection
- Technology and technology transfer agreements
- Timing for the project (often faster than is practicable)
- Use of local content

The second reason to form the core team early is to be able to appoint the project director, who is very likely to be the only person in the entire sponsoring organization that may actually stay with the project from beginning to end. Between the time that the core team is named early in front-end development until the project is sanctioned, there will usually be a high level of turnover as personnel come on to the project, do their bit, and then move on to another project. Having the project director and a few of the director's reports on the project early helps to glue the endeavor together. The project director needs to develop a working relationship with the business director very early on because their relationship is among the most important for the project's success.

Team Size Matters

The most common attribute of megaproject teams is that they are too small at every point in the evolution of the project: from the earliest scope development to controls in the field in execution, we find that the most common set of initials on the organization charts are TBD (to be determined) or a person named Vacant. Unfortunately, both TBD and Mr. or Ms. Vacant are hard to locate on the job and don't ever seem to get very much done. Although their salaries are low, their cost to the company in the longer run is enormous.

How do we define the "core owner team"? The core team consists of "functional leads." The functions we count as part of the core team are listed in Figure 8.1. Thirty-seven positions are listed, some of which may have more than a single lead. For example, if a megaproject is composed of three subprojects, each of the subproject managers is a member of the core team. The core team, as the designation suggests, is a subset of the full project team. For a typical $2 billion project, the core team is about one-third of the total owner project team, if the project is fully staffed.

Complexity is the primary driver of the required core team size and has several dimensions. Oil and gas development megaprojects generally

Figure 8.1
Members of the Core Owner Team

Business	Project Controls	Procurement
• Project Business Sponsor(s) • Lead Project Financial Modeler	• Project Controls Manager • Lead Cost Engineer • Lead Scheduler/Planner • QA/QC Manager	• Procurement Coordinator(s) • Supply Chain Manager(s) • Materials Supervisors
Project Management	**Construction**	**Finance**
• Project Director • Project Managers • Interface Management Coordinator(s)	• Construction Managers • Labor Relations Specialists	• Economics and Investment Representatives • Financial Advisors
Professional Services	**Contracts**	**Local Government/Authorities**
• Legal • Project-Savvy Human Resources	• Contracts Manager	• Government/Authorities Relations Manager • Government Liaison • Customs Specialist
Engineering/Process	**Environment, Health, and Safety**	**Operations/Maintenance**
• Engineering Manager(s) • Discipline Lead Engineers • Process Lead(s) • Principal Geophysicist* • Principal Geologist* • Principal Petrophysicist* • R&D Leads (Where Applicable)	• Environmental Lead • Permitting Lead • Safety Specialist • Health Specialist • Site Security Advisor (Where an issue)	• Production/Operations Manager • Operations Coordinators (Each major area) • Maintenance Representative

* *Team Members for Minerals or Petroleum Development Projects.*

require larger teams because they are actually composed of at least three technical teams: the reservoir team, which is responsible for characterizing the reservoir and planning how to drain it; the facilities team, which is responsible for the development, design, and construction of the platforms or other necessary facilities; and the wells construction team, which plans, drills, and completes the wells. Minerals mining and processing projects have analogous complexity. In the case of new technology projects, regardless of industrial sector, a cadre of R&D personnel will have to be added along with additional process design personnel.

The biggest driver of increasing core team size requirements is the number of subprojects involved in the development. It is not the project size per se that drives team size; it is the subprojects. For example, a $2 billion liquefied natural gas (LNG) train addition at an existing site without new upstream gas supply requirements is a fairly simple project and can be handled by a core team of 20 to 35 people. Increasing the project cost by building two new trains instead of one does not increase the personnel requirements. Conversely, a $2 billion grassroots chemical complex using new technology for one of the primary units may require 50 percent more people. The project will likely be broken into at least two subprojects, which increases the core team size by about 10 to 12, and an R&D cadre will be required that increases the core team by 5 to 10.

So what do the team sizes actually look like in megaprojects, and what difference does it make? We counted the team size as the projects approached authorization and asked when the incumbents had been named. We also asked whether there had been turnover in the positions since the first person was named. Included in our count were any functional leads that appear in Figure 8.1. They were not counted if the position was vacant (TBD). No administrative personnel were included in our counts. If joint venture personnel were seconded to the project *and* had real jobs rather than oversight and liaison, they were counted. Independent contractors filling the positions were counted, but we noted they were not actually owner personnel. When employees of one of the contractors working on the project filled the position, they were not counted.

After controlling for complexity, the degree of stepout in the technology, and being schedule driven, all of which decrease the chances of a successful project, each member added to the core owner team increases the probability of having a successful project by more than 3 percent ($P > |z|$ .02).

There are several compelling reasons why larger owner teams tend to deliver better megaproject results. Larger owner project teams are able to respond to crises in execution, whereas smaller teams are not. Let me give you an example. This was an onshore oil field development project located right in the middle of nowhere (technical term). The terrain was rugged, and the local population was generally hostile to the project because they had poor experience with prior projects. The area was also environmentally sensitive. In what is somewhat unusual for the oil industry, the lead sponsor decided to execute on an EPC-reimbursable contract basis and forced a reluctant partner to agree.

The contractor got into serious trouble with the local population when building roads and transporting materials to the site, whereupon the lead sponsor immediately replaced all of the contractor's field leadership with his own people. They were able to reassure the neighbors that the problems were over and proceeded to complete the project without incident. That was possible only because of an abnormally large sponsor team and the willingness to intervene quickly. Whenever I hear grumbling about a megaproject being overstaffed, I immediately think we might have a successful project on our hands.

Larger teams on the front end drive better practices. They are much more likely to have no key owner positions vacant, and we call these owner teams "integrated." All of the functions needed to fashion the project are present. To qualify as an integrated team, the functional leads on the team must be able to speak authoritatively for their function. For example, the operations member of the team can make decisions on operational issues without checking back with anyone in higher authority. For a project of average complexity, the integrated core team was twice as large on average as the nonintegrated team ($P > |t|$ .03).

Integrated Teams Generate Better Projects

Developing an integrated team, one in which no key functions are in absentia, is the single most important project management practice for a megaproject. Unfortunately, less than 60 percent of megaproject teams in our database are integrated during front-end development.

All of the functions listed in Figure 8.1 are important, and missing any one of them can end up sinking a project. But some of the functions are critical to fashioning comparative advantage for a project. Chief among these are technology, scope developers (the process people), and operations and maintenance. These functions provide the input that makes the project distinctly reflect its primary owner. Of these, the function that is most often missing is operations.

Once while closing out a failed chemicals megaproject, I asked the project director what he would have done differently. His answer was surprising in its simplicity: "I have thought about that question a good deal, and the only thing I should have done differently is to have shut the project down when I couldn't get a single op rep [operations representative] during FEL-2. When they finally arrived during FEED, we had to make change after change and we were like a dog chasing its tail; we could never catch up. They might have fired me for shutting it down, but it would have been the right thing to do!"

Developing an integrated team might seem like an easy enough task, but it actually can be like pulling teeth. For example, a typical megaproject may need 3 to as many as 20 operations people during all of the front end (Phases 2 and 3). Furthermore, these folks need to be the best that the operations department has. Operating facilities are short of people and have no doubt been "burned" when providing people for scope development for projects that were never authorized. Furthermore, under the best of circumstances, there is little or no benefit to the loaning organization.

Responsibility for team integration usually resides with the project director and his direct reports, the subproject managers. It shouldn't. Primary responsibility should reside with the *business* director. Business directors have more clout in most organizations than project directors. The operating organization reports to the businesses, not to engineering, as do most of the other functions whose people have to be pulled into a project. Gaining and ensuring cooperation in owner team development outside the project organization personnel should routinely be a business responsibility. The project director's responsibility should be to accurately develop the staffing requirements from

Figure 8.2
Integrated Teams

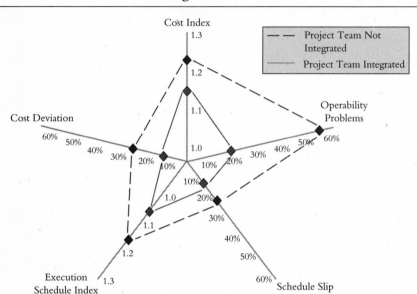

nonproject functions, including R&D and reservoir/ore body, and make them known to the business director in a timely way.

I cannot overemphasize the importance of an integrated team for a megaproject. First, as shown in Figure 8.2, projects have much better outcomes when all functions were actively involved. Every difference shown in Figure 8.2 is statistically robust. Only 22 percent of the projects that lacked integrated teams were successful, versus 51 percent of projects with integrated teams.* (The 51 percent is not exactly heartwarming, which tells us that more than team integration is needed to produce successful projects.)

As shown in Figure 8.3, when we are missing one of the critical functions during front-end loading, it damages the quality and completeness of the front-end work. We discuss front-end loading and its measurement in detail in Chapter 10, but suffice it to say at this

---

*Difference based on Pearson chi-square is significant at .001.

Figure 8.3
Team Integration Drives Front-End Loading

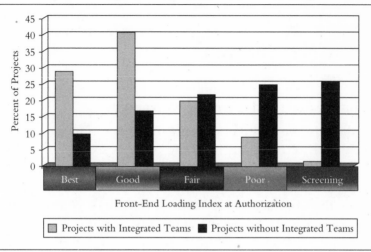

Front-End Loading Index at Authorization

☐ Projects with Integrated Teams ■ Projects without Integrated Teams

point that the quality of the FEL is the most important single driver of megaproject results. Team integration is almost a necessary condition for effective FEL. When teams are not integrated during FEL-2 and FEL-3, projects are unlikely to be well defined at sanction and likely to be at a level of definition associated with still being in scope development or even earlier. The FEL index is made up of dozens of pieces of information. On average, integrated teams rate better than noninte- grated teams on every item that makes up the index.

We mentioned some of the functions, such as technology and pro- cess design and concept selection, that are essential for fashioning comparative advantage for the sponsor(s). There is another set of func- tions that is equally essential for reasons of moral hazard and control. Cost estimating, scheduling/planning, and controls in the field are all activities subject to conflict of interest when executed solely by con- tractors.[2] These functions, more than all the other traditional owner functions, have been subject to significant downsizing since the mid- 1980s in most companies in Europe, North America, Australia, and Japan. As a result, most megaproject sponsors have difficulty staffing these positions internally, and many even have difficulty supervising outsiders doing this work. I remember challenging one megaproject director at a major oil company about his need to staff the controls function for his project. He replied, "The 12 people needed to staff controls for my project would be more controls people than we have in the whole company around the world."

Team Integration and Owner Involvement

One of the surprising features of many megaprojects in the past 20 years is the low level of involvement in the project's execution by many of the sponsor teams. More than half of the teams reported that their intended (and actual) stance toward their project was to step back and allow the contractors to do the project. In practice, a passive stance means that the sponsor team is not guiding the performance of the contractors at each step. They are not intervening actively when problems start to develop, and they do not take responsibility for managing the interfaces, particularly the contractor-to-contractor interfaces, on the project. They hold extended (owners and contractors) meetings less frequently.

Integrated teams were 60 percent more likely to take a highly involved and proactive stance than nonintegrated teams. In part, this merely reflects the reality that nonintegrated teams tended to be seriously understaffed. One can't be highly involved without having the people. Also, because nonintegrated teams were going into execution with much less firm information about the project from good-quality front-end loading, they were often simply not in a position to take an active role.* For example, how can you take an active role in cost and schedule control if you do not have a high-quality, control-grade estimate and a resource-loaded schedule?

Interestingly, the level of owner involvement was unrelated to whether the execution was being done on an EPC lump-sum basis.† In fact, the "alliance" type of reimbursable contractual arrangements

---

*Indeed, the front-end loading index is much worse on projects with low levels of owner involvement, averaging in the "poor" range on the scale shown in Figure 8.3. The high-involvement projects averaged in the "good" range. The difference $(P > |t|)$ was significant at .0001.
†The Pearson chi-square probability was nonsignificant at .28.

were overwhelmingly associated with low levels of sponsor involvement. (We return to this subject in Chapter 11.) However, taking a passive stance toward the execution of a project does suggest that the teams believed they had transferred execution risks to the contractors, regardless of the contractual approach taken.

Low involvement by sponsor teams is particularly prevalent in the petroleum industry. Almost two-thirds of the teams in upstream petroleum industry megaprojects took a "hands-off" stance toward their projects in execution, versus 36 percent of the rest of the industry. Recall from Chapter 3 that the petroleum industry production (i.e., "upstream") projects also fared the worst of any other sector in terms of failed projects. By contrast, more than 80 percent of chemical industry project teams took a highly involved stance toward the projects.

There is a heavy price to be paid for being unwilling or unable to be proactively involved in the execution of the project. Only 16 percent of projects with low-involvement teams were successful. If the teams were also not integrated, the success rate falls to a paltry 10 percent. And if the FEL index was not at least "fair," success disappears almost entirely.

Where Do We Get All These People?

Adequately staffing industrial megaprojects in the early twenty-first century is one of the great headaches of project organizations. A number of factors have converged to make staffing extraordinarily difficult:

- There are more megaprojects than ever before.
- Twenty years of downsizing owner engineering organizations have left the cupboard empty.
- The aging of the workforce in the OECD countries has thinned out the remaining personnel and continues to do so as the baby boomers retire.

As a result, only a few megaproject sponsors around the world are able to adequately staff most of their large and complex projects. Those are the companies that made a strategic decision during the 1980s and 1990s not to radically downsize their project organizations.

Attempts by several large companies to significantly increase the ranks of their project organization in the past decade have largely failed. One company that succeeded in adding a large number of people in the past decade discovered that the people hired were of such low quality that they were forced to undertake a global purge of the poor performers.

Any thought that the contractor ranks can be used as a reservoir of talent for owners should be dismissed. The major international contractors from the OECD countries also face severe staffing problems. As a result, sponsors find themselves having to cobble project teams together and too often end up leaving critical positions vacant.

Individual independent contractors (ICs) and so-called agency staff* can usefully augment owner people. ICs and agency staff are often highly skilled, but they come with a problem: continuity. ICs need a steady stream of project work. This means that they start looking for a new position about six months before the current position is due to expire, usually because the project is ending. When the market is tight, as it is going to be for the foreseeable future, they often leave their current position before the work is done. Staff from agencies are subject to the same limitation, as their employer will often want to move personnel to a more lucrative contract and substitute less skilled personnel. From the owner's viewpoint, this lack of continuity in functions such as cost control is a serious problem. When IC and agency controlled staff leave early, the owner ends up with absolutely no idea of where the money went or why a schedule slipped. The sponsors then find themselves easy prey for spurious contractor claims because they have lost the people and the records necessary for claims defense.

If ICs and agency staff are going to be used, they must be contractually tied up for the duration of the project. For ICs, this means providing a significant (four to six months of salary) end-of-project payment. For agency staff, the situation is more difficult. Generally, owners will seek to tie particular agency personnel in their contract with the firm, but in my experience, this is rarely completely successful. I believe that bonus payments would be more likely to succeed, but this has been resisted by owners.

---

*Agency staff are employees of specialist consulting firms. These firms offer services such as scheduling or field controls.

The most common owner response to a lack of project personnel is to employ a project managing contractor (PMC). The PMC is usually hired to, in effect, replace most of the owner team. The PMC will engage the other contractors on the project and exercise cost and schedule controls in place of the owner. For companies hopelessly short of project management skills, the PMC approach is probably the only way they can act as lead sponsor for a megaproject. However, using a PMC is fraught with difficulties. When used in the traditional way, a PMC adds a thick additional layer to the organization, usually starting in FEED (FEL-3). The use of a PMC increases the cost of the project. The problem is less the cost of the PMC, although that can be substantial, and more the reaction of other contractors when a PMC is employed. Working for a PMC is viewed as a significant risk by other contractors. This is especially true because the PMC is usually given a substantial piece of the EPC work on the project. When that is the case, other contractors add an average 30 percent premium to their bids to account for the added risk. (That often results in the PMC being given even more of the EPC work at a price that is below the bids but much higher than a competitive price.)

When a PMC is necessary, I recommend that the PMC be used as a source of personnel who will augment and complement the personnel of the sponsors. Control must be maintained by the sponsors if an effective project is going to result. Many contractors that act as PMCs resist this kind of fully integrated owner-PMC team because it reduces their control and profit opportunities.

Agency staff, ICs, and PMCs are nothing more than stopgap measures. If a company expects to be in a commodity business for the foreseeable future, then the process of rebuilding project management and other engineering disciplines from the bottom up is the only long-term solution. It cannot be done quickly, it will provide little added value for at least five years, and it will not reach its full potential for a decade. However, it is the only viable route in the long term.*

---

*I should be clear that I do not expect more than a few companies to adopt such a strategy simply because it is a long-term solution. Among many of my clients, there is very little corporate interest in any long-term issues. Regrettable, but true.

If outside hiring is going to be attempted to fill in missing skills for a project or series of projects, specialized project resources recruiting talents are needed. Many human resources (HR) organizations are not geared to find and vet project skills. People who like to work on large projects are not looking for the types of positions that HR normally fills. They are often far more likely to be enticed by a really difficult and ambitious project than by a comfortable, stable position behind a desk. If the HR organization is going to be used for recruitment of project resources, project professionals already on board should actively consult in the process. Hiring bodies is relatively easy; hiring skills is much more difficult.

Absorptive Capacity: A Key Dimension of Team Success

As I have stated several times now, projects teams are very peculiar organizations. They are deliberately temporary, which makes that recruiting task much more problematic and peculiar, and they are very dynamic. By dynamic, I mean that they add people—often in large numbers—at several points in the evolution of the project while shedding other personnel who have performed their tasks and are no longer needed or are no longer needed full-time. Figure 8.4 can help explain what I mean.

The team should be formed mid to late FEL-1. The teams generally stay small until a decision is made to start scope development. Then the team may need to double and then double again a few months later. Depending on the lead sponsor's capability, contractors may start to join the project early in scope development. If the owner has strong capabilities, the contractors may not mobilize seriously until the start of FEL-3 (FEED, define, or feasibility). When the contractor(s) joins, there is another step change in team numbers. Members start leaving the team as early as FEL-3. In particular, it is important that the process designers have completed their work and stop making changes as FEL-3 gets seriously under way.

Expansion of the team can give rise to a whole series of potentially deadly problems. The most common problem is that the person needed is simply not available. Often, certain individuals are all but essential to moving a project forward. Sometimes, it is the particularly

Figure 8.4
Changing Team Composition

The Project Team Changes Its Size and Composition
as the Project Progresses

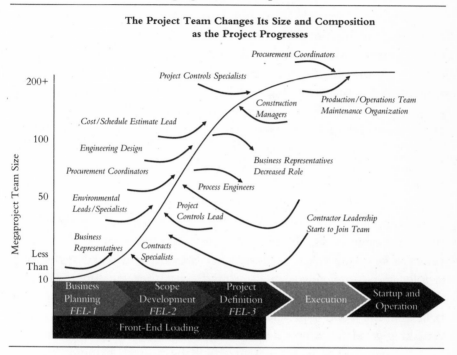

talented project director. More often, specific technology experts are needed for process design. And, of course, sometimes a great many people are not available because insufficient people exist in the company. Sometimes joint venture partners can be persuaded to part with skilled people even when they are not the lead sponsor. I always encourage lead sponsors to recruit joint venture partner people because I find it helps solidify the partners. It can also alleviate skill shortages.

One characteristic of front-end development work is that the schedules tend to be rather fluid. It is in the nature of scope development to be iterative and therefore hard to precisely schedule. Also, because the shaping process is ongoing during scope development, work may need to be slowed or accelerated to meet changes in shaping. Recall that letting the project development get ahead of the shaping process is very problematic because the sponsor's negotiating position will tend to deteriorate.

The schedule uncertainty fosters bringing people on before the project is ready for them. This can be as much a problem as not having people available when needed. People who are added when there is nothing for them to do are easily disgruntled and can demoralize the team members who are fully employed. Most problematic is bringing contractors on board before the project is fully ready to absorb them and put them to useful work. When contractor organizations join a project in FEL, they want to run with the project. Although this is understandable from the contractor's perspective, it can be a disaster from the project's perspective. When a contractor joins a project prematurely, work very quickly gets out of sequence. Before anyone joins the team, the team leadership needs to be very clear on what work they will do and that the numbers being added match the workload.

The points in the evolution of the project when the project team must be expanded significantly are times of potential peril to the project. The key issue when expansion needs to occur is whether the team is fully and completely aligned around what they are supposed to be doing. Does the team believe that the project is strong? Does the team believe in the technology selected? Does the team believe that leadership is making good and timely decisions and keeping the project moving?[3]

If the team is not in agreement about the project, bringing on new team members explodes the discontent and unhappiness. Those taking one side or another in an ongoing disagreement within the team will recruit new members to their point of view. What were workable disagreements become factions within the team, which will probably require a change in team leadership to correct. Strong team alignment, plus carefully worked out assignments for new members, generates good absorptive capacity by the project team. In those circumstances, the new members help propel the project forward. If those two conditions are not met, the new members set the project way back.

One final note on adding team members: Megaprojects often involve areas of scope with which sponsors are completely unfamiliar. That scope development is often given over to a specialist consulting engineering firm to develop without ever really integrating those people into the project team. This is a mistake because the communication between the team and the consulting organization will be weak, and the opportunities for disconnects will be abundant.

The Role of Megaproject Team Leadership

I noted at the beginning of this chapter that the literature is in violent agreement that team leadership is important. I want to add my voice to that chorus, but I would also like to add some specifics about what constitutes leadership. I have met a great many megaproject directors, and superficially at least, they do not seem to have much in common. For every one that fits the mold of the strong military-type leader, there is another who better fits the mold of the quiet, thoughtful professor. I even know one megaproject director who started his major projects career as a "kick ass and take names" type and then mid-career completely switched to a "touchy-feely, team-building" type. And he was equally successful in both modes! (He was nicer in the second incarnation but always generated respect.)

There are some qualities that go beyond the superficial that successful megaproject directors seem to share. First, they are generalists. Megaproject directors must often work closely with partners, regulators, and politicians. They need to focus upward and outward, whereas the subproject managers can focus downward and inward. Most started their careers within the sponsor company outside project management. Many started in the functions, such as R&D, petroleum engineering, or geology, all of which are responsible for Basic Data development. Being able to reach across functions is a necessary quality.

Second, successful project directors are politically savvy within their own company organizations. They have a network within the company that can provide assistance when the project runs into difficulty. Especially important is the ability to get other functions to make good quality people available when they are needed. This means that the successful project director often has friends and allies in the businesses or in the top management of the company. It is a shame that this is necessary, but it often is.

Third, they are good communicators and especially good at communicating upward. They tend to be able to take complex issues and simplify the decision making of their business superiors. For example, they can explain in layperson's terms why the schedule acceleration desired by the business cannot be achieved without unacceptable sacrifice in cost or quality.

Whether a megaproject leadership is able to hold the trust of the project team depends above all else on its ability to insulate those at the working level from interference from outside the project. If people outside the project team do not cooperate with the project director, respect for his or her leadership erodes. Project professionals are willing to work on megaprojects because the projects themselves are interesting and exciting. If the leadership cannot keep the project momentum up, it is very difficult to maintain team morale. Only the very best project directors can succeed when the opportunity shaping process is not going well.

The Importance of Continuity

My final team topic is the importance of maintaining continuity in team leadership. Because project teams are temporary organizations with constantly changing membership, turnover in leadership positions is particularly damaging. Unlike permanent ongoing organization, projects cannot have much in the way of institutional memory. Most damaging is the departure of the project director anytime between FEL-2 and project completion.

We have long noted the connection between turnover in the project leader and project problems for projects of all sizes. Some argue that the cause is that project leaders are replaced when projects are going poorly. However, this is rarely the way causality flows. Only occasionally are sponsor project directors replaced for (perceived) poor performance. Usually much more mundane things like retirement, promotion, or reassignment generate the turnover. Megaprojects are so long that maintaining continuity is difficult. Just more than half of our megaprojects experienced a turnover in their leader. Even worse, the great majority of those turnovers were not planned.

From a statistical perspective, the link between failure and turnover of the project leader is unmistakable. Even after controlling for every other factor that affects success, turnover of the project director is associated with a higher failure rate.* As Table 8.1 shows, every measure of project quality suffers when there is turnover.

---

*The $P \, |z| < .004$ on a probit regression with success as the dependent variable.

Table 8.1
Turnover of Leader Drives Failure

Outcomes Measure	Without Project Director Turnover	With Project Director Turnover
Cost overrun (%)	11	30
Cost competitiveness	1.09	1.30
Execution schedule slippage (%)	10	23
Schedule competitiveness	1.06	1.16
Projects with poor operability (%)	24	42
Successes (%)	57	23

How does the loss of the project director result in so much damage? Of course, some of the relationship between turnover and poorer projects is actually generated by other factors. Project systems that have less turnover tend to be better staffed and better managed. It is not surprising they produce more well-staffed projects, better team integration, better front-end loading, and better projects overall. However, even after accounting for those things, we see the deleterious effects of turnover. The reason is that turnover in the project leadership becomes an opportunity for lots and lots of changes.

When the project leadership turns over, it seems to trigger a loss of memory among some functions and organizations that borders on total amnesia. Agreements between operations/manufacturing and the project about design features come unstuck. The business may decide this is a good opportunity to add a product to the mix or otherwise change scope. And most important, every informal agreement between the project director and the contractors may suddenly disappear.

I vividly remember a minerals megaproject in which the project director and the leading contractor project manager had a long and successful relationship doing large projects together. Because they had worked together and developed a good deal of trust between them, their current project was being done on a reimbursable contract basis with no penalties for delay. Because product had been forward sold, it was, however, very important for the project to be completed on time. The project director was promoted to vice president and went off the project, and all the informal agreements between the project director and the contractor disappeared without a trace. The contractor slowed the project down and then demanded an additional $100 million in fees to restore the original schedule. It may have been unethical and unconscionable, but it was effective; the sponsor paid and the project was completed on time. The lesson there is that trust is a very valuable thing. But like all valuable things, one should seek to economize on the need for it. All of the agreements should have been in writing.

SPECIAL CHALLENGES FOR MEGAPROJECT TEAMS

Megaproject teams have some challenges that are unusual in smaller projects, among which are geographic dispersion, dealing with joint venture partners, and managing many interfaces.

Geographic Dispersion

Megaproject teams, especially during FEL-3 and engineering, are likely to be spread out around the world. It is not uncommon for two or three contractors to be working on FEED, and part of the sponsor team needs to be in each of those offices. Multiple contractors may do engineering and fabrication and construction, and again the team is dispersed to many locations.

Geographic dispersion makes coherent management much more difficult despite all of the modern tools of rapid communication. The simple fact is that people sitting next to one another can communicate more easily than those separated by 5 to 10 time zones. There is really no solution to the problem because contractor availability and quality do not follow a simple geography. The more time zones and the more nodes, the greater the complexity in managing the team. The desire to minimize these often leads to suboptimal contractor selection by taking one that is local, even if its skills and availability do not fit the situation.

It appears that dividing up engineering into multiple offices, complete with the use of low-cost engineering centers, is a cause of late engineering. I say "appears" because causation is difficult to establish. Did we divide up engineering among more contractors because there was a shortage, which really caused the engineering to be late, or did the added nodes cause the tardiness? Or is it simply a matter of larger numbers of contractors meaning more opportunities for someone to fall behind? Late engineering is one of the primary causes of project failure. We return to this subject in Chapter 12.

Integrating Joint Venture Partner Personnel

Joint venture partners can be a blessing or a curse. Partners who want their people assigned to the project solely for oversight purposes are clearly the latter. When a partner assigns people to the lead sponsor's team for the purpose of checking up, they are a drain on the resources of the team. The team spends their time answering questions rather than getting useful work done. Some joint venture partners insist that their personnel not be assigned regular team membership tasks. This is one of those issues that should be hammered out as part of the initial discussions between partners, not left to evolve on its own. Joint venture partner secondees should be fully and completely integrated into the project team. Where they have experience, they should be given appropriate leadership positions. Joint venture partner personnel who have regular team positions gain a much deeper understanding of how the project is going. They are much less likely to be negative about the project team's performance because they have a deeper understanding of the issues than the "drop-in, drop-out" liaisons can.

Some of the most difficult joint venture situations are "equal partner" projects. In these cases, the project director will come from one of the partners and the deputy director from the other. They may even switch positions as the project evolves. These situations can be very difficult to negotiate unless the project director and deputy can genuinely cooperate.

When they cannot, we tend to see highly dysfunctional teams. Perhaps the worst example I have ever seen occurred on a recent project. A U.S. company and a national host company were 50/50 partners on a big complex project. The scope development was being done at the American company's location, and the process of creating a unified team had been working—and working well—for nearly a year when the new deputy director was introduced one morning to the collected project team. Instead of saying the usual pleasantries and words of encouragement, he said, "I will now meet with *my* people," meaning, of course, those from his company. Twelve months of hard work on generating mutual understanding were wiped away with seven words.

The problem with 50/50 joint venture situations is that they beg for nobody to really be in charge. At the beginning of this chapter, I noted that strong project work process with everyone trained was an essential element in a successful megaproject team. There is a temptation in equal partnership ventures to try to "blend" the work processes of the two companies. Like most temptations, this one should be vigorously resisted. When work processes are blended, it ensures that no one knows what they are doing, rather than just half. There will be no training material available on this new hybrid process. Even worse, there is a tendency to combine the worst features of both systems. Poor features of project work process do not occur randomly. They are there because somebody influential wanted them there. When the work processes are combined, those features are likely to survive for the same reason.[4]

Interface Management

Finally, megaprojects always contain a large number of interfaces. An interface occurs whenever independent or even quasi-independent functions or organizations come into contact. Interface management is an issue for even small projects, but it is a major issue for megaprojects. By the time a typical megaproject is completed, there will have been hundreds of organizations involved in varying degrees. In many respects, the task of megaproject management is a task centered around the effective management of the interfaces. The interfaces are opportunities for conflicts and misunderstandings to occur. They are the places where things tend to "fall between the cracks." As we see in the next chapter, the team needs to be organized in ways that facilitate rather than hinder effective interface management.

CHAPTER 9

ORGANIZING MEGAPROJECT TEAMS

Whether we like it or not, organization is a necessary part of any discussion of projects. Teams do not spontaneously come together and everyone somehow magically knows what to do and when. Rather, individuals are drawn into a structure with reporting lines, rules, and norms.* It is important to understand that good organization does not cure poor project fundamentals. There is no perfect organizational form. Each approach to organizing a big project has drawbacks. Organizations always provide some opportunities for people to misbehave. Organizations will always have some features that retard rather than enhance the work process.

That being said, some forms and approaches to organizations are clearly better than others. Those organizations:

- Define and communicate who is supposed to do what and when
- Hinder workflow as little as possible—never perfectly
- Put people next to each other who must communicate the most often
- Try not to have people who must cooperate intimately report up through different lines

---

*Behind every project, there is some form of project management organization that recruits, develops, and assigns individuals to projects. This book is not the place to tackle this huge topic, but it is a safe assumption that if the organizations behind the project cannot recruit, train, and qualify individuals to join the megaproject teams, the chances of success are greatly diminished. Pulling owner team members "off the street" rarely results in a successful project.

- Above all else, avoid incentives that are at war with the goals of the project*

As we think about the appropriate way to organize megaproject teams, one principle should stand above all the rest: the key to a successful project team is the flow of information to the right people at the right time. Remember that the entire front end of a project and its engineering is nothing but information. Nothing physical happens until a shovel goes in the ground or the first steel is bent. Yet every project professional knows that by the time the shovel goes in the ground, the outcomes of almost every project are already determined.

Complexity Is the Nemesis of Megaproject Organization

If information flow is the key to good organization for all projects, it is doubly important for megaprojects. By their nature, megaprojects are complex, and some of them are extremely complex. Complexity is the enemy of good flow of information. Let's consider the various types of complexity in megaprojects and how that affects organizational performance.

First, the shaping process described in Chapters 4 and 5 and all of the stakeholders and partners that are typical of megaprojects add substantially to complexity. Although the business side of the lead sponsor should take the leadership role in dealing with the stakeholders, their work involves a constant exchange of information to and from the project development team. If the stakeholders include joint venture partners, as they do about three-quarters of the time, that may add yet another set of tasks to be performed, especially if the partners want to oversee rather than contribute to the work. Often, the joint venture partners have very different project cultures and may therefore require a lot of explanation for why the project is being developed

---

*This is the biggest problem of trying to do projects with functionally based teams instead of cross-functional teams. Each function has its own organization with its own organizational imperative to thrive and grow. When the project is handed to the functional organization to do its part, the work is interpreted in terms of the organizational imperative instead of what is best for the project. Most project systems around the globe discarded this approach about 40 years ago. A number of national petroleum companies continue to be organized in this fashion, probably as a legacy of being public organizations following the bureaucratic organizational model. It profoundly handicaps their ability to do large projects well.

and executed as it is. Occasionally, the joint venture partners deliberately throw "sand in the gears" because they have objectives that are not consonant with the lead sponsors'.*

Second, megaprojects usually have a number of distinct scope elements, and often each major element becomes a subproject. For example, a gas to liquefied natural gas (LNG) development will usually have a gas production element with several scope elements and, of course, a facilities and wells construction component, a substantial pipeline project carrying gas to the LNG facilities, the on-plot gas plant and LNG plant, a supporting utilities project, and a major port project. Refining and chemicals projects often have several areas of on-plot scope, the supporting utilities, and various off-plot items such as ports and pipelines. Grassroots minerals projects have mine development, processing facilities, and often a major rail or slurry transportation project, and finally port facilities. The most complex megaproject we have seen was a project with 10 subprojects, each one of which easily qualified as a megaproject! Every subproject is an opportunity for something to go wrong. The organization must be structured so that the subprojects that need to talk to each other can do so easily at the appropriate times.

Finally, most of these projects have a number of contractors, often including multiple prime contractors responsible for different areas of scope and a host of subcontractors. Even more vexing is that the contractors are often scattered around the world. Figure 9.1 is a real example of the geographic complexity many projects suffer. The project shown has eight nodes, not including the lead sponsor's home office. In this case, as in many others, the coordination requirement is truly global.

Generally, responsibility for the equipment vendors will be left to the engineering contractors to worry about, so no owner team members are resident at vendor offices. However, if there is specialty equipment involved for which the sponsor is the expert, that generalization will not hold. During busy market periods, equipment vendors will almost always be on the critical path schedule, not only with respect to

---

*We have seen this occur in a number of oil and gas developments when a partner in a development owns adjacent blocks. The partner may, for example, want its existing platform to be used as a host for the field instead of supporting a stand-alone development. Or it may wish to delay the one project so that another project, which would be more lucrative for its company, can be developed first. These are examples of shaping issues that come to interfere with the success of the project development.

Figure 9.1
Scattered Team Members Increase Complexity

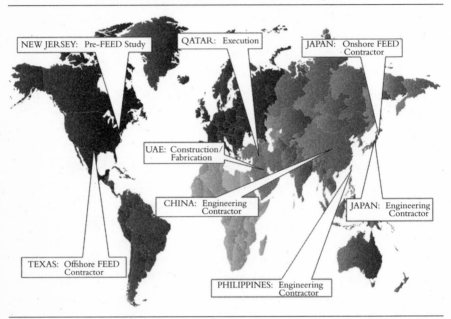

eventual delivery, but also with respect to the timely arrival of drawings that pace the engineering effort during FEED and early execution.

THE ROLE OF ORGANIZATION CHARTS

Organization charts are really important yet worthless most of the time. They are important because they can help newcomers understand who is responsible for what. They are even better if they indicate how communication should be effectuated. But they are worthless most of the time because they are not properly maintained, which confuses new team members rather than helps them. If there are too many TBDs on the charts, then, of course, they are worthless except to remind everyone how understaffed the effort is.

I am always surprised at the number of organization charts that are still maintained on paper in megaprojects. Or if they have been transferred to electronic form, very little of the data warehousing that is possible in electronic format has been used. Electronic organization charts have the ability to provide a great deal of information to team members about who is doing what. They should be searchable by keywords so that when someone needs to know with whom they should be communicating, the information is readily available.

THINKING ABOUT ORGANIZATIONAL APPROACH

Of course, organization charts, good or bad, don't make much difference if the organization itself is a mess. So let's step back and think about the problems that megaprojects pose and then have that thinking lead us to how we should approach organizational design.

What characterizes megaproject organizational problems?
- The volume of work is prodigious.
- A large number of people must be effectively recruited, trained to some extent, and acculturated into the team.
- Much of the work must be executed in parallel.
- The work is heterogeneous, which requires people with different expertise, backgrounds and disciplinary language, and training.
- The heterogeneous functions must be working in parallel and constantly exchanging information about setbacks, changes, and progress.
- In most cases, only the engineering and project management work is subject to disciplined and systematic work process.
- The cross-functional communication is retarded by a lack of common knowledge, vocabulary, and shared worldview.
- Often, joint venture partners with different languages and cultures are an integral part of this mix.

As organizations get larger, communication within the organization gets progressively more difficult. In permanent organizations, the usual response to this situation is to progressively formalize and structure communication and develop layered roles and responsibilities. This is what we usually call bureaucracy. The bureaucratic form, although much maligned, is actually quite serviceable, which is why it is nearly universal. The bureaucratic form works in permanent organizations because the work is largely repetitive. But bureaucracy for a project organization is a killer because it is inherently slow and the work is not merely nonrepetitive—you largely get only one opportunity to get something right. Large and complex megaprojects organized as traditional hierarchical organizations almost always end up bogging down and being restructured on the fly.

STRUCTURING MEGAPROJECT ORGANIZATIONS

Most megaprojects are actually designed in largely the same manner as smaller projects but with some accommodations. Most are set up in the "strong project manager" mode with a project director taking that lead position. Beneath the project director are a set of subprojects (e.g., on-plot scope, utilities scope, and off-plot scope), each of which is organized as a traditional project with its own project manager, lead engineer, disciplinary engineers, and so on. Some activities either can be centralized under the project director to gain economies of scale, whereas some need to be centralized to prevent chaos from breaking out. Human resources (HR) and procurement are usually centralized, and sometimes estimating and scheduling are also centralized.

This traditional structure only applies to projects in which most of the project work is executed by a project management organization. So, for example, in petroleum production projects, only the facilities team is organized in this fashion under the single project director. The reservoir team that develops much of the key Basic Data and the operational plans for depletion of the reservoir and the drilling teams may be organized completely differently and are only rarely fully integrated into a single project organization with the facilities team. Note there is no compelling reason why they couldn't be matrixed-in the way others are. It just isn't done.*

---

*I have heard lots of reasons that a matrixing of the reservoir function into projects should not be done, but the one I hear most is that doing so would lead inevitably to the weakening of the function. The function is so central to the success of an oil company, the argument goes, that its weakening would have catastrophic consequences. Although I cannot agree to the inevitability of the argument, the weakening of the project functions over the past 25 years lends credence to the argument. We have seen instances in which full functional integration has occurred within petroleum developments, but those have been mostly accidental, as, for example, when the reservoir, facilities, and drilling functions are colocated in remote areas and integrate spontaneously. In those cases, markedly better project performance resulted.

Most of the way that petroleum projects are organized is merely a historical accident that has been institutionalized by turf-protecting organizational behavior. Teams should do projects; functions should provide the expertise to the teams. By organizing the functions as teams instead of organizing cross-functional teams, the petroleum industry inadvertently encourages poor alignment. The lack of functional integration that characterizes the oil industry, and to only a slightly lesser degree the minerals industry, comes at a very high price. It makes doing large, complex projects particularly difficult because it maximizes the opportunities for the functions to be misaligned and misunderstand each other. It makes it possible for different functional elements to follow completely disjointed work processes. It also retards the ability to accommodate new information, for example, from the reservoir engineers, quickly and easily. The unwillingness of the oil industry to organize its projects with a matrix that incorporates all of the functions into a single team is surely one of the root causes of its abysmal record on these large projects. One would imagine that a 78 percent failure rate would be a compelling rationale for change.

ALTERNATIVE ORGANIZATIONAL MODELS

I see three basic models, but of course with variations, that should be applied to megaprojects as a function of their complexity:
- The traditional project model
- The hub and satellite model
- The organic model

For purposes of applying the models, I am defining complexity in terms of the number of separate teams, not including the "center" or top management, that are needed to organize the project work.

1. **The traditional model**

    If a project is large but simple, there are no particular reasons why the traditional model cannot apply. This approach works best with one or two teams reporting to a project director, who reports to the project business director (although these two should view each other as equals). The usual difficulties are the ones discussed in the previous chapter: not enough people and not enough cooperation from the nonproject functions.

There are several important advantages to the traditional model. It is simple. Lines of authority are clear. Downward communication is easy and quick. Upward communication may suffer the same problems as any other hierarchical structure—unwillingness to communicate bad news—but the organization is small enough that upward communication can be encouraged. Decisions can be made very quickly by the project director as long as other functions and stakeholders are "well behaved."

If there are more than two or three subproject teams, the traditional model begins to falter because integration starts to become problematic. The need to manage the interfaces among teams (and the collections of contractors they will tend to bring along) becomes too big a job for the traditional project leadership. The project director now needs a coordinating team, and the coordinating team transforms the traditional model into a different model.

What happens too often is that the organization starts out as a traditional organization and then morphs into something like a Model 2 organization without having been planned carefully from the beginning. What activities end up where is a matter of expedience and what is not working rather than an articulated model. It is far better to assess the complexity of the venture at the outset and plan the model that is going to be needed because it helps the project director better anticipate staffing needs, as well as the structure of the organization.

2. **Hub and satellite model**

When the project involves three or more teams with different scopes, I consider the project at least moderately complex. Command and control systems will begin to break down under the weight of the interface management and the sheer number of decisions being passed up to the project director to make. This prompts the need for a different model. That approach is usually the hub and satellite approach as shown in Figure 9.2. Each area is an area of scope. This should not be confused with a

Figure 9.2
Hub and Satellite Model

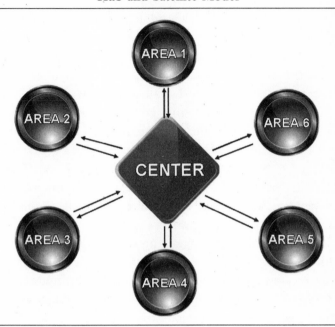

petroleum production project having separate teams for different functions. Each of the area teams in a hub and satellite model has its own full scope of work to do.

Hub and satellite is an improvement over the traditional command and control model in these situations for several reasons. First, the center's capabilities are beefed up. The safety program will be run from the center. Estimating, scheduling, contracting, and controls will likely be staffed at the center. Recruiting, training and orientation, and logistics will all be part of the typical center's activities. Often some procurement activities, especially for long-lead items, may be included as well. Second, decision making is pushed down to the areas for everything that does not have implications for other areas. And finally, the hub and satellite approach may make geographic dispersion of the team easier to manage. Because each area is being managed largely as a separate smaller project, maintaining geographic cohesion by area is easier.

Hub and satellite arrangements are not without problems. The boundaries for each area need to be very carefully drawn. As we say in New Hampshire, "Good fences make good neighbors." The hub and satellite model depends on having as few ambiguities about where one area ends and another starts as possible. Anything that must be managed as an interface between areas is a headache. Also, any interfaces between an area and scope outside the project are problems. For example, if one of the areas has to feed a third-party project or is fed by a third-party project, that interface has to become part of the area's scope. The other problem for the hub and satellite model is it can become very slow as the number of decisions referred to the center increases. The center is a complex organization itself; if it does not function very well, everything slows down.

Hub and satellite arrangements are the most common organizational form for complex megaprojects. The hub and satellite model is considerably more scaleable than the traditional model, but it too can reach a point in terms of complexity in which the model breaks down. The biggest barrier to scalability is extensive interdependencies between areas. We evaluated a project recently that was in FEL-2 (scope development). It was a very complex and tightly integrated project with 10 areas. The center was suffering from such extreme information constipation that the area teams didn't even know what the cost estimates were for their areas because the center could not get the information out to them. Decisions that should have been turned around in a day or less were taking weeks. When the hub and satellite model breaks down, our final model is the only viable solution.

3. **The organic model**

What I call the organic model is illustrated in Figure 9.3. This model seeks to maximize the number of decisions made at the teams' level by encouraging the teams to manage the interfaces among themselves and other teams that are affected by their decisions. I call this model "organic" because the development of the project occurs in much the same way as an organism develops. The center (brain) outlines the master plan and distributes the plan out to all of the teams to carry out. Surprises and changes are managed largely at the area level.

Figure 9.3
Organic Model

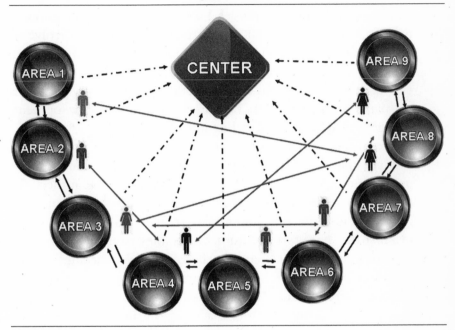

The keys to making this approach work are in the little stick figures shown in the diagram. Each team has one person, probably full-time, who is responsible for communications to and from the team. For example, if area 3 makes a change that affects areas 2, 4, and 9, the area 3 "integration manager" disseminates that information and gets the feedback from the teams affected. If area 3's changes are not easily assimilated by the other areas, the areas get together and try to reconcile. The integration managers also meet regularly together and with the center to ensure everything is coordinated. The extremely complex project I mentioned above moved to this sort of organization after it became clear that hub and satellite model was not going to scale. The change enabled them to move the project forward.

To my knowledge, this was first developed and articulated by Alan Mullaly in the development of the Boeing 777, which would have to be classed as an extremely successful complex megaproject. The genius of the model is that it was designed to fit the problem, rather than trying to fit the development problem to an organizational model. Like many other complex megaprojects, the development of a commercial airliner involves a large number of concurrent development teams, each working on some piece of the airplane. The big problem is that at the end of the day, it all has to fit together perfectly. Integration is the name of the game.[1] As the director of the 777 development, Mullaly called himself the "chief integrator."*

Like every other model, the organic model has strengths and weaknesses. When properly implemented, it can produce quality and speed in the front-end loading of the project. In the 777 case, the development time was cut in half from prior planes because the teams were able to work fully concurrently, making the necessary adjustments as they went. There were an astounding 200 concurrent design teams working on the 777 development. The model is clearly the most scalable of the organizational models we have seen.

There are a couple of drawbacks to the organic model. It is a better front-end development model than execution model. Whether it could even be adapted for execution (detailed engineering and construction/fabrication) is an open question. The integration manager position in each team is very important. One of the staffing weaknesses in a good many megaprojects is that the "interface managers" are often junior people who have very little clout. To make the organic model work, these positions have to be staffed by experienced people who are excellent communicators. Such people are in short supply.

What about Programs?

Sometimes the response to a megaproject being very complex is to transform the project into a program—a series of related projects executed over a substantial period rather than all at once. Sometimes the

---

*Yes, it is very curious that this very successful model was not employed for Boeing's next airplane. Perhaps the explanation is that Mr. Mullaly had moved on to Ford Motor.

program format is used to spread the cost of what would have been a single megaproject over a longer period to conserve cash. Sometimes, the tightness of the EPC market is also cited as a reason to go to a program format.

Whether a program is a viable solution depends on whether the scope of the overall effort is really a single project with respect to both the logistics and the economics. When megaprojects are carved into pieces for whatever reason, the results have been miserable indeed. The sum of the program's projects have surely cost much more than the megaproject would have. Even worse, some of the pieces of the program often end up stranded with no rationale because the pieces they depended on were never built.

Programs should not be viewed as an alternative to a project organizational model. If phasing of a megaproject is desired, that can work as long as each phase is economically justified independent of the others. Programs only make sense when the work is actually programmatic in nature, which means that the various pieces are not intimately linked.

CHAPTER 10

PROJECT DEFINITION
GETTING THE FRONT END RIGHT

For want of a nail the shoe was lost.
For want of a shoe the horse was lost.
For want of a horse the rider was lost.
For want of a rider the battle was lost.
For want of a battle the kingdom was lost.
And all for the want of a horseshoe nail.

Because megaprojects are frag-
ile, even little things matter. Let me offer an example of a seemingly
trivial oversight in project preparation that brought down what could
otherwise have been a great project.

The project was a greenfield chemicals joint venture megaproject
executed in a nonremote, project-friendly area. The shaping process
developed without any problems, and the scope was fully defined at
closure. The project team did an excellent job defining the project.
Our evaluation of its front-end work gave the team an almost perfect mark. Their undoing was the "almost." A single item was not
completed before the project was tendered for EPC lump-sum bids: a
HAZOP* evaluation of the design. The HAZOP, of course, not only
finds potential hazards in the design but also tends to find any errors
and omissions in the piping and instrumentation diagrams. The team
elected not to do HAZOPs because it decided to put the task in the
requirements for the winning contractor. I believe that when the team

---

*HAZOP stands for hazards and operability study. It is a rigorous examination of the design, especially
studying what happens when the plant is started up, shut down, or experiences an upset such as sudden
loss of power.

made the decision, they already had a good idea of who the winning contractor would be and they knew it to be a technically strong organization. It was considered a minor shortcut by the team, but they were pressed to meet their sanction date and HAZOP is one of the very last tasks in front-end loading phase 3 (FEL-3). So instead of a perfect 4.00 score on their FEL index, they received a 4.25.

Several months into execution, the team asked its contractor to show it the results of the HAZOP. The contractor responded that it didn't think the sponsors *really* meant for them to do the HAZOP, so it hadn't done it. The owner team demurred, saying that the complex would handle huge hydrocarbon inventories and the HAZOP was not optional. So the contractor stopped work, performed the HAZOP, and found a significant number of errors that had to be corrected.

Because design had been progressing rapidly for several months with both the contractor and a licensor participating, the changes were very disruptive to engineering, and engineering fell seriously behind. The engineering contractor had bid the project using the most highly respected international construction contractor in the region as its subcontractor. When informed that construction would have to begin nearly a year later than planned, the construction contractor voided its agreement with the engineering contractor, as it was permitted to do by its agreement. The construction firm had other projects to which it was committed that now conflicted with our project.

As a result, the lead contractor was forced to look for alternatives and finally had to settle for a number of smaller construction firms, several of which turned out to be hopelessly incompetent. Construction hours spiraled out of control, which ended up overrunning the contractor's bid estimate by more than 25 million field hours! The whole project fell still further behind, and when the project was finally delivered, the result was a shoddily constructed, marginally operable complex. All this despite the fact that the contract was a "lump-sum turnkey" with penalties and was awarded to one of the world's premier engineering contractors. The plant took a year and half to start up and in my opinion will never operate satisfactorily. "All for the want of a horseshoe nail."

For a number of reasons, the sort of debacle just described would not happen on a smaller project simply because the HAZOP was postponed. Because the engineering effort would be smaller, it would probably be possible to catch up. The market for competent construction firms would not be as constrained for a smaller project. And in the case of a smaller project, the HAZOP, which caused the problem to begin with, probably would have been executed by the team because it would not have been that time-consuming. Because megaprojects are fragile, they are terribly sensitive to seemingly small mistakes.

The definition of a project, from the formation of the core team until full-funds authorization is achieved, is what we call the FEL process. After 30 years of showing the data, badgering, cajoling, and whining to the industry about the criticality of FEL, I believe there is now virtual consensus among project professionals within the community of industries we serve that FEL is the single most important predictive indicator of project success. There are very few project professionals in the process industries who do not agree with the basic principle that definition and planning drive success, and those who don't should probably be in some other line of work. In more than 300 megaprojects, only a few had project directors that considered FEL not very important. All were inexperienced project directors, which is unusual for megaprojects, and all were disastrous failures.

The basics of what later became the IPA FEL index were published in 1981.[1] Of course, the formalization of the process did not start there. Exxon Research and Engineering had a work process as early as the 1960s that in structure is very much like the stage-gated process that is now standard within the oil, chemicals, pharmaceutical, and minerals industries. I have encountered a number of "inventors" of the process over the years, and I have never doubted that the process was invented in parallel any number of times. It is indeed such an obvious process that parallel invention would be expected.

We have succeeded so well in getting agreement that defining a project thoroughly is a good thing that we are starting to see a backlash and complaints that we have "too much of a good thing."[2] Of course, one can do too much FEL; it is perfectly obvious. This is why IPA has always spoken in terms of "best practical" FEL, not "best possible." As soon as the investment in planning gets large enough to create a forward-going economics trap, you are doing too much. For megaprojects with difficult shaping situations, one also has to be aware of the problem of FEL getting in front of the shaping negotiations and distorting negotiating positions due to sunk costs. Yes, I know that sunk costs are sunk, which is to say they should be forgotten. However, sunk costs are often still too real psychologically to be dismissed. Unfortunately, we are nowhere near the point of having too much definition for industrial megaprojects. Indeed, quite the opposite is true.

WHAT IS FRONT-END LOADING?

FEL is the core work process of project teams prior to authorization. The work process is typically divided into phases or stages with a pause for an assessment and decision about whether to proceed. The gate assessments should examine both the economic/business and technical aspects of the project at that point. Those decision points are generally called gates. A basic rendition of the FEL process is shown in Figure 10.1. The number of gates in a system is not terribly important, although I believe that three is the minimum for a coherent process. There needs to be at least one gate at which the business case can be assessed, a gate when the scope is closed and the implications of the scope can be evaluated, and finally, a gate that triggers the full commitment of funds. But I know one (very good) project system that has an astounding 32 gates, although only a few are actually used as key decision points.

One of the most important misunderstandings within industrial firms is the purpose of the gates in the work process. Many business professionals assume that because the engineering and project management organization is the steward for the stage-gated process, the process is structured to meet an engineering purpose. In fact, however, the gates serve not an engineering purpose but a business purpose. That business purpose is to allow points in the development process to make decisions to stop, recycle, or proceed. The work process without the gates is a combined business-engineering process that starts out very heavily business focused and acquires its technical and engineering focus along the way. The engineers would gladly forego any gates and follow a seamless process all the way through, but that would be a disaster for the businesses.

Figure 10.1
In Staged Process Each Gate Addresses Different Issues

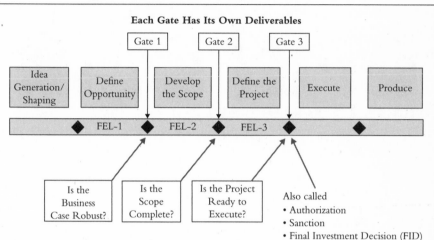

It is very important to the health of the business's capital program that those decision points in terms of the development of the projects be the same for every capital project brought to a gate. Without commonality of FEL for all projects at each decision point, effective governance of the capital portfolio is not possible. The loss of governing control occurs because projects at different levels of FEL provide very different levels of reliability for cost, schedule, and production attainment. As we will see, this general observation about all projects is especially applicable to megaprojects because they are extremely sensitive to FEL status.

In the three-phase format shown in Figure 10.1, the first gate is designed to produce an inspection and evaluation of the health of the business case for the capital project. The way IPA assesses FEL-1 quality is shown in Figure 10.2. Each of the bulleted items in each major category is the subject of a number of questions. The scores from each item are aggregated to score for the main area (e.g., "Business Case" and then the main areas are added on a weighted basis to create the FEL index for Gate 1). That index is a very good predictor of the ratio of the actual net present value (NPV) achieved after 30 months

Figure 10.2
FEL-1 Is about the Business Case

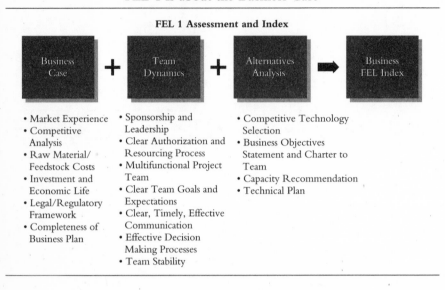

FEL 1 Assessment and Index

Business Case **+** Team Dynamics **+** Alternatives Analysis ➡ Business FEL Index

• Market Experience • Competitive Analysis • Raw Material/ Feedstock Costs • Investment and Economic Life • Legal/Regulatory Framework • Completeness of Business Plan	• Sponsorship and Leadership • Clear Authorization and Resourcing Process • Multifunctional Project Team • Clear Team Goals and Expectations • Clear, Timely, Effective Communication • Effective Decision Making Processes • Team Stability	• Competitive Technology Selection • Business Objectives Statement and Charter to Team • Capacity Recommendation • Technical Plan

to NPV promised at full-funds authorization. For megaprojects, the opportunity shaping process should subsume all of the items in Figure 10.2 and many more. In an effective megaproject development, there will be a lively interchange of information between those attempting to shape the project and those responsible for developing the technical scope of the project. The information needs to flow both ways. For example, the technical team needs access to the site of the project very early. The shaping team has to ensure that access is available. At the same time, the shaping team will be anxious to understand the likely cost and schedule of the project, but unfortunately, at Gate 1, the cost estimates and schedule forecasts don't mean much.

Cost estimates made at this point are little better than educated guesses because the physical scope that will be required to create a real project has not yet been defined. But guesses or not, there will be at least one cost "estimate" for the project. The problem with early cost forecasts is not just that they are usually too low. It is that they are too low by a completely unknowable amount. The cost number that was thrown out might be 80 percent of the eventual project cost, or it might be 30 percent. That means bias cannot be removed from the early numbers simply by applying a factor. For example, doubling the early numbers would kill some very good projects while doing little or nothing about the truly terrible ones.

The best approach at this juncture in a project is to take a set of projects that are broadly similar and ask whether this one has characteristics that would make it tend to be lower or higher than those projects on a capital cost per unit output basis. If, for example, your project is petroleum production, ask how much capital per barrel are we spending on projects with similar sized reservoirs? Is this project in deeper or shallower water? Does it have easier or harder logistics? Is the resource owner easier or harder to work with? The same sorts of questions can and should be asked for minerals and chemicals projects. Nonetheless, the cost numbers at this early stage are not really estimates in the usual sense; they are at best indicators of cost. The same general rubric applies to schedules as well. At this point they are indicative only—and usually too short.

The corporate governance problem is created when cost and schedule numbers from a project that is still early in gestation are compared with those from a project that has been fully and carefully developed. The latter will lose because of the inherent low bias in the cost and schedule forecasts for poorly defined projects. Having the poorly defined project win out distorts behavior and encourages misrepresentation of projects by rewarding the poorly defined projects with money. If you create a situation in which liars win, sooner or later, that's all you will have.

It is unfortunate that Gate 1, the business gate, is by far the weakest in most organizations. Too many projects pass through the gate without much assessment. This in turn creates too many projects in FEL-2, which consumes the most creative technical people in the organization. Often, they are doing work that has no possibility of becoming a real project. Because Gate 1 is weak, many bad business ideas start scope development. Some of them inevitably become real projects. Unlike Gates 2 and 3, there is nothing approaching an industry standard in terms of deliverables for Gate 1. Businesses have been unwilling to subject themselves to the sort of strict standards that would make Gate 1 meaningful.

Megaprojects with very weak business cases are much more likely to be single-owner sponsor ventures or to have a dominant lead sponsor and a small, passive cosponsor. Joint venture partners seem to have the effect of checking irrational enthusiasm. However, when the business case for a megaproject is weak, there are some telltale characteristics. First, the projects tend to enter FEL-2 (scope development) with a large number of possible options. This is highly problematic because prior research has shown that entering FEL-2 with more than two or three scope options results in FEL-2 not being complete, even when it is declared done.[3] Second, the projects with weak business cases are likely to come under intense pressure to cut costs during FEL-3, which leads to project failure. And third, weak business cases are associated with aggressive schedules because a more aggressive schedule will make cash flow appear to be better.

ASSESSING FEL-2

FEL-2 develops and articulates the scope of a project to a point where we can be confident that all elements of scope are accounted for. FEL-2 is the most important phase in the development of any project, including megaprojects. Early in FEL-2, the basic technology approach to the project must be selected if it was not done earlier. As we discuss later, the scope development must be informed by and be sensitive to the project context profile that has been developed by the country advance team (see Chapter 4). For example, finding out during FEL-3 (FEED) that your environmental impacts mitigation strategy will not suit the country requirements is a recipe for disaster.

How IPA assesses FEL-2 is shown in Figure 10.3. The lists on the figure are tailored to process facilities, but analogous data are required for other types of projects.*

Scope development in FEL-2 must be comprehensive. Every part of the scope—on-plot, utilities, off-plot, infrastructure, waste treatment facilities, community development, everything—must be accounted for. The heat and mass balances must be closed, the process flow

---

*There are separate FEL indices for petroleum production projects, mines and minerals, pipelines, and pharmaceutical facilities projects. Modifications are made to the diagrams shown for power projects.

Figure 10.3
FEL-2 Is about Scope Development

FEL-2 Assessment and Index

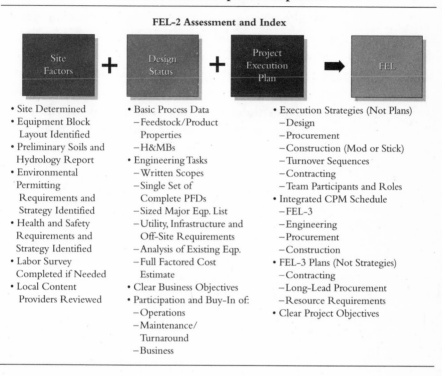

- Site Determined
- Equipment Block
  Layout Identified
- Preliminary Soils and
  Hydrology Report
- Environmental
  Permitting
  Requirements and
  Strategy Identified
- Health and Safety
  Requirements and
  Strategy Identified
- Labor Survey
  Completed if Needed
- Local Content
  Providers Reviewed

- Basic Process Data
  - Feedstock/Product
    Properties
  - H&MBs
- Engineering Tasks
  - Written Scopes
  - Single Set of
    Complete PFDs
  - Sized Major Eqp. List
  - Utility, Infrastructure and
    Off-Site Requirements
  - Analysis of Existing Eqp.
  - Full Factored Cost
    Estimate
- Clear Business Objectives
- Participation and Buy-In of:
  - Operations
  - Maintenance/
    Turnaround
  - Business

- Execution Strategies (Not Plans)
  - Design
  - Procurement
  - Construction (Mod or Stick)
  - Turnover Sequences
  - Contracting
  - Team Participants and Roles
- Integrated CPM Schedule
  - FEL-3
  - Engineering
  - Procurement
  - Construction
- FEL-3 Plans (Not Strategies)
  - Contracting
  - Long-Lead Procurement
  - Resource Requirements
- Clear Project Objectives

diagrams must be complete, and every last piece of major equipment must be accounted for. The equipment list will then be priced and become the basis for the development of a *reliable* capital cost estimate for the entire project. Any piece of scope that is not found and included now will have two deleterious effects on the project: (1) it will increase the estimated cost (and possibly extend the schedule) when the scope omission is realized, which may cause serious stakeholder problems, and (2) it will cause a change to the project at a time when change is disruptive.

If FEL-2 is complete, then the cost estimate will be centered around the actual cost of the project in real (constant currency) terms.[4] Barshop and Giguere (2006) finds that the most important single measure of FEL-2 closure is whether the process flow diagrams

(PFDs) are complete. When the PFDs are complete, projects tend to experience no cost growth during FEL-3. When the PFDs are not complete, or when alternative scopes are still under consideration, significant cost growth occurs, and the probability of project failure increases significantly.

At the end of FEL-2, we should have closure of the shaping process, closure of the project scope, and reliable cost and schedule forecasts. By "reliable," I mean that they are centered around what the eventual actual values are most likely to be and the distribution around the most likely value is known and real, not the figment of somebody's imagination. But the forecasts are not yet highly precise, which is to say the distributions around both cost and schedule will typically be on the order of $-15/+25$ on a single standard error. At this point, the stakeholder-investors will have to make a decision about whether to do the project. It is unlikely that any more information will be forthcoming. The last option on the project is about to expire.

Some will object at this point that the final decision has not yet been made. Full-funds authorization will not come until after the FEL-3/ FEED/feasibility phase is complete. Surely, we get one last chance to decide on the project, so this end of FEL-2 decision is less important! That interpretation of the FEL process is, I believe, profoundly incorrect. FEL-3 is necessary and important, but it culminates not in a decision about whether we *will* do the project but rather a decision about whether we are *ready* to do the project. The decision about whether the project should be done has to be made at the end of FEL-2. FEL-3 is far too expensive to be canceling projects after completing it. FEL-3 activities only become important to the decision about whether to do the project if FEL-2 activities were incomplete or otherwise defective. FEL-3 should not be important to the go/no-go decision.

Occasionally other circumstances will lead to project cancellation when FEL-3 is under way or even complete, but they are peculiar. For example, a megaproject was killed after FEL-3 when one of the major investors suffered a reversal of fortune in its general business and no longer had enough money to proceed. The project will go forward at some point, but another partner will have to be found. We know of a few projects that were canceled because an announcement by a competitor changed the market opportunity dramatically. Sometimes, megaprojects are canceled because the market for the product turns down sharply during FEL-3. However, unless something structural has changed in the market, a downturn should not cause cancellation unless the sponsors no longer have the cash flow or ability to borrow to sustain the project. Market timing should be irrelevant for mega-projects. By the time the project is up and producing, the market may well have changed again anyway.

ASSESSING FEL-3

FEL-3 is all about preparation to execute the project. FEL-3 is about filling in all of the details. All the items that were rated as "prelimi-nary" at the end of FEL-2 need to become "definitive" at the end of FEL-3, meaning complete and final. The framework for the FEL-3 assessment is shown in Figure 10.4.

We characterize FEL as having three big blocks of work. The first is getting the project established and adjusted in its site. Examples of the kinds of issues that need to be tackled are shown in the figure. For onshore projects, the labor supply is particularly critical. For offshore petroleum projects, this is just as important and, in some respects, more difficult. Offshore project teams must understand the site in terms of ocean floor and the metocean conditions.* When moving into new ocean territory, fully understanding the metocean condi-tions can be difficult because there may be no records that cover the location adequately. For example, when BP pioneered the move into the area west of Shetland off of the UK coast, it encountered some of the most difficult ocean conditions ever seen. As a result, one of its vessels there, the Schiehallion, has been battered to the brink of destruction and is being replaced far sooner than ever envisioned.[†]

When local content is an issue, understanding the capabilities of the local materials and service providers is an essential part of the site fac-tors work. It needs to be addressed early enough so that the informa-tion can be included in any invitations to tender.

---

*Metocean = meteorological and oceanographic.
[†]The Schiehallion's sister ship, Foinaven, was saved from a similar fate because it was a converted ice breaker and therefore rugged enough for the conditions.

Figure 10.4
FEL-3 Is about Readiness

FEL-3 Authorization Gate Front-End Loading Index

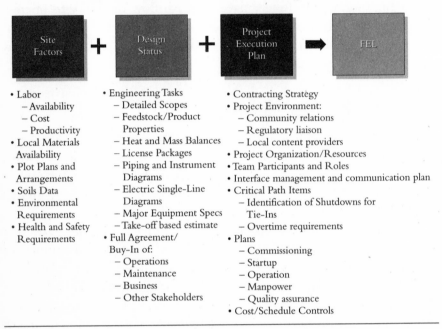

- Labor
  - Availability
  - Cost
  - Productivity
- Local Materials
  Availability
- Plot Plans and
  Arrangements
- Soils Data
- Environmental
  Requirements
- Health and Safety
  Requirements

- Engineering Tasks
  - Detailed Scopes
  - Feedstock/Product
    Properties
  - Heat and Mass Balances
  - License Packages
  - Piping and Instrument
    Diagrams
  - Electric Single-Line
    Diagrams
  - Major Equipment Specs
  - Take-off based estimate
- Full Agreement/
  Buy-In of:
  - Operations
  - Maintenance
  - Business
  - Other Stakeholders

- Contracting Strategy
- Project Environment:
  - Community relations
  - Regulatory liaison
  - Local content providers
- Project Organization/Resources
- Team Participants and Roles
- Interface management and communication plan
- Critical Path Items
  - Identification of Shutdowns for
    Tie-Ins
  - Overtime requirements
- Plans
  - Commissioning
  - Startup
  - Operation
  - Manpower
  - Quality assurance
- Cost/Schedule Controls

Provided that the FEL-2 work was brought to closure, the design tasks for FEL-3 are relatively straightforward but require a great deal of work. The goal is to bring all aspects of the design up to a level from which rapid production design can commence. There are some subtleties in this process that deserve mention. Some parts of what would normally be considered "detailed" design, which is normally a postsanction process, may be required to support the ordering of long-lead time equipment that is on the critical path schedule. This has to be done without letting the contractor(s) "run away" with the project during FEL-3.

If the sponsorship of the project is a joint venture with more than a single lead sponsor being active in guiding the project, great care has to be taken not to confuse the FEED contractors during this period. Unless the joint venture team is so well blended that it is truly seamless—that does happen, but very occasionally—then any disagreements between partners about how to proceed with FEL-3 are likely to manifest in conflicting instructions to the contractors. Those conflicting instructions can result in making a hash of FEL-3. Let me give you an egregious example. This was a 50/50 joint venture with both partners actively involved in the management of the front end. One of the partners was very anxious for the project to proceed into FEED, believing (probably correctly) that if they could get FEED going, it would force the other partner to commit earlier than the partner wanted. So with scope development (FEL-2) about half done, the deputy director of the project simply hired the FEED contractor without consultation or permission of the director! That is extreme, but the lesson is important: If your contractors are given two orders—"go" and "don't go"—they heard "go."

The "best practical" rating for engineering design is what we call an advanced study design. We are frequently asked how this translates into the more conventional measure of "percent design complete." I resist giving a simple answer because the two measures are related but hardly the same. Design complete is generally calculated as the portion of expected engineering cost that has been spent. That measure suffers a number of problems. It is a percentage of what may be a completely fictitious denominator, as engineering costs tend to overrun more than any other single line item. Of even greater concern is that the design may be advanced too far in some areas and barely begun in others, and the "design complete" number will still sound perfectly reasonable.

The better way to measure is to ask what engineering tasks are complete. Three tasks, when taken together, constitute the acid test of whether the design is ready for sanction: *Adv. study*

1. The piping and instrumentation diagrams (P&IDs) are complete, reviewed, and approved.
2. The major equipment specifications are completed and the long-lead time items are ordered.
3. The cost estimate was developed with take-offs of all material quantities from the P&IDs.

If all three conditions are met, the design is very likely advanced study. If "no" or the more common "well, sort of," the design is limited study and the project is not yet ready for sanction. Of the successful projects, 80 percent had achieved advanced study versus 40 percent of the failed projects $(P > |\chi^2| < .0001)$.

Engineering is an area in which one can do too much prior to authorization. Our "best practical" rating of advanced study is substantially short of the best possible "full design specification." An interesting aside here is that none of the successful projects achieved a full design specification prior to authorization, but three of the failed projects did. These were projects in which the engineering effort continued despite major shaping problems. The sponsors were overcommitted to the projects and continued when they should have quit.

The third big element of FEL-3 at authorization is completion of the project execution planning. The development of the execution plan should start with the project itself at the start of FEL-2. By the time sanctioning of the project is near, the execution plan should be quite detailed. Many aspects of the execution plan must be decided no later than the start of FEL-3. For example, the decision whether the construction strategy will be modules or stick-built should be made as early as possible because it affects how the design will be developed in FEL-3.

It is tempting to postpone some aspects of execution planning on the theory that the needs are far enough in the future that there is plenty of time. This usually turns out to be a mistake. For example, it is tempting to delay the first draft of the commissioning and startup plans until sometime during execution, especially on long projects. The fault in that logic is that the turnover sequences for megaprojects are often complex. The turnover sequence defines the order in which various units should be commissioned, started up, and turned over to operations. Most of the turnover sequences are required, not discretionary. After they are finally worked out, you may realize that you cannot achieve the desired sequence because you failed to order a few pieces of long-lead time equipment way back in FEL-3.

The local content providers need to have been identified and qualified well before any bid packages go out to prime contractors so that the local content risk can be reduced in the eyes of the potential bidders. The outlines of the contracting strategy should have started back in FEL-2 because how and who is contracted to assist with FEL-3 will depend on how you intend to contract the execution. As discussed in the next chapter, if the execution strategy is going to be lump-sum, hiring one of the desired lump-sum bidders to do the FEED work is not a good idea.

Especially for ventures in new geographies for the lead sponsor, the building of the operating organization must be planned during FEL. One of the sadder projects among our megaprojects was a grassroots refinery. The project was doing extremely well, being completed on time and on budget at a competitive cost. However, because the plant-manager-to-be did not believe the refinery could possibly be done on time, there was absolutely no operating organization to commission, start up, and operate the refinery when it reached mechanical completion. It took nine months to cobble an organization together to run a couple of billion dollars worth of investment that had been sitting on the ground rusting.

The most difficult single aspect of execution planning is the development of a high-quality schedule. Developing a good schedule is difficult not only because it simply takes a lot of work but also because too many companies no longer have the depth of scheduling expertise required or the data needed to properly resource load the schedule. Resource loading of the engineering and construction provides deep insight into whether the schedule you would like to meet is achievable by mere humans. We return to the importance of schedule later in this chapter.

The relationship of the measurement schemes for FEL-2 and FEL-3 are shown in Figure 10.5. The numbers shown are the points in the index where we break from one category to another. Both FEL-2 and FEL-3 are measured on the same scale but with quite different expectations for how much work has been accomplished by the time the gate at the end of the phase is reached. Note that in both cases, it is possible to overdefine. Too much definition means that the project is no longer synchronized with other critical activities. For FEL-2, it means that we have moved into FEED (feasibility for minerals) before achieving shaping closure. Recall that shaping closure should be coincident with passing through the gate at the end of scope development. Overdefinition for FEL-3 means that we have moved into execution

Figure 10.5
Single Scale Defines FEL

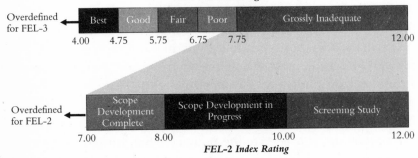

Front-End Loading Index
Both FEL-2 and FEL-3 are Reported on a Single Scale

of the project without passing through the sanction gate, which means we never stopped to check whether we were ready to execute the project.

Best practical FEL-2 is when the scope development is complete and all elements are accounted for, all site elements are preliminary, and the pieces of the execution plan that will be needed for FEL-3, including the construction strategy and the basic contracting strategy, have been settled. If the project were authorized at that point, the FEL would be rated as "poor" with respect to sanction, although "best practical" with respect to Gate 2. In general, the costs to the end of FEL-2 are no more than about 0.5 to 1.5 percent of eventual total cost. If recycle has been necessary, or if the shaping process has slowed progress, the costs will be toward the high end of that range. If all has gone smoothly, the low end of the range will usually suffice. In any case, remember that none of the money spent in FEL-2 for either shaping or project development is project investment; it is information acquisition money.

To go from the end of FEL-2 to a ready-to-sanction project is considerably more expensive: another 2 percent to as much as 4 percent of eventual total capital cost may be required to complete FEL-3.

FEL-3 for a megaproject will always involve the mobilization of contractors to do the details of the site and engineering definition and to assist in the execution planning. FEL-3 costs are and should be considered project capital investment.

WHY IS COMPLETE FRONT-END LOADING SO IMPORTANT? – CAPTURE Value Id'd

Once we launch the execution of a project, our goal is to maintain whatever business value has been created in the opportunity shaping and scope development processes. That means we have to deliver on whatever promises have been made in the authorization package that was reviewed and approved by top management, often including the main board of directors. Maintaining value means that the project will be on or close to its sanctioned budget and schedule and will produce as promised after startup. So let's review the importance of FEL to achieving those goals.

FEL and Cost Performance

Figure 10.6 plots the relationship between the level of FEL that had been achieved when the project was given the go-ahead for execution and how much growth in capital cost was seen, in real terms, to the end of the project.* The shading around the median trend line represents a standard deviation above and below the mean. Consider this chart in the context of risk assessment. If your FEL work is best practical, you will, on average, underrun by a few percent. The distribution around that slight underrun is about −15 percent and +25 percent.

In this case, the reality is even better than the numbers appear. A handful of projects were rated as best practical FEL but experienced huge (>70 percent) cost overruns for peculiar reasons. Two of the anomalous projects were overdefined, and shaping problems caused major disruptions after authorization. In one case, an inexperienced project director ceremonially dropped all the project definition work

---

*Cost overruns are measured as the ratio of the actual total capital cost in inflation-adjusted, constant currency terms to the cost estimated (contingencies included) at full-funds authorization measured on the same adjusted basis.

Figure 10.6
FEL Drives Cost Predictability

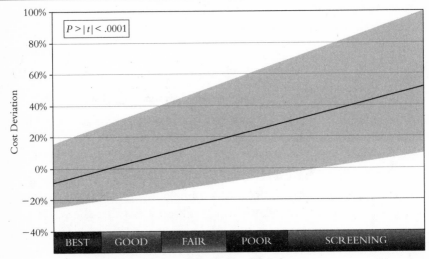

Front-End Loading Index
Shading represents +/− standard deviation

in the waste bin after authorization, saying that the project would be done "my way!" And in a couple of cases, well front-end loaded projects were directed to undertake major cost cutting after authorization, which made a shambles of the front-end work. When the outliers are discarded, the distribution around the slight underrun for best practically front-end loaded projects is about 10 percent. In other words, if the FEL is best, megaprojects are not particularly risky from a cost perspective!

By sharp contrast, if the FEL is "poor" at sanction, one is about equally likely to come in on budget or have a 60 percent (real) overrun. Now that is risky! If an outside observer—bankers, please take note—is trying to understand the cost risk for a megaproject, the very first measure should be the quality of FEL. If the FEL is poor, the project is a bad bet to back. If the FEL is "best practical," the project is odds-on to be fine with respect to cost.

The same basic relationship between FEL and cost growth is found in all projects and is equally strong statistically. However, the slope of the relationship for megaprojects is more than twice as steep as it is for

Figure 10.7
FEL Drives Schedule Predictability

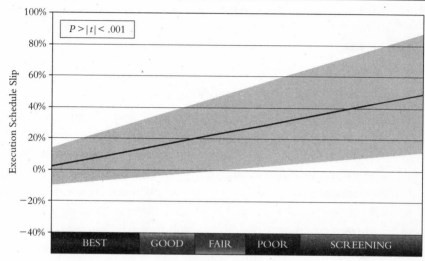

Shading represents +/− standard deviation

projects of less than $500 million (based on the 2003 U.S. dollar). In other words, the same principles apply to all projects, but those principles are much more important for megaprojects.

Poor schedule = ? completion

FEL and Schedule Performance

Let's turn now to the risk of slipping our execution schedule* in Figure 10.7.

The pattern for schedule slippage is very similar to that for cost growth. The best practically front-end loaded projects usually achieved their schedules. When projects were rated "poor," they slipped by about 30 percent, which for the average project in our database means that first production would occur 13 months later than promised and 13 months later than the economic forecast for the project. Even more important from a risk perspective, the poorly

---

*Execution schedule is defined as the point of full-funds authorization to mechanical completion (in principle ready-to-operate) of all required kits. For petroleum production projects, the period ends at first production.

front-end loaded project is equally likely to be 26 months late to completion. Put in stark project management terms, if a project is "poor" on the FEL index at sanction, the only honest answer to the question, "When will this thing be done?" is a very unsatisfactory "I have no idea."

FEL and Production Performance

The third big promise made at authorization, and the promise upon which all cash flow from the project ultimately hinges, is operability. As described in Chapter 3, we classify a project as an operability failure if it has severe and continuing production problems into the second year after startup. The projects so classified averaged about 40 percent of planned production in months 7 through 12 after startup. The amounts spent to attempt to recover operability will never be known.

Figure 10.8 shows the relationship between the incidence of operability failure and FEL. When the level of FEL was "good" or better, the number of operability failures is under control. As soon as the

Figure 10.8
FEL Reduces Operability Problems

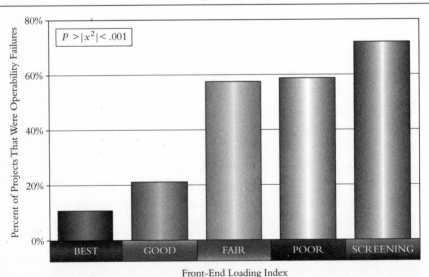

$P > |x^2| < .001$

Percent of Projects That Were Operability Failures

BEST   GOOD   FAIR   POOR   SCREENING

Front-End Loading Index

FEL index moves into the "fair" range, operability collapses. Projects that did not achieve at least "good" FEL were odds-on to fall short of meeting expectations. There were a number of underlying causes of the operability disasters. Some projects were so schedule driven that corners were cut in both Basic Data development and FEL. In some cases, the poor FEL triggered numerous changes during execution, and those changes caused quality to suffer. In some cases, poor FEL resulted in failing to fully understand the environmental permitting requirements, which in turn led to the facilities being shut down by the authorities for being out of compliance.

The failure of a project to produce at or close to the rates that were promised at sanction is debilitating to the economics of the project. If product prices remain constant, the early years' production are the most valuable the project will ever have. When a sponsor's assets consist largely of the project being developed, the failure of the project to be completed on time and then to produce at the expected rates often means bankruptcy or a "fire sale" of the company assets. The bondholders and banks must be paid.

FEL and Safety Performance

For projects generally, project execution planning is a major contributor to better construction safety. When I restrict my sample to countries that have strong reporting standards, I find the same relationship for megaprojects. Figure 10.9 shows how safety problems increase as execution planning degrades. The median recordable incident rate increases in a linear fashion as execution planning moves away from a "definitive" rating. The more serious accident rate, involving days away from work, restrictions on work that can be performed, and injuries forcing a job transfer (the so-called DART rate), does not show an increase until execution planning degrades to "assumed." It then doubles. Both relationships are statistically significant.*

---

*Because safety statistics have a sharp skew that is difficult to transform, I use a number of techniques to check my results, including Poisson regression, glm, and robust regression. All showed statistically significant results for both types of injuries. Although the statistical results are strong, I would not overinterpret the nonlinear result for the DART rate. Because the DART rate is more volatile than the recordable rate, the loss of observations is a potential problem.

Figure 10.9
Execution Planning Improves Safety
(Truncated Sample)

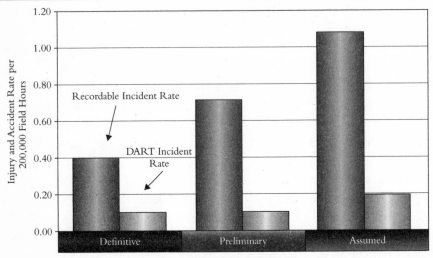

Project Execution Planning

That better execution planning drives better safety should surprise no one. Better planned sites are more orderly sites. Better execution planning is associated with less aggressive schedules and much less schedule slippage. When schedules begin to slip, safety begins to suffer. Projects with poor execution planning averaged almost a 30 percent slip in their execution schedules and almost twice as many recordable injuries than projects with "definitive" or "preliminary" execution planning. The DART injury rate correlates with execution schedule slip for countries with reliable reporting so strongly that nearly a third of the variation in serious injuries is explained by slip in the project schedule ($P > |t| < .0001$).

So, again, why is FEL so important? It is important because it is a prime driver of almost every project outcome that we care about: cost, schedule, operability, and safety. Figure 10.10 summarizes the relationship between the FEL index and successful projects. Almost two-thirds of the projects that achieved "best" FEL delivered what was promised at authorization. Among those projects that failed with best practical FEL, only a couple simply had bad luck. For example,

Figure 10.10
FEL Increases Likelihood of Success

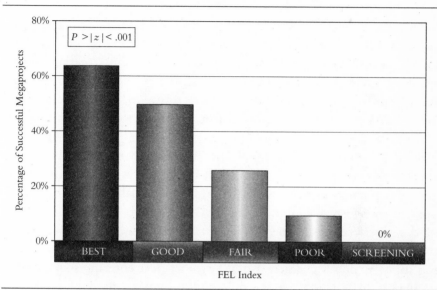

one of them failed because a third-party (government) project did not get done anywhere close to schedule. Two suffered repeated failure of major equipment despite conventional technology and well-established equipment fabricators. A few well-defined failures were highly innovative projects that overran badly but ultimately worked and proved the technologies, which may make money on future projects. A few others failed because they "gave away the store" to their lump-sum contractors. They were so anxious to get the projects done and on a lump-sum basis that they were willing to pay 50 percent and higher-risk premiums.

As soon as the FEL index moves down to "fair," the success rate falls below one project in four, and at the worst level of FEL, success disappears altogether. Every relationship we have reviewed in this chapter holds for smaller projects as well. But in every case, the relationship is more dramatic and severe for the megaprojects than it is for their smaller cousins. This brings us once again to the peculiar bimodal character of megaproject results.

HOW WELL ARE MEGAPROJECTS FRONT-END LOADED?

Megaprojects are the most important projects in any industrial company's portfolio. When they succeed, the company is strengthened for the long term. When they fail, massive amounts of shareholder wealth can be made to evaporate in a single project. Almost every project professional agrees that better, more thorough FEL means better project results. Logic, therefore, would suggest that almost all megaprojects would achieve "best practical" FEL before the investors' money is committed. As Figure 10.11 shows, however, that is not the case. In fact, only one megaproject in five achieves best practical FEL, and as explained previously, that number is actually somewhat exaggerated by those that undid their FEL work early in execution. Half of the megaprojects achieve "fair" FEL or worse. Fifteen percent of the megaprojects have a level of FEL that is the equivalent of a screening study, which is characteristic of projects just entering scope development rather than projects at full-funds authorization.

Figure 10.11
How Well Are Megaprojects Defined at Authorization?

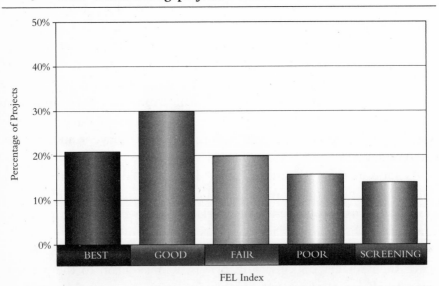

FEL Index

There are no statistically reliable differences in the level of FEL by industrial sector. Liquefied natural gas (LNG) is a little better than average, but not systematically so. Pipeline megaprojects are a little worse than average, but not systematically so. The real question is, Why isn't FEL much better than it is for all industrial sectors?

WHY ISN'T FEL BETTER?

The FEL story pulls together much of what we have discussed in the previous chapters of this book. Although failing to do excellent FEL is a primary proximate cause of megaproject failures, it is a symptom of a set of deeper problems. The relatively poor FEL for megaprojects is an extension of projects generally. When looking at our overall database of more than 14,000 projects, there is a systematic and undeniable relationship between larger size and poorer preparation. If we restrict our sample to only major projects that exceed $100 million (based on the 2003 U.S. dollar), the result does not change.* Megaprojects are merely at the far end of the cost spectrum and are, therefore, the most poorly prepared of projects on average.

What this means is that the more important a project is to the health of the modern industrial firm, the less likely we are to do the things absolutely necessary to make the project succeed. This perverse state of affairs starts with a lack of the people needed to do the work, which is due to the massive downsizing of owner engineering organizations that started in the mid 1980s. IPA asks megaproject directors at the end of FEL whether they had adequate numbers of staff to get their work done. A total of 61 percent answered yes, and 39 percent answered no. When they answered no, the FEL index was much poorer ($P > |\chi^2| < .0001$). But that is only the start of the problem. When the staffing was deemed adequate, 82 percent of the FEL teams were integrated. When the staffing was not described as adequate, only 25 percent of the teams were integrated. To some extent, these two

---

*The statistical results here are overwhelmingly strong. When I regress the FEL index against the natural log of estimated cost (in constant 2003 U.S. dollars), the t-ratio around the coefficient is greater than 11, meaning that one would need to go 11 standard deviations to the left of the coefficient before the relationship disappears. The probability that the relationship could be generated randomly is tiny indeed.

Figure 10.12
Team Integration Is the Critical Enabler

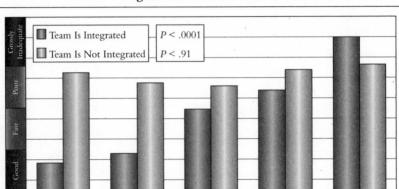

issues are tapping the same thing, but they are also tapping different realities as well. When the teams were not integrated, gaping holes were left in the FEL, whether or not there were enough people in total to get the work done. When the teams were integrated and the staffing was considered adequate, the average FEL was solidly in the "good" range. When neither condition was met, FEL was "poor."

But that is not the whole story. In Chapter 8, I discussed how having clear objectives and understanding the trade-offs among key outcomes was necessary to building strong teams. In Figure 10.12, we show that improving FEL depends not only on knowledge of the trade-offs, which subsumes having clear objectives, but also on team integration. When a team is integrated, understanding objectives and trade-offs drives much improved FEL. But when the team is not integrated, nothing helps. The team may perfectly understand what it is supposed to do, but if it is not adequately staffed or is missing one or more of the functions on the team at the right time, the FEL effort fails anyway.

Late arrival of Basic Data also degrades FEL, and this effect is not washed out when we control for team integration and staffing adequacy. Part of the reason for this is that Basic Data problems are associated with the FEL duration actually being *shorter* than it would otherwise be. That result, in turn, is an artifact of Basic Data problems being greatly exacerbated by pressure to drive the FEL schedule. This almost always happens because the entire project is being driven to be completed at a breakneck schedule. When corners are cut in Basic Data development, corners are likely to be cut in FEL and every other measure of project quality as well.

Sometimes problems encountered in the shaping process create problems in achieving good FEL. In a joint venture, which is the norm for megaprojects, partners may have very different ideas of what constitutes acceptable FEL. As the joint ventures are being formed early in the shaping phase, the businesses of the two (or more) partners may be discussing front-end work with little or no input from the project organizations. Because FEL issues are typically of low salience for business professionals, fundamental disagreements about how much FEL should be done or how long it should take may exist but not surface. When they do surface, as they must eventually, it is far too late to realize that you have the wrong partner.

Often the formal joint venture agreements are very slow to materialize. Usually, prior to formal agreement on the joint venture, there is a certain amount of confusion about who is willing to pay for what. We often encounter cases in which one partner is paying all of the FEL costs because the joint venture agreement has not been signed. As the FEL continues without a signed joint venture agreement, the business folks in the lead owner can start getting very anxious about the amount of money that is at risk and start slowing spending.

Some partners use FEL as an integral part of their shaping negotiating strategy. This may appear clever, but it really isn't. They want the other partner to spend as much "out of pocket" as possible because it bolsters their position. This is not materially different than demanding an upfront cash payment, which is another negotiating ploy but one very easily recognized as such. Encouraging the other partner to go as far out on the limb in funding FEL as possible works because the two partners now have an asymmetrical loss situation in the event that the project does not go forward. The reason this strategy is not clever is because it encourages too little FEL to be done. The resulting losses associated with project failure make everyone losers.

My very strong recommendation when in joint venture situations is to confront the FEL funding issue immediately when starting negotiations on the venture. Make the willingness of the other partner to fund FEL a simple matter of goodwill. If they are unwilling to fund their share, you must understand you are at an immediate disadvantage if you go forward in the shaping phase.

Sometimes insufficient FEL is done simply because the lead sponsor is excessively frugal (cheap) and doesn't want to spend the 2.5 to 5 percent required to get first-class definition of the project. We hear things like, "Why should it cost so much money? I once front-end loaded a big project on a napkin over a beer." If you are the project director, now would be a good time to post your resume.

More common, however, is that business management is driving the overall schedule for the project to first production. This is a problem we have already discussed in other chapters at some length, but one point needs to be revisited in this context: If as the project director, you respond to overall schedule pressure by shortcutting work on the front end, you are making a bad situation much worse. Poor FEL drives execution schedule slippages, startup time, and poor operability. Most important, poorly front-end loaded projects end up being slower overall.

Finally, there is the belief in some quarters, even among some project professionals, that the amount of FEL required will be less for certain contracting strategies. In particular, there is a belief that if the project will be executed on an EPC lump-sum basis, the execution planning is not really needed or is not needed to the degree it is for other contract forms. Not only is the belief without empirical foundation, it is precisely wrong. FEL has more effect in restraining cost growth and schedule slippages in lump-sum projects than it does in other contract forms. The reason is not hard to fathom. FEL reduces changes during execution. Owner changes during execution are major sources of profit for lump-sum contractors. You will get hit, quite appropriately, with the costs of the changes and the cost of the schedule delay that the changes cause. Then at the end of the day, the project operability will suffer because changes degrade quality.

FRONT-END LOADING AND THE PROJECT CONTEXT

In the discussion of shaping in Chapter 4, I said that the first step in a healthy shaping process was to explore the attributes of the project context. That information is needed both by the business leadership, who is trying to make a difficult decision about whether to go forward into the shaping process, and by the project team, who will need to mould its FEL activities to meet the challenges that the project context provides. The failure to fully explore the project context early in the evolution of the project puts the project team at a disadvantage. Before they can proceed, they will have to find sources of information about the context or risk getting things terribly wrong.

Three areas of the context are particularly important for the project team to understand very early:
1. Challenges of the physical location
2. Availability and quality of the construction labor
3. Permitting difficulties

I discuss each of these areas in turn.

THE LOCATION: DEALING WITH REMOTENESS

We classify our projects into three groups: very remote, semiremote, and nonremote. Very remote locations are more than 200 km from any major population center (greater than 50,000). The actual projects in our database that are classified as very remote average 400 km to the nearest population center.* Examples of very remote sites are around much of the Caspian Sea, the North Slope of Alaska, Central Africa, interior North Africa, much of Papua New Guinea, some parts of Australia, and so on.

Semiremote projects are closer to a major population center, but that center is far too small to provide labor or large amounts of

---

*We are not entirely rigid about these definitions. For example, if the site is less than 200 km from a population center but is separated by 100 km of dense jungle without access, we would classify it as very remote.

support to the site. For example, we classify areas of Western Australia south of Perth as semiremote even though interior areas north of Perth are mostly very remote. We classify most coastal sites along the Arabian Gulf as nonremote, but inland sites in some areas would be very remote.

Offshore petroleum development projects pose another sort of challenge to classify. Areas with extensive prior development are classified as nonremote. For example, most of the North Sea, the U.S. Gulf of Mexico, and much of offshore Nigeria, and so forth, are classified as nonremote. However, the far northern frontier of the North Sea and the newly opened Atlantic margin are classified as very remote. If exploratory efforts are successful and they are further developed, they will be down-rated for future developments.

A little less than 20 percent of our sample is classified as very remote; about 35 percent, as semiremote; and the remainder, as nonremote. The projects are roughly the same size, with remote projects tending to be a bit larger. All three groups are widely scattered around the world, with every inhabited continent represented in all three groups.

What does remoteness do to the FEL effort? It makes it much harder. Table 10.1 provides some of the key differences in projects as a function of remoteness from population centers. The first thing to note is that teams are smaller. Holding size and complexity constant,

Table 10.1
Remote Sites Increase Difficulty of Projects

Factor[1]	Nonremote	Semiremote	Very Remote
Core team size	35	27	18
Integrated teams	60	55	36
Adequate staffing	66	65	38
Sponsor new to region	9	35	57
Problems with government	11	19	30
Major infrastructure needed	10	36	75
Labor must be imported	22	45	63

[1]All numbers are percentages of sample except for the first row, which is number of people (full-time equivalent).

the average core team for nonremote projects is twice as large as for very remote projects.*

When a project is remote, the cost of team members increases. People cannot be borrowed for short-term assignments from local facilities. And it is far more difficult to recruit team members for projects in very remote areas than in nonremote areas. Potential core team members know that they are likely to be posted to the site for two to three years as the project progresses. Even if their families will be permitted to accompany them, that is simply not very attractive to many two-income households these days. Because of the added cost, there is often pressure to keep team size down in remote projects.

Project directors must develop strategies for recruiting and retaining high-quality core team members for semiremote and very remote projects or for any megaproject that may be viewed as undesirable for any reason. There are obvious things like premium pay, but money is a limited incentive. The corporation needs to support the project directors by providing clear signals that willingness to serve on these difficult projects will be career-enhancing.

One of the most common approaches to recruiting and retention for remote megaprojects is rotational assignments, often in the form of alternating 28 days on and 28 days off. Each job is then shared with another person. Unfortunately, this approach is both very expensive and quite problematic in terms of effective teams.

The smaller team sizes are reflected in lower rates of team integration, especially for the very remote projects. One or more of the essential FEL owner functions is missing for about two-thirds of very remote projects. This result is merely echoed in the project director's assessment of the adequacy of the team size overall.

Although the project team is shrinking, the amount and difficulty of work is increasing. As remoteness increases, prior sponsor experience in the area declines and the percentage of projects experiencing difficulties with the host governments increases. Problems with the host governments are things such as being unable to move material across ports, being delayed by local police looking for "consideration," delays in processing workers into the country, and endless spools of

---

*The differences in team size are statistically significant $(P > |t| < .01)$.

red tape. Very remote projects were more likely to be in politically unstable environments and have security concerns.

As remoteness increases, the chances that the project will be required to install major new infrastructure—roads and bridges, power, potable water, community development, even airports—increases. In and of itself, infrastructure is not a problem. However, it is not the type of scope that most industrial sponsors execute very often, so it is unfamiliar. Perhaps more important, infrastructure is traditionally a government responsibility or the responsibility of a government-owned entity. When a project must provide infrastructure, it is likely stepping onto someone else's turf. In the worst case, part of the infrastructure will actually be developed and executed by the host government. Then the project has all of the concerns created by being dependent on third-party projects.

Finally, as remoteness increases, the chances rise that some or all of the labor will have to be provided from outside the country. Like infrastructure, that is not necessarily a problem, but it can be, especially if there are social and ethnic tensions that may be exacerbated by the imported labor or construction supervision.

The upshot of all this is that very remote megaprojects are front-end loaded significantly less well than less remote projects. Their average FEL at sanction is "poor." We left FEL-2 with open scope only 9 percent of the time for nonremote projects but 35 percent of the time for very remote projects. This is another example of the glaring irrationalities we find in megaprojects. The more team size, team integration, and FEL are needed, the less we tend to do. The result is that only 22 percent of very remote projects succeed.

All outcomes tend to degrade as remoteness increases, and they degrade rather sharply for very remote projects. But the outcome that is glaringly poor for very remote projects is operability of plant. This difference, which is highly statistically significant, is true despite the fact that very remote projects employ less new technology than their nonremote and semiremote counterparts. About 60 percent of very remote projects were classed as operability failures, versus about 30 percent of the remainder of the sample. In reading through the case histories, two things stand out. First, there were many, many quality control problems and the accompanying endless fixes. Second, there were numerous infrastructure problems, such as poor power reliability, lack of water supply, and inability to get things to the sites in a timely way for repair.

LABOR SUPPLY ISSUES

By their very nature, megaprojects strain the supply of construction labor, particularly in the highly skilled crafts. Shortage of craft labor should be considered the norm, not the exception, for megaprojects. In some parts of the world, severe shortages of labor are normal even for smaller projects, and from time to time, most parts of the world with significant construction activities have experienced shortages.

Determining the appropriate field staffing rates for megaprojects entails a complex optimization process that must juggle the following considerations:

- Availability by craft
- Productivity by craft
- Availability of craft versus wage rate
- Productivity of craft versus requirements (productivity tends to decline and may decline sharply as requirements increase)
- Availability and productivity versus the desired project construction schedule

It is the last item that is usually the most important consideration for megaprojects.

A labor shortage occurs when the numbers of qualified workers required to execute a given project in a given period of time cannot be found or cannot be found at prices the project can afford. As the schedule is shortened, the number of workers required at any given time increases rapidly. Just more than 30 percent of megaprojects experienced labor shortages, and those projects experienced a dismal 14 percent success rate, which is significantly poorer ($P \mid \chi^2 \mid$ < .006).

Labor shortages are only very rarely the root cause of megaproject failure. Rather, it is the recognition of the labor situation and how the project responds that determine success or failure. There is a set of front-end activities that relates directly to whether a project copes

successfully with labor availability issues: the work of the country
advance team in anticipating the labor situation, the use of labor surveys early in FEL, and the development of schedules with the number
of craft required assigned to each task, which is called resource loading. When resource loading was completed as part of FEL, longer,
more situation-appropriate schedules were set.

I return to this subject in Chapter 12 in the context of execution.
Some of the most spectacular megaproject failures have occurred
when the labor situation interacts with project requirements and weak
controls to produce a collapse of field progress.

PERMITTING PROBLEMS

The permitting process is a large part of the nexus between the project and the governments in whose jurisdictions the project will reside.
Note that I use the plural here, but it is unusual that only a single government is involved. The central government will always have some
role in authorizing megaprojects, but local and regional governments
also often play a role and in many cases are more influential for your
prospects than the central government.

In places with strong institutional environments, the permitting
process is not only structured but is also bound by rules. If you fully
comply with the rules, you will sooner or later receive your permits. Whether it is sooner or later depends very much on whether
there is strong social support for the project or significant opposition.
But even where there is strenuous opposition, if your project is fully
within the rules, the permits will eventually be granted.*

It is also important to understand that a country may have a strong
institutional environment overall, but the particular jurisdiction in
which you want to execute the project does not. In those cases, the
strategy should always be to try to get central government involvement and, in the best case, preemption of local prerogatives.

Twenty percent of the projects in our sample encountered significant problems in obtaining some or all of the permits that were

---

*When there is strenuous opposition in strong institutional settings, sponsors will sometimes elect to
abandon the project because they believe there will be too much collateral damage to other things they
may want to pursue or to their reputation.

Figure 10.13
Permitting Problems Create Havoc

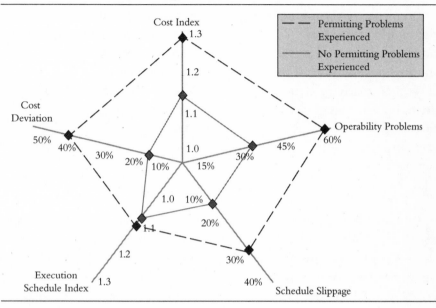

required to execute the project. (Remember, many more megaprojects encounter permitting problems, but many of those are never sanctioned and, therefore, do not make it into our sample.) We say a problem occurs when a permit is denied after appropriate application or if the permitting authorities sit on the application for six months or more beyond the promised decision date. The effects of permitting problems on project results are summarized in Figure 10.13, and they are not pretty. The solid line in the interior shows the outcomes of projects that did not experience permitting problems. They were not all great projects, but they are manifestly better on average than the projects that had permitting problems. Those projects averaged a 43 percent cost overrun, and 60 percent experienced operability problems. Note that they were about the same speed as the projects without permitting issues, but they had a very large slip in their execution schedules. What this tells us is that their schedules were much more aggressive than the projects without permitting problems. Again, speed kills.

Problems obtaining permits are not randomly distributed around the world. Less than 15 percent of projects in Europe, Australia, South America, Canada, or the United States experienced permitting problems. All the countries involved have (or did have at the time) relatively strong institutional frameworks for projects at the central government level. Permitting problems among the projects in the Middle East were almost unknown, with only a single project encountering difficulty. In most cases, the governments were sponsoring partners in those projects, which no doubt helps. But it is also true that the permitting frameworks in most of the Middle East are relatively clear.

By contrast, almost a quarter of the projects in Africa experienced problems, and that number is depressed by several cases in which there were no permitting problems because no permits were needed because there were no regulations. Eventually, as those countries create regulatory frameworks for their projects, things will change. More than 40 percent of the megaprojects in Asia experienced problems, and Central Asia tops the list with permitting issues in more than 70 percent of the projects. If we use Transparency International's Corruption Perceptions Index (CPI) as a measure of institutional strength, we find that the CPI correlates with permitting problems $(P > |z| < .02)$ in the expected way.

Only one industrial sector stands out as having more permitting problems $(P |\chi^2| < .04)$, and that is petroleum production. One oil and gas project in four suffers serious regulatory issues. These problems are not entirely confined to areas with weak institutional environments. Petroleum projects are more likely than other projects to encounter regulatory difficulties in Australia, in South America, and in countries with strong institutional environments.

The real question is whether the projects that suffered permitting problems were merely victims of the circumstances or whether they actively collaborated in their own demise. The answer is some of both. One element of FEL that we measure for every project is the level of definition of the permitting requirements and the actions that have been taken on permits. We expect the project teams to have explored the details of the permitting regime from an early point in FEL-2. We expect that the permitting process has been fully integrated into their FEL and execution schedule. We expect that a dialog started with the regulators early on and that the discussions continued as the project evolved so the regulators would not be surprised by the scope and its implications when the permit applications were received.

For projects generally, we consider a "preliminary" rating on permits to be the best practical status at authorization. This means that the team has fully explored the requirements and has submitted valid applications for all permits required. The rating only changes to "definitive" if the permits have been received or the authorities have signaled back that the applications are acceptable and the permits will be issued. That amount of assurance is not generally needed for projects, but it clearly is for megaprojects, even in areas with strong institutional settings. Figure 10.14 shows why.

When projects achieved a definitive rating on the permitting definition, they experienced permitting problems only 6 percent of the

Figure 10.14
Permitting Definition Is Good Investment

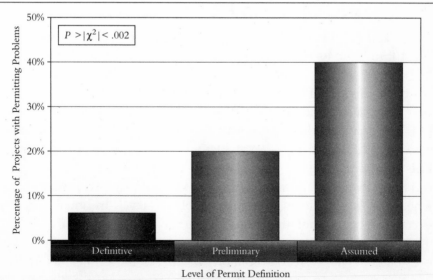

$P > |\chi^2| < .002$

Percentage of Projects with Permitting Problems

50%
40%
30%
20%
10%
0%

Definitive   Preliminary   Assumed

Level of Permit Definition

time. When they had achieved what is "best practical" for projects generally, 20 percent had problems, and when they blithely assumed they would get their permits on time, the number jumped to 40 percent. The shocking thing is that 17 percent of projects overall and about a quarter of petroleum development projects were in that "assumed" category!

Projects that were "preliminary" rather than "definitive" had much more aggressive schedules ($P > |t| < .009$) and were much less likely to have done a thorough job on the development of the project schedule ($P > |\chi^2| < .0001$). So one has to conclude that a good many of our permitting problems are self-inflicted. Too much drive for speed, too little attention to permitting requirements, and too little detail in the schedules to understand what needs to be done on permitting combine to generate many of the problems.

Ultimately, however, the best way to reduce permitting problems is to delay authorization until all necessary permits are received. Simply applying for the permits does not appear to make much difference. Making the permits an essential prerequisite to authorization does. We had only 3 percent of projects that encountered permitting problems when the permits had been received before project sanction.

How Long Should FEL Take?

I am asked often enough how long FEL should take for a megaproject that I know the issue must be addressed even if I would prefer to skip it. I would like to dismiss the question because I don't have a very satisfying answer. The period in question here is from the formation of the core team to start scope development through the end of FEL-3 (FEED). If there were pauses during the process, for example, between FEL-2 and FEL-3, the hiatuses were removed in calculating FEL duration.

There is no ideal duration for FEL except to say that it should end when FEL is completed to a "best practical" level. In other words, it is critically important that progress, rather than the calendar, determine how long FEL is. That means a certain amount of flexibility is essential. The typical $2 billion (based on the 2003 U.S. dollar)

Figure 10.15
Relationship between FEL Duration and Megaproject Costs

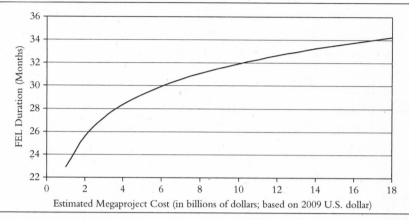

$2l_1 = 25 \text{mos}$

megaproject took about 25 months for FEL-2 and FEL-3, with FEL-3 consuming an average of 55 percent of that time.*

As expected and shown in Figure 10.15, the average FEL time increases as a function of project size.[†] The rate of increase is not terribly dramatic. Minerals projects on average took seven months longer to front-end load than other projects, although at least one minerals company stood out as quite fast at FEL (often with poor quality).

The interesting relationship is between FEL duration and FEL completeness. If FEL is very poor, FEL is on average several months faster than it would otherwise be controlling for size, type of project, and so on. This is to be expected. Not doing much doesn't take that long. If FEL is best practical, FEL duration is only slightly faster (two months) than would be expected. Otherwise, *there is no relationship at all between time and completeness of FEL.* This is as it should be.

---

*I have elected to cut the FEL durations at 60 months. No project with an FEL longer than five years actually took that long to work on defining the project. Rather, the shaping process was not going well, and a number of stops, starts, and reconfigurations were involved. In some instances, the projects were clearly searching for a business case during FEL-2.

[†]I am showing the estimated rather than actual costs because those readers planning a megaproject's FEL might have some idea of the former but little or no idea of the latter.

Any change in business objectives during either FEL-2 or FEL-3 is associated with an average eight-month extension of the FEL duration $(P > |t| < .007)$. Even with the delay, the objectives change tends to degrade FEL quality and decrease the chances of success $(P |z| < .0001)$.

Often the time required for FEL-2 (scope development) is very much a function of the progress and ease of the shaping process. When the shaping process is smooth, FEL-2 proceeds as rapidly as the staffing of the effort permits. But if there are significant shaping issues, FEL-2 should be slowed to stay synchronized with the shaping effort.

The time required to execute FEL-3 (FEED) varies only slightly with the size of the project. About 15 months are required, regardless of whether the project is larger (>$5 billion) or smaller (<$2 billion). When projects are larger, the feed is often done by two or more contractors in parallel. Only when projects are extremely large (>$10 billion) do we see a statistically reliable relationship between size and longer FEL-3. Then the FEED duration increases to nearly 20 months.

There is one FEL factor that is associated with shorter FEL-3 durations: doing a poorer job on that critical permitting definition factor that we discussed earlier in this chapter. We "save" about two months as permitting definition degrades from "definitive" to "preliminary" and another two as it degrades to "assumed" $(P |t| < .002)$. This underscores my earlier conclusion that time pressure was the driving force behind not doing an effective job in defining the permitting requirements. But if we encounter a permitting problem as a result of our shortcut, all of the "saved" time is given back, plus a 50 percent penalty.

WHY DO PETROLEUM DEVELOPMENT MEGAPROJECTS FAIL SO OFTEN?

We have now reached the point at which we can address a question raised in Chapter 3: Why do oil and gas development projects—also referred to as "E&P projects"—suffer such a disproportionate failure rate? (We will use the terms *petroleum development* and *E&P* [exploration and production] interchangeably. *E&P* is a bit of a misnomer in our case because we are referring only to the production portion of the process, not to exploration.) Almost four of every five petroleum development megaprojects fail, versus about one of two for all of the

Figure 10.16
E&P versus Other Megaproject Results

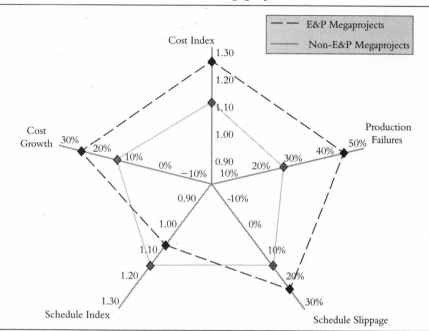

other sectors. I needed to wait until now to address the issue directly because FEL (as well as a number of other subjects we have covered) is an important part of the story.

There really can't be any question that the petroleum projects suffer more problems; the probability that the distribution of success that we see could be generated randomly is considerably less than 1 in 10,000. Figure 10.16 tells the story.

The average petroleum development megaproject is worse than megaprojects in other industrial sectors on cost overruns, cost competitiveness, production attainment failures, and schedule slippages. The only measure on which petroleum projects look better is the measure of schedule effectiveness, and that is an important part of the story.*

---

*The difference in schedule effectiveness is not statistically significant at a .05 cutoff probability value using a two-tailed test ($P |t| < .074$).

Table 10.2

Petroleum Development Projects Are Not Inherently More Difficult

Area of Potential Difficulty	E&P Megaprojects	Other Megaprojects
Size (actual cost in 2009 U.S. dollars)	3.6 billion	2.7 billion
Average FEL-2 and FEL-3 duration (months)	27	27
Execution duration (months)	44	41
With substantial new technology (%)	7	7
With Basic Data problems (%)	16	18
In very remote locations (%)	13	15
In labor–short locations (%)	27	33
With weather problems (%)	41	43
With a lead sponsor who is new to the area (%)	26	28
Government involvement (%)	34	46
Political violence in location (%)	7	13
Formal local content rules (%)	58	49
Adequate staffing (%)	66	57

One possible explanation of the difference in success rate could be simply that petroleum development projects are intrinsically more difficult than other megaprojects. But that hypothesis doesn't withstand close scrutiny. Table 10.2 lists 13 factors that might reasonably be considered potentially problematic for megaprojects. Many of the issues listed are in fact associated with poorer project outcomes. However, there is virtually no difference between petroleum development and other megaprojects on any of the measures, and in a number of cases, the nonpetroleum projects look more difficult. Petroleum development projects are larger at the end of the day, but most of the difference is because they overran more. They look a little longer, but that is because they slipped more. Even from a technology perspective, it's impossible to make a good case that petroleum development projects are more difficult. Both groups use the same amount of new technology. Both suffer the same rate of problems with Basic Data. And the average engineering content of the nonpetroleum projects is much greater.

The petroleum development sample was a little more likely to have formal local content requirements, but these requirements were not associated with a higher failure rate for the projects ($P\ |z|\ <\ .47$). But there is a fascinating difference here: nonpetroleum projects with formal local content requirements were, on average, 18 percent less expensive, whereas local content requirements were associated with no difference in cost for petroleum projects. For petroleum projects, local content requirements are associated with a sharp increase in the instances of reported problems with host government authorities and an increase in permitting problems. For nonpetroleum projects, local content requirements were only weakly associated with an increase in problems with host governments and were associated with a *decline* in permitting problems. The results for the nonpetroleum projects fit with what many megaproject managers have reported to me: When properly managed, local content is often inexpensive and seems to reduce opposition to the project from the host government and other stakeholders.

I find the international oil industry generally very hostile to formal local content requirements and generally intent on rolling them back whenever possible. In some instances the local content requirements are very difficult for petroleum companies to meet. This is especially true when the local content requirements are specific about what must be secured locally rather than how much. In these cases, the industry resistance is entirely understandable. In other cases, however, the resistance appears more ideological than logical. The industry needs to learn something from their colleagues in other sectors and genuinely embrace local content whenever it is feasible to do so. Despite differences in the treatment of local content, this issue explains very little of the difference in failure rate in petroleum projects. We must look elsewhere to understand it.

One of the intriguing features of petroleum development megaprojects is the extreme separation between the successful and unsuccessful projects. As shown in Figure 10.17, the 22 percent of petroleum development projects that were successful were spectacularly so. They had no cost growth, they were inexpensive, they operated as planned with an average production in the first year ahead of plan, and they experienced no schedule slippage whatsoever. The only respect in which they were less than extraordinary was in schedule performance, where they were merely average for projects with their characteristics. That one average result is, of course, no accident. The successful projects started execution with an average (that is, achievable) schedule and met it.

By sharp contrast, the failures were dismal failures. They overran their sanction estimates by more than a third, they cost 37 percent

Figure 10.17
E&P Successes versus Failures[1]

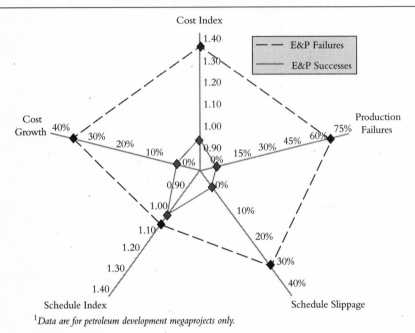

[1]Data are for petroleum development megaprojects only.

more than they should have, two-thirds experienced serious production problems, and their schedules slipped by more than 30 percent. The one outcome on which they fared reasonably well is schedule. There is no difference, statistically or practically, between successes and failures regarding schedule competitiveness. Again, this is no accident, and we will return to it shortly.

There are three big drivers of failure in petroleum development megaprojects. These three factors work individually and interactively to causes petroleum megaprojects to fail:

1. The completeness of FEL at authorization
2. Turnover in the project leadership
3. Schedule aggressiveness

I discuss each in turn.

Figure 10.18
Complete Front-End Loading Is More Important for Petroleum
Development Megaprojects

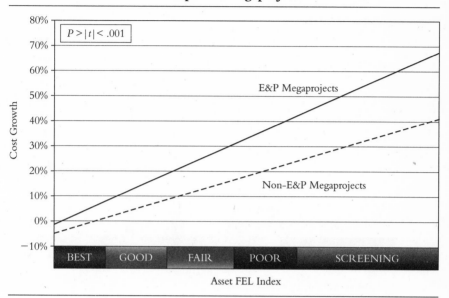

Poor Front-End Loading Devastates Petroleum Development Projects

We have emphasized the importance of FEL for all projects and especially megaprojects, but it turns out that petroleum development megaprojects are even more sensitive to even small lapses in FEL than other megaprojects. Two dimensions of outcomes are particularly hard hit when the FEL is anything other than "best practical": cost predictability and production attainment. The effects are shown in Figures 10.18 and 10.19. We measure FEL across three big areas for petroleum development projects: the reservoir, the facilities, and the wells construction. The combination of all three areas we call "asset FEL." In Figure 10.18, note that cost growth rises faster with asset FEL for oil and gas projects than for others. Note also that the relationship is stronger statistically as well. Figure 10.19 shows the relationship between production failures and asset FEL for E&P projects. What is

Figure 10.19
E&P Megaproject Production Attainment Depends on Front-End Loading[1]

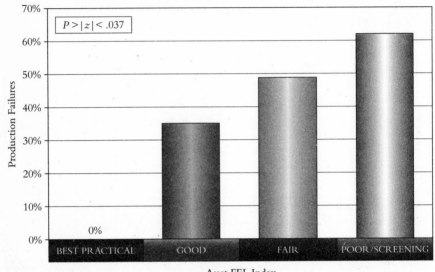

$P > |z| < .037$

Production Failures (y-axis): 0% to 70%

Asset FEL Index (x-axis): BEST PRACTICAL (0%), GOOD, FAIR, POOR/SCREENING

[1]*Data are for Petroleum Development Megaprojects only.*

striking is the sharp discontinuity between "best practical" FEL with no production attainment failures and "good" FEL, which jumps to more than one in three classified as production attainment failures.

Although E&P megaprojects tend to be less well defined than other megaprojects on every common measure, there is one measure on which E&P projects are very noticeably deficient: definition of the permit requirements. Figure 10.20 contrasts the level of permitting definition for the two groups. The statistical test results show that E&P is clearly different along this dimension. A "definitive" rating on this variable means that all key permits have actually been received. "Preliminary" means that applications have been submitted and discussions have been held with the regulators about the requirements. "Assumed" means literally that the teams assumed that the permits would be forthcoming in a timely manner but at sanction had still not made application. One E&P project in five assumed that everything was going to be alright, and about the same number had permits

Figure 10.20
E&P Permitting Is Deficient

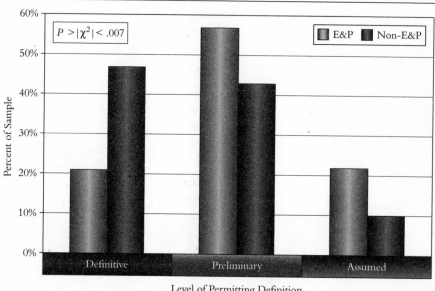

Level of Permitting Definition

in hand. By contrast, almost half of non–E&P projects had received their permits. In fact, many non–E&P companies refuse to sanction a project before the key permits are in hand. This bit of prudence is driven by the reality that permits are a signal that the government is on-board with the project. Permits are almost never withdrawn after they are granted unless there is a clear violation of the premises on which the permit was granted.

I was so surprised when I saw the number of "assumed" values on this scale for E&P that I went back to the source material and read the analysts' notes taken at the presanction interview. The attitude toward the permits was blasé; "they won't be any problem" was the most common comment from the teams.

Figure 10.21 suggests this confidence was misplaced. Lack of definition around the permit requirements was associated with cost growth for all megaprojects but was especially acute for E&P projects. Although part of this effect is explained by other factors, especially

Figure 10.21
Poor Permitting Definition Drives Cost Overruns

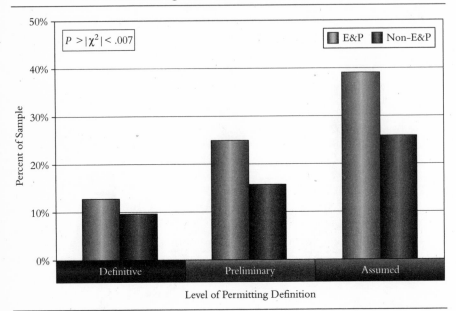

schedule aggressiveness, the link between poor definition of permitting and cost growth remains for E&P projects even when all other factors are controlled. Lack of permitting definition drove the failure to collect the permits in a timely fashion, which, in turn, was associated with delays, work-arounds, and overruns. The lack of definition of permits is a symptom of a "roll-the-dice" attitude that many E&P companies appear to take toward their projects.

TURNOVER IN PROJECT LEADERSHIP

The second important cause of E&P megaproject failure is turnover of the project director one or more times between the start of FEL-3 and the end of the project. (Turnovers made very late in execution when the project was substantially complete were not counted.) The project director, who may be called the project manager or facilities project manager in some systems, is the highest ranking project professional on a megaproject. E&P projects replaced that person at least once in 63 percent of projects versus 49 percent for non–E&P megaprojects.

Recall from our earlier discussion of turnover in Chapter 8 that most turnovers are not caused by project difficulties but rather by the needs of the sponsor, reassignment, or retirements or voluntary resignation. Turnovers in the project leader are rarely turnovers that involve only the one person. Most project directors have a small cadre of professionals with whom they work, and if the project director is reassigned, that cadre usually goes with him or her and a new cadre of people comes in with the new director. Turnovers in the project leader tend to damage all megaprojects, but they are devastating to E&P megaprojects. For non–E&P projects, the turnover of the project director was associated with a decline in the success rate from 62 percent to 39 percent. For E&P projects, the decline was from 48 percent to 7 percent! That's right, 93 percent of E&P megaprojects with a turnover of the project director failed.

Of course, turnover of the project director does not really explain all of those failures. Many bad things and poor practices tend to go together and reinforce one another. When project leadership turns over, FEL tends to be poorer, the team is more likely to be inadequately staffed, team integration is more likely to be absent, and the schedule tends to be more aggressive. However, even when all else is accounted for, turnover of the project director is still strongly associated with E&P project failure.

Why is project director turnover disproportionately damaging for E&P projects? Because E&P projects are usually organized in a manner that inadvertently renders the project directors critical to success and therefore leave the project very vulnerable to discontinuity in that position. Most non–E&P projects are organized with all of the technical functions reporting directly to the project director. The only important functional interface is between the project and the business. Although this interface is often fraught with difficulty, it is also often manageable.

Most E&P capital project organizations, and especially the large ones, are organized into at least three large technical functions: reservoir characterization and depletion planning, facilities engineering, and production wells drilling and completions. Even if E&P project teams describe themselves as integrated, the reality is that integration is fragile and depends heavily on the strength and whole asset view of the project director. Outside the project director, there is no individual with purview of all aspects of the development. There should be an asset development manager assigned by the business, but there almost never is. Therefore, that role falls inevitably to the project director.

In the parlance of organization theory, most E&P projects are weak to mid-strength matrix organizations. The functions maintain a fair degree of control of their personnel when they are assigned to projects. Very effective project directors pull the functions toward a "strong matrix" format. Most megaprojects that fail do so because of poor communication somewhere along the line. Weak matrix organizations are prone to communication failures, and when the project director turns over, the disconnect between functions becomes acute. This is most often manifested in E&P projects in production attainment failures because production attainment success is most dependent on full-functional integration. When there is no project director turnover, only 32 percent of E&P projects experienced production attainment failures. When the position changed hands, 60 percent did. For non-E&P projects, turnover of the project director was much less important to production attainment because all of the functions were more likely to have been fully integrated into the project team. This failure to strongly integrate the technical functions is the core pathology of E&P megaprojects.

Schedule Aggressiveness of E&P Projects

Another manifestation of risk taking in petroleum development is schedule aggressiveness. Schedule aggressiveness is measured as the ratio of the promised schedule for execution time made at sanction to the industry average actual schedule for a project of that size and type—the "benchmark schedule." E&P projects have much more aggressive schedules on average than do non-E&P megaprojects. The average difference is 15 percent of execution time, and the relationship is very powerful statistically ($P |t| < .0001$).

Schedule aggressiveness helps explain the failure of E&P projects to wait until permits were in hand to authorize the projects. More fundamentally, schedule aggressiveness is associated with Basic Data errors both for the reservoirs and for facilities. As discussed in Chapter 7, recovery from Basic Data problems is rarely possible.

One possible explanation of schedule aggressiveness is that projects primarily producing natural gas rather than oil are subject to commercial competition for gas sales. Project directors on gas projects often complain that those making the commercial deals did not consider project constraints when striving to close a deal, only to leave the project hopelessly schedule driven. By contrast, oil is purely a commodity and is only very rarely subject to niche market constraints.* The "gas hypothesis" for petroleum project schedule aggressiveness is flatly wrong. The oil projects have *more* aggressive schedules than do gas projects by 13 percent ($P |t| < .021$). The argument against driving schedules for pure commodity projects was discussed in Chapter 5 but is particularly compelling for crude oil projects. Schedule aggressiveness damages every outcome except schedule itself, on which it has no effect. From a business perspective, the strategy only has merit in the odd case in which the arrangements with the resource owner have distorted the goal of configuring the project so as to maximize NPV.

Remember that what appears totally irrational at the corporate level may be entirely rational at the individual level, which is the only level at which rationality actually applies. Much of the schedule aggressiveness in E&P projects is driven by the desire of business unit leaders to meet production goals that are the basis of their incentive compensation. This often involves attempting to advance production from one or a number of projects. Let me offer an ugly but not terribly unusual example.

The project involved the development of an oil reservoir with the expected ultimate production of 200 million barrels. The reservoir had no natural drive. Therefore, recovery depended on drilling water injection wells around the periphery of the reservoir and then producing wells toward the center. The project was a great success on cost and schedule up to the point at which drilling was set to begin. Then the business unit director ordered the team to drill the producers first and move up first production to fill a "hole" in the business

---

*The only exceptions are when the crude in question is particularly difficult to process, such as highly acidic crudes that can be processed in only a few refineries.

Figure 10.22
The ABCs of E&P Megaproject Failures

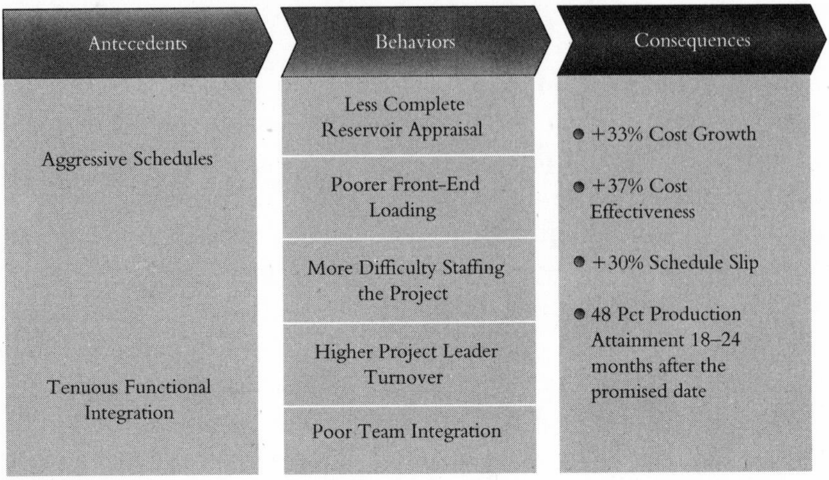

Antecedents	Behaviors	Consequences
Aggressive Schedules	Less Complete Reservoir Appraisal	+33% Cost Growth
	Poorer Front-End Loading	+37% Cost Effectiveness
	More Difficulty Staffing the Project	+30% Schedule Slip
Tenuous Functional Integration	Higher Project Leader Turnover	48 Pct Production Attainment 18–24 months after the promised date
	Poor Team Integration	

unit's production profile. The team objected vehemently, citing the potential for reservoir damage. They were overruled. They drilled the producers and started production. With fewer than 50 million barrels produced, the reservoir collapsed and production was halted forever. The capital investment was suddenly deeply NPV negative.

Figure 10.22 summarizes the flow of problems on E&P mega-projects, and many smaller projects as well. The problems start with aggressive schedules and the difficulties of integrating functions that have strong separate identity. Both of these antecedents separately and together are associated with a set of decisions and conditions that depress the chances of success. Aggressive schedules mean that we are less likely to start the project with a strong appraisal of the reservoir. This restricts the quality and completeness of the Basic Data package upon which all else will be based. Schedule aggressiveness and difficulty integrating the functions generates poorer FEL. Schedule aggressiveness also makes projects less attractive to staff and to project directors who realize they have been set up to fail. The consequences are clear enough: a project failure rate of almost 80 percent.

A Final Comment on Megaproject FEL

The failure to complete FEL on megaprojects is costing industrial firms and their shareholders hundreds of billions of dollars of value. This has been understood for some time now, and yet there are no signs of improvement. This can only mean that the business leadership of industrial firms fundamentally does not understand the relationship between FEL and success or that they have established incentive structures within the firm that render that understanding moot.

I believe that those charged with the education of business professionals, especially in the Untied States and Europe, bear a good deal of responsibility for the failure of business professionals in industrial firms to understand the connections here. Curriculums that fail to fully distinguish between the management of commodity industrial firms and other types of manufacturing or financial services do not prepare business professionals to understand the essential roles of technical professionals to the survival of the firm.

CHAPTER 11

CONTRACTING

If I had to select a few terms to describe megaproject directors and managers, *practical, hardheaded,* and *not given to magical thinking* would come to mind—except in one area: contracting. Contracting for the services needed to engineer, procure materials, and construct megaprojects is an area of intense disagreement and almost religious-like fervor among project professionals.* Individual experiences with single projects, good or bad, come to shape views for a career. Every approach to contracting appears to have both ardent adherents and steadfast opponents. I do not expect the following discussion to change either of those groups, but I hope some facts will aid those still searching for what to do.

Contractors tend to do good projects well and bad projects poorly. By that I mean that contractors almost always succeed when the project has a strong business case, fully aligned stakeholders, bought-in sponsors, an integrated owner team, and best practical front-end loading (FEL). Conversely, when the sponsors are fighting among themselves, other stakeholders are sniping, the business case is marginal, the owner team is missing key functions, and the FEL is mediocre, the contractors always look moronic. We tend to exaggerate the importance of contracting approach to project success or failure. No contracting approach guarantees success; most contracting approaches can succeed. Contracting is a second-order concern.

That being said, some contracting approaches are fraught with more dangers. Some are unsuitable for certain situations. Some strategies work for some owner organizations but fail miserably for others

---

*The reader who is unfamiliar with the many special terms used in contracting in industrial projects should refer to the Glossary before reading this section.

because the strategy depends on owner strength. Some strategies help a well-developed project deliver on its promise while failing on a project that is less well prepared. Every contracting approach brings with it uncertainty and possibility. Contracting is difficult, and it is situational. Perhaps that is why so many owner project and business professionals want to believe they have found *the* answer. But in reality, *the* answer probably does not exist. There is, however, one rule that always seems to apply: if sponsors decide to engage in contracting games, by which I mean trying to get the better of contractors, they will always lose. Contractors always have been and always will be better at contracting games than owners. Their lives depend on it.

Before moving into alternative approaches, I need to address who should be involved in contracting decisions. The basic contracting strategy must be addressed as part of the project shaping phase. Disagreements among partners on this issue can be so violent that the project can come apart. The business leaders who will be fighting out any issues must be informed by their project management teams, and the view of the project director should weigh very heavily in the discussions. After all, it will be the project director who must ultimately make the strategy work.

When it comes to the actual selection of contractors, that decision should absolutely be made by the project director and the team. Any involvement by business leadership in the selection of individual contractors is inappropriate and could be viewed as a breach of trust by partners. Any involvement of the lead sponsor's purchasing (procurement or sourcing) organization in the selection of contractors is likely to be catastrophic. The selection of the right contractor often comes down to the selection of the right contractor team. That needs to be a team that the sponsor team can work with creatively. Purchasing does not have to live with the selection made and only rarely has the expertise required to even assist.

CONTRACTING APPROACHES

There are four basic types of contracts for megaprojects with endless variations. I define each in this chapter and then show the relationships between success and the use of the different approaches. In addition, I discuss some fundamentals of successful contracting for large complex projects.

EPC Lump-Sum (Fixed-Price) Contracting

EPC lump-sum contracts are the most common form of megaproject contracts and involve a single contractor being responsible for engineering, procurement, and construction for the whole project or for some portion of the whole project under a single contract. This basic form has a number of variations.

1. All parts of the project are under the single EPC contract, including installation for offshore projects. If commissioning and startup are included, the contractual form is generally considered "turnkey," which is to say that an operating facility is turned over to the owner/sponsors. The contractor will often subcontract for fabrication/construction and for various other activities. This single prime contractor form is unusual for large megaprojects because single contractors rarely have enough people and the full range of skills to devote to a very large EPC lump-sum contract without creating lumpiness* problems in their project portfolio. In some cases, contractors have formed joint venture consortia that offer a single EPC lump-sum contract for a large megaproject. These consortia often focus on a single technology package.

2. A second form of EPC lump-sum contracting involves multiple prime contractors reporting to the owner/sponsors. Multiprime arrangements are common on very large megaprojects where a single prime contractor would be reluctant to take the risks associated with the entire project. Multiprime arrangements require a good deal of owner/sponsor competence to manage the interfaces between the contractors.

3. "Conversion" to lump-sum contracts is a strategy that starts the project with reimbursable engineering and procurement and

---

*In this context the term *lumpiness* refers to an unbalancing of desired portfolio risk due to a single element in the portfolio being unduly large.

then provides an option for the sponsor and engineering and procurement contractor to convert to a whole project lump-sum contract at some point during engineering.

4. Occasionally, there will be some portions of the project done on a reimbursable basis. If most of the total cost is in an EPC lump-sum contract, I classify the project in that category, although I discuss some ingenious mixing of lump-sum and reimbursable contracts later.

Ⓑ

Reimbursable EPC and EPCm   *↗ most Flexible*

Under this form, a single contractor is responsible for all (or the great majority) of the project under a contract that reimburses the contractor based on the quantity of services and materials provided. The details of how the contractor is reimbursed are very important. Alternatives include a percentage fee, fixed fee, fixed fee and fixed overhead, and various incentive forms.

The key attribute of reimbursable EPC is that the engineering and procurement contractor controls the construction/fabrication as well. That provides both opportunity and lots of problems for the owner/ sponsors. The precise manner in which the contractor is reimbursed interacts with the control of the field to determine the incentive structure under which the contractor actually is operating, which may be quite different from the incentive structure under which the sponsors think they are operating. We return to this subject later in this chapter. The fee structure for reimbursable contracts is very important and the subject of a great deal of misinformation.

Reimbursable EPC can also be operated with a multiprime arrangement, much like multiprime EPC lump-sum contracts. Lump-sum and reimbursable EPC contracts can be run on the same project and are sometimes even run on the same site, but with generally very poor results. The poor results are driven by the fact that the contractors with reimbursable contracts are able to take resources away from the lump-sum contractors, resulting in (quite justifiable) large claims by the lump-sum contractors. In one case, a contractor with a lump-sum contract actually quit a major project under these circumstances, resulting in a complete disaster.

A hybrid of this model is EPCm—engineering, procurement, and construction management. In this case, the engineering and procurement contractors hire the constructors/fabricators and manage their work. They may hire the constructors on any form of contract—reimbursable, unit rates, lump-sum, or whatever—but the full costs of construction are passed directly to the owners/sponsors without risk to the EPCm contractor(s). I group EPCm with EPC reimbursable contracts for a very simple reason: they behave the same way. The key characteristic is that the engineering contractors control the construction activities.

Alliance Contracts

Alliance contracting is a particular form of reimbursable incentivized contracting that was pioneered in the petroleum industry in the UK North Sea in the 1990s. It is not to be confused with long-term multiproject relationships between an owner and a contractor, which are sometimes also called frame agreements. My use of the term *alliance* here refers to a grouping of all (or almost all) of the contractors working on a megaproject under a single compensation scheme. The grouping of contractors takes place for the particular project; this form is not to be confused with a contractor consortium or contractor joint venture. The primary goal of the alliance contracting approach is to align the goals of the contractors with those of the owner/sponsors through a "shared destiny" approach. The schemes involve some form of bonuses or gainshare (usually in the form of splitting underruns among the owner/sponsors and contractors) in the event that the project performs better than targets, usually on cost. In the event of an overrun, some alliance schemes have the contractors share some portion of that overrun up to some cap.

Mixed Contracts

Mixed contracting is a strategy that involves reimbursable engineering and procurement, including, in some cases, the procurement of some lump-sum package items, followed by lump-sum contracts for construction or fabrication by constructors or fabricators that are independent of the engineering and procurement firm(s). The construction lump-sum contracts can be a single lump-sum contract to a construction management organization or a series of lump-sum con-tracts by craft discipline. However, the strategy does not apply in cases in which the engineering firms procure the construction or fabrica-tion work. That strategy would be an EPCm arrangement. The key characteristic here is that the constructors and fabricators are indepen-dent of the engineering contractor(s), which is to say they are prime contractors to the sponsors.

Frequency of Use on Megaprojects

One of these four basic contract types, with variations, of course, was followed by all of the megaprojects in our database. Figure 11.1 provides the breakdown of the contract types in our sample. Lump-sum contracting in a number of variations is by far the most com-mon approach to contracting large projects. Although EPC lump-sum contracts predominate, they are actually less common than they were in the 1990s. Some parts of the world, notably Canada and Australia, moved away from lump-sum contracting as their project markets heated up in the past decade because EPC lump-sum arrangements

Figure 11.1
EPC Lump-Sum Contracting Predominates

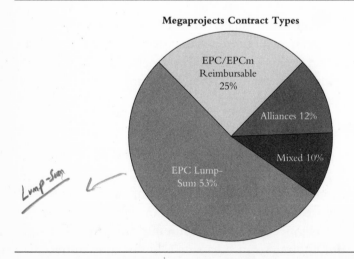

Megaprojects Contract Types

tend to become less cost-effective for owners/sponsors, or even alto-gether unobtainable, when the market for EPC services is overheated.

There is little or no pattern by industrial sector. No chemicals sec-tor projects were executed with an alliance-type contract, but every contract type was found in all industrial sectors. Contract type is, however, clearly influenced by geography. EPC lump-sum con-tracts dominated the megaproject contracts in the Middle East, South America, Asia, and Africa. This is largely an artifact of the involvement by government-owned companies as sponsors or cosponsors of proj-ects in these areas. Governments tend to prefer whole project lump-sum contracting the world over; more than 80 percent of the projects in which the lead sponsor was a nationally owned company used an EPC lump-sum contracting strategy, versus about 45 percent of other megaprojects. We return to the subject of government involvement in the contracting process, which we argue is rarely helpful, later in this chapter. Alliances were used predominantly in OECD countries, except in Japan. The other contract forms were used in every region.

There is no pattern between estimated project cost (inflation adjusted) and type of contract. Every type of contract had some "ele-phant" projects in their set. The alliances ended up larger, but that is due to overruns, not intent.

CONTRACTS AND PROJECT OUTCOMES

Figure 11.2 shows the success and failure rates for our four basic con-tract types. The results will not be particularly surprising to anyone who has followed our research on contracting for industrial projects over the past 10 years. The EPC lump-sum projects had a success rate that was about average for the megaprojects overall. Given that they constitute more than half the sample, that result is surely to be expected. The reimbursable projects fared a little worse than the lump-sums. However, if we control for other factors that affect project out-comes, the reimbursable projects are not statistically different than the EPC lump-sum in terms of results. Reimbursable contracting is by far the most flexible approach for owners/sponsors. The owners/sponsors have complete control over schedule and quality. The greater control also, of course, implies a very hands-on approach to the project.

Figure 11.2
Alliance Contracting Hurts Performance; Mixed Contracting Helps

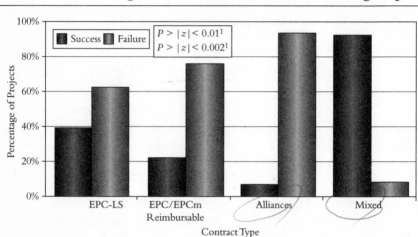

Contract Type
[1]After Controlling for Team Integration and Front-End Loading

Two contract types clearly influence project results, albeit in oppo-site ways. The alliance arrangements were in almost every case disas-trous. The mixed strategy projects were disproportionately successful. To test whether contract type has an independent effect on project results, I first controlled for team integration and the completeness of FEL because they are major drivers of success and failure and are far more important to explaining variation in success than contract type. Projects using alliance contracts and those using mixed contracts are both statistically significantly different than the average in terms of success rate.*

The patterns of outcomes are different for different contract types. Figure 11.3 provides some greater granularity around the outcomes of projects by contract type. The projects using EPC lump-sum con-tracts averaged only modest overruns of about 13 percent, but they suffered an unacceptably high rate of failure in production attainment. The danger of this trade-off is inherent in lump-sum contracting. If the contractor is not in a loss position, quality will be reasonably

---

*Results are based on logit regression z coefficient probabilities.

Figure 11.3
Patterns of Outcomes Vary by Type of Contract

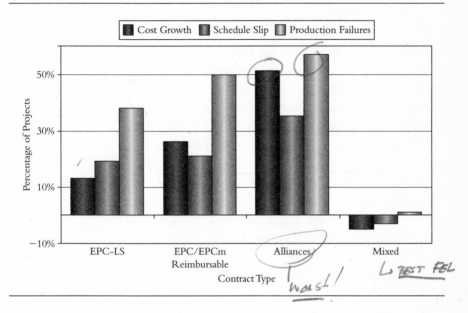

good if owner/sponsor controls are good. If the contractor is in a large loss position, quality will be poor. The high incidence of production attainment failure in the EPC reimbursable class was mainly driven by a higher incidence of the use of new technology and the higher use of reimbursable forms in highly remote locations. Those two factors together account for most of the differential production attainment failure rate. Highly remote locations are more likely to end up with reimbursable contract forms because obtaining cost-effective EPC lump-sum bids is difficult when the uncertainties around logistics are high. The production attainment result is not a reflection on the use of reimbursable contracting; the reimbursable contracts were selected in part based on the uncertainty associated with the technology and location. The result does remind us about the importance of solid Basic Data.

The results of the alliance projects are dismal with respect to every outcome, but cost overruns and production shortfalls are particularly so. The average alliance-contract project experienced more than 50 percent cost growth, and nearly 60 percent of the projects were

production attainment failures. Only a few alliance-contract projects were successful. Our results regarding alliance contracting flatly
contradict the views of a number of published articles on the subject. Miller and Lessard, for example, believe that "Substantial gains in
costs, schedules, and project delivery . . . can be made by the adoption
of generative owner-contractor relationships," that is, alliance-type
arrangements.[1] As I discuss later, however, these arrangements actually increase instability in project execution. I would like to be able to
report that this contracting strategy is dead, but that is not the case. It
continues to be used, often by companies using it for the first time.

The projects using a mixed strategy fared by far the best of any
contractual approach. One reason for this was that, for whatever reason, the projects using mixed contracting were the best front-end
loaded of any group; they averaged a "best practical" FEL index.
However, excellent FEL was not the only reason for their success.
Even after I control for FEL and team integration, the mixed-strategy
projects fared significantly better. I discuss the reasons for their success
later in this chapter.

Not surprisingly, how sponsors rated the performance of their prime
contractors correlates very strongly with how the projects came out.
The differences by contract type are shown in Figure 11.4. We asked the
owner's team to rate the overall performance of the prime contractors on the project on the simple three-point scale: good, about average, and poor. The contractors with EPC lump-sum contracts were the
only normally distributed group; a little more than a quarter were rated
"good" and "poor," with the majority in the "about average" category.
The ratings of the contractors who had lump-sum contracts were reflec-
tive of the quality of the facilities more than any other outcome. Neither
cost growth nor schedule slippage was important, but quality associated
with facility performance accounted for nearly half of the total variation
in the contractor ratings.

For the reimbursable contracts, what the ratings are picking up
most strongly is slippage in the execution schedule. Although many
of the facilities had operability problems, the sponsor teams are not
blaming that outcome on the contractors.

For those who had alliance and mixed strategy contracts, there is so
little variation in the ratings that it is impossible to quantitatively link

Figure 11.4
**Sponsors View Contractor Performance Negatively in Alliance and
Reimbursable Contracts**

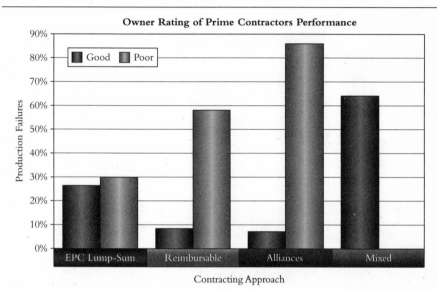

Owner Rating of Prime Contractors Performance

the teams' unhappiness and happiness, respectively, to any particular outcome. We know from the case studies that the sponsor teams were genuinely outraged at the attitude and performance of their contractors on the alliance-contract projects. As I show later in this chapter, I think they really have mostly themselves to blame.

Having now described the relationship between contractual approaches and project results, I want to explore the strengths and weaknesses of each approach suggesting what promotes success with each strategy.

THE CENTRAL ISSUES IN CONTRACTING STRATEGY

As we discuss contracting strategy in this section, there are three important considerations that need to be kept clearly in mind: the capabilities of the sponsors, the nature of the project, and the state of the EPC services markets. All three must be carefully and honestly

Figure 11.5
Contract Selection Decision Making

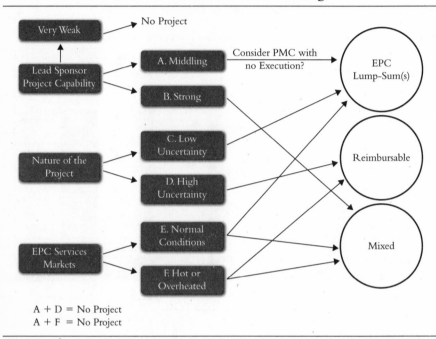

$A + D$ = No Project
$A + F$ = No Project

assessed if a reasonable approach is going to result. The way these issues should push the contracting decisions is shown in Figure 11.5.

Sponsor Capabilities Influence Contract Approach

The following questions need to be addressed:

- Has the lead sponsor undertaken large projects before?
- Does the lead sponsor's business leadership understand the owner's role in project management?
- Does the lead sponsor have a mature project work process? By *mature*, I mean a work process that has been used many times before by the sponsor project organization, with proper training of its people on the use of the work process.
- Can the lead sponsor (with assistance from partners if they are willing) staff FEL with all of the needed functional leads?

WHERE IS PEARLY?

- Can the lead sponsor develop a detailed estimate and schedule for a megaproject?
- Does the lead sponsor have a procurement organization that can order long-lead equipment during FEL prior to authorization?
- Can the sponsor field a strong controls organization that can fully monitor and control engineering and construction?

If the answer to most of the questions above is "no," the company is not ready to take on a leadership role for any megaproject. If the answers are mixed and "sort of," this should push the company toward an EPC lump-sum contracting strategy, perhaps with independent contractor support for certain missing skills sets. The focus will be on the preparation of a strong invitation to bid (ITB) package followed by strong quality assurance/quality control (QA/QC) in execution. These middling answers also make the use of a project managing contractor (PMC) more attractive, but as I discuss later, projects with PMCs did not fare well. Sponsors that can answer all of the questions with an unqualified "yes" can use whatever strategy they prefer.

The Nature of the Project -- *RISK PROFILE*

Some projects must carry more uncertainty into execution than others. New technology is one main source of uncertainty. Highly remote areas are another. Such projects are inherently more difficult. Greater difficulty translates into a higher incidence of late changes, especially during engineering. The probability of late changes influences the relative merits of different contracting strategies.

If change during execution is highly probable, even with excellent FEL, the contracting strategy is pushed away from EPC lump-sum contracting and toward a strategy with reimbursable engineering. This is because changes rapidly undermine the cost-effectiveness of EPC lump-sum strategies. It does not follow, however, that construction or fabrication work must be reimbursable.

The State of the EPC Services Market

When the markets for engineering services, vendor-fabricated equipment, and craft labor are overheated, the chances of obtaining a cost-effective EPC lump-sum bid are reduced. The contractors view the circumstances as risky for them, and given the state of the market, they can afford to bid conservatively. If a lump-sum strategy is going to be pursued in a hot market, the sponsors need to remove as many of the risk elements from the contractor as possible. For example, prices can be indexed, currency risks hedged or otherwise reserved to the owners, and equipment ordered during FEL on owners' novation.

Nonetheless, if the markets are hot enough, it may become simply impossible to obtain EPC lump-sum bids or the bids may be high enough to render the project uneconomic. If the sponsor group cannot manage a reimbursable format, at least for engineering, the appropriate action may be to cancel the project.

During the long period of oversupply of EPC contractors up to 2003, weaker owners were able to have some successful megaprojects because the contractors could in effect bail them out of trouble and, given the lack of alternatives, were highly motivated to do so. EPC lump-sum contracts were more common in that period and more likely to be successful than they are now.

THE ROLE OF EXTERNAL FINANCING ON CONTRACT APPROACH

When banks finance projects, they routinely require that the project be contracted via EPC lump-sum contracting and often even require that a single lead contractor be responsible for the entire project. These requirements, as well as the behavior of government entities, are the primary reasons that EPC lump-sum contracting predominates in megaprojects.

It is regrettable that banks insist on lump-sum contracting for two reasons. First, lump-sum contracting of very large projects is expensive, and the larger the project, the larger the penalty, especially when market conditions are tight. Second, EPC lump-sum contracting has absolutely no bearing on the risk profile of the project. Bankers, like some sponsor businesspeople and lawyers, fail to understand that lump-sum contracts are not a ceiling on the cost of the project. Indeed, they are a floor on the cost because surely no less than the contract price will be paid. Furthermore, although cost performance

Act Ks a Floor

is important, it is not nearly as important as operability, and when lump-sum contractors start to bump up against that contract "ceiling," the first thing to suffer is operability of the facilities. Given that banks are repaid via the cash flow from production, it behooves them to start understanding project risk at a first principles level.

WHAT DRIVES SUCCESS AND FAILURE IN EPC LUMP-SUM CONTRACTING?

EPC lump-sum contracting is a perfectly acceptable way to contract for megaproject execution. Many successful projects have been completed using some form of this basic contract vehicle. There are some important pitfalls to be avoided, and there are some erroneous beliefs about lump-sum contracting among many sponsors that tend to push us into making disastrous mistakes. It is these pitfalls and mistakes we need to review, as well as some creative uses of this vehicle. EPC lump-sum contracting is a risk-averse approach to contracting from the owners' perspective. Ironically, it is an approach that tends to work well only when inherent risk in the project is low anyway.

Some Key Pitfalls In EPC Lump-Sum Contracting

Much of the benefit of EPC lump-sum contracting derives from competitively bidding the work. The process of preparing the ITB, prequalifying a set of contractors that will be invited to bid, and then evaluating the bids themselves provides the sponsors with a great deal of information that can be used to help guide the project to success. The key to success lies as much in the process of competitive bidding as the results in terms of low bid value. The competitive bidding process provides the sponsors with excellent information about how much the project should cost if (and only if) they interpret the bid responses correctly. What this means is that there is very little value to sponsors in sole-source EPC lump-sum contracting. Our research shows what others have shown as well: sole-source lump-sum contracting is an expensive option.[2]

Sole-source EPC lump-sum contracts sometimes are used because a technology license that the sponsor wants comes bundled with an

EPC contractor. That arrangement is enormously bad for sponsors' wallets. Such tied-sale contracting arrangements clearly are a restraint of trade, even if they are not universally illegal.

Other situations that generate sole-source lump-sum contracts can be at least as bad. The worst case is when the primary FEED contractor is going to be allowed to bid the project in a lump-sum competition. This often has the effect of discouraging other qualified firms from bidding, resulting in the FEED contractor receiving the project by default. Let me provide an egregious example.

The project was in a remote area that suffered serious security concerns. The FEED contractor, who was experienced in the area while the lead sponsor was not, carefully built the hourly labor rate. The labor would be sourced from an expensive area and the labor would have to be flown in and out of the sites daily. The security costs would add greatly to the rate, and so on. The final expected hourly cost was well north of $100 U.S. per hour. The FEED contractor, as he had fervently hoped, was the only bidder; no one else was interested, primarily because the FEED contractor was being allowed to bid. The contractor then took home almost $100 on every hour as a low-cost source of labor was "discovered" and the local army was suddenly willing to provide security (for a small consideration), all of which resulted in an extra $500 million in profit to the contractor.

Still another route to the sole-source EPC lump-sum contract is the "convertible" lump-sum contract. This form starts as a reimbursable engineering and procurement contract with an option to convert to a lump-sum contract at some point during engineering. In principle, there is nothing wrong with this approach and a lot to like. In principle, it means that almost all of the potential cost growth and schedule slippage will have been discovered by mid-engineering and there will be very little remaining risk to the engineering and procurement contractor in taking the project on as a lump-sum contract with a minimal premium.

In practice, convertibles usually turn out very differently. Because the owner expects the contractor to choose to convert, the owner is not prepared for any other outcome. The field controls organization needed to continue the project on a reimbursable basis is not there, nor has the sponsor done the things needed to bid the construction to a set of prequalified construction management organizations. The engineering and procurement contractor, who is expecting to do construction on whichever basis he or she believes will be more lucrative, would not cooperate with another construction management organization anyway. If the contractor believes more money can be earned through lump-sum contracting, he or she goes with lump-sum; otherwise, the contractor stays with reimbursable. It is one more contracting game sponsors can't win.

Schedule Incentives and Liquidated Damages

EPC lump-sum contracts always include powerful incentives to minimize cost. Any money saved is profit earned for the contractor. However, the same structure creates incentives to float the schedule to whatever duration will assist in minimizing cost. Fortunately, good cost performance on EPC lump-sum contracts correlates very strongly with good schedule performance ($P \mid r \mid < .02$) and limited schedule slippage (.01). The addition of incentives to achieve schedule has no relationship with better schedule performance. Directionally, the statistics point in the opposite direction! When schedule incentives were included in lump-sum contracts, they were associated with an increase in the frequency of production attainment failures ($P \mid \chi^2 \mid < .03$) in all industrial sectors. What is going on is quite apparent: at the end of the project, when the contractor company could see the possibility of gaining the schedule incentives by acceleration, it cut corners on quality so substantially that operability was damaged well into the second year after startup. Any time they actually saved toward the end of the project was minimal, but the damage to the project's value was huge. Schedule incentives should not be used.

Sometimes schedule incentives have the effect of reducing schedule slippage but do so simply by lengthening the forecast schedules. The most extreme form of this game involves the FEED contractor insisting on a percentage of any sales of product that can be made due to early completion of the project. Being the FEED contractor, he or she is in a position to manipulate the schedule promised and then profit handsomely from this pessimism.

Liquidated damages are a contract provision that imposes a penalty from the contractor if a project is late. In some cases the penalties are quite substantial. Liquidated damages generally are not applied until a project is several months beyond the expected target completion date. Of course, liquidated damages cannot be applied if the sponsors were responsible for the delay or if force majeure can be claimed successfully. Liquidated damages appear to have only a negligible effect on the low bids for projects, although they are so intensely disliked that some contractors may choose not to bid. In some cases, liquidated damages are essential because there are very large downside consequences to the sponsors of the project being late. These circumstances include cases in which the production has been forward sold with penalties for nondelivery and cases in which a large value stream is dependent on the completion of the project, such as a petroleum field's production depending on the completion of a gas plant. Unlike schedule incentives, liquidated damages appear to work. The average schedule slippage on lump-sum projects with liquidated damages was only 6 percent. However, when I control for FEL, the relationship between liquidated damages and schedule slippage disappears.

Sponsors must understand that the schedule is the most common source of contractor claims. In some cases these claims are entirely justified. But schedule claims are a major source of abuse by contractors as well. There are so many forms of claims games relating to schedule, I cannot hope to cover them all. Fortunately, that has already been done.[3]

Taking the Very Low Bid — *Contractor wants to $$ RECOVER ---*

We have already discussed at several prior points what happens when a significantly low bid is accepted. (We defined a significantly low bid as one that is $100 million [in 2009 terms] less than the next lowest bid.) Acceptance of such a bid guarantees that the bidder does not fully understand the project or has made a disastrous bidding error. Either way, the sponsor will lose. Occasionally sponsor greed drives acceptance of such a low bid. More often, however, the involvement of a government-related partner requires that any low bid will win.

All of the EPC lump-sum contracts that were won on significantly low bids—that is, $100 million or more lower than the next closest bidder—failed. When the "winning" contractors realized the magnitude of their low bids, they immediately started to try to recover their losses. They floated the schedules longer to minimize costs believing (correctly in most cases) that they could avoid liquidated damages. Even if the liquidated damages would be triggered, the amount of money contractors paid in liquidated damages would be relatively unimportant in the bigger scheme of things. The most damaging aspect of their behavior, however, was to cut quality corners at every opportunity. The sobering aspect of this is that the strength of the sponsors' controls organization for the project had no mitigating effect on the ability of the contractors to cut corners on quality when they were facing cost overruns on lump-sum contracts. The operability results were simply unaffected by controls for the lump-sum projects. (For non–lump-sum projects, however, higher quality controls in execution were clearly associated with fewer operability problems.) There is also no reliable relationship between turnkey provisions in the lump-sum contracts with regard to operability. The contractors on turnkey projects appear to be increasing their bids enough—about 5 percent—to absorb any losses associated with performance guarantees.

When EPC lump-sum contractors are facing a significant loss on a project, they routinely take several actions that further damage the project. They start squeezing their subcontractors and suppliers and slowing down payment. That causes the subcontractors to go into defensive mode, looking for claims opportunities. The losing contractor will also start thinning out his or her management people on the project in an attempt to save money. This often extends right down to the general foreman level for fabrication or construction. The staffing levels need to be articulated down to the general foreman level in the bids, and then the sponsors need to try to hold the contractors to those levels as the project proceeds. I say "try" because it will be very difficult to do.

Acceptance of significantly low bids is so strongly associated with bad results that I believe that the procedure for handling them needs to be addressed between partners as a shaping issue. If addressed as a shaping issue that requires a full investigation of a seriously low bid, there will be at least some possibility of getting the bid rejected or allowing the contractor to amend. One might imagine that given the overheated state of the megaproject market since 2003, no one will have to worry about very low bids. This is not so; serious bidding errors were made right through the boom market.

When Governments Control Contracting

In many countries in the world and for almost all nationally owned companies, the government controls the contracting process. In almost all cases, the government rules require competitive bidding of essentially all contracts. Often, as mentioned before, the rules will require that the contracts be lump-sum, fixed-price arrangements. In some cases, the rules do not actually stipulate that fixed-price contracts be let. However, they require specific government approval for all transactions over a certain amount. In one important case, the amount is $10,000. What this means is that the project would have to return to the government to secure approval every time it spent much of anything, which would be not only impracticable but wide open to abuse. The solution is to make a single expenditure for the entire project amount.

Governments almost always require that low bids be accepted. Acceptance of significantly low bids almost always triggers project failure. This means that prequalification of bidders is the most important single step in the contracting process. Not only must the prequalification process be thorough, but it must be done with an eye on the possibility that the government will seek to add bidders that, for whatever reason, it wants to win the competition. Remember, this is not just a Third World phenomenon. It happens everywhere.

The most important single change that could be made in the usual low-bid acceptance procedure is a provision for an investigation of any low bid that is substantially separated from other bids. The definition of *substantial* can be either a dollar amount (I would suggest $100 million) or a percentage amount (I would suggest 10 percent). Ideally, the investigation would enable the low bid to be rejected in the event that it is based on a misunderstanding of the requirements or an estimating error.

One common government provision that causes misunderstandings with bidders are rules forbidding anything but written communication between bidders and the project in the period between the issuance of the ITB and the award of the work. Although this may seem reasonable to ensure a level playing field, it greatly hinders effective communication. Very early in project development, discussions need to start to amend these rules to allow a series of face-to-face (or telephone conference) meetings between the evaluation team and all of the bidders during the bid preparation. These occasions would allow the bidders to ask any questions in the presence of everyone.

There also needs to be allowance for the team to verify a bidder's representation of qualifications when questions arise during the bid evaluation process. One of our megaprojects failed because one of the bidding companies exaggerated its experience with the 3D computer-aided design (CAD) system. (They owned the system but had never actually used it!) When their bid was evaluated, some members of the evaluation team raised questions about whether the bidder really understood the CAD system, but they were precluded from verifying the bidder's qualifications at this point. The result was that a critical part of the design was six months late, equipment was late being ordered, and materials were incorrect. The project spiraled out of control.

Some government rules concerning secrecy of company cost estimates have the ability to cause a significant amount of trouble. The government concern is that information about the estimate will be brokered to contractors and provide an unfair advantage. But in some cases the secrecy provisions become absurd. For example, one national company keeps the sanction estimate secret from the project teams! The effect is that they have no idea of the relationship between what they are scoping and what things cost.

The usual assumption is that government rules are immutable and must be accepted. That is, of course, usually true. However, we did have a few projects that successfully argued with the governments for rule changes that would allow more flexibility. The project directors started discussions with the government about the contracting rules very early, sometimes more than two years before the ITBs were sent out. They made their successful arguments for greater flexibility by explicitly linking contract flexibility to more effective local content. In particular, what they sought was permission to contract directly for local content using whatever contracting vehicle would give the local provider the best chances to actually succeed in developing their skills, rather than just dumping money into the local economy. The persistence of these project directors achieved two excellent benefits: they received high quality and inexpensive local content, and they eliminated very large risk premiums by taking the local content requirements out of the ITBs for the international contractors. The lesson is do not automatically assume that the government agencies will not consider strong arguments for added flexibility, especially when those arguments are couched in terms of their goals.

Creative Use of EPC Lump-Sum Contracts

When EPC lump-sum contracts are used, sponsors often think that they have very limited control over the execution process. This view is reinforced by corporate legal staff who worry that any sponsor intervention in an EPC lump-sum situation will make it impossible to hold the contractor liable for poor results. (These folks believe in the myth of risk wholesale transfer, which I discuss shortly.)

In fact, some of the most successful EPC lump-sum projects involved owners being hands-on during every facet of execution. The best EPC lump-sum projects were usually multiprime arrangements. This involved careful carving out of pieces of the project that could be executed almost as a parallel stand-alone project. Where I am from in the United States, we have an expression, "Good fences make good neighbors." This expression certainly applies to how the pieces of multiprime EPC lump-sum projects are defined. Parts of a project that are too intimately linked from either a design or construction perspective must be included within the same contract. Pieces that can be designed based on a requirements and specification statement without reference to the details of the design of other bits can be contracted separately. For example, onshore portions of offshore petroleum production projects are usually contracted with separate EPC lump-sum contracts. As long as the oil and gas composition data were correct from the reservoir appraisal, this arrangement works well.

A Good Example

One of the more ingenious uses of EPC lump-sum contracting occurred in a chemical complex built in a developing country environment.

The primary units consisted of an olefins cracker, a large power plant, and a number of olefins derivatives units. The cracker and the power plant were tightly coupled, feeding streams to and from each other, so they were grouped in a single contract. Each of the derivatives units were contracted separately, each with a different EPC lump-sum tender. The result was five prime contracts.

The contracting strategy was developed during FEL-2 as the scope was being developed. Knowing that the site offered some real challenges in access and logistics, they laid the units out so that separate access was available to each portion of the complex as they intended to contract it. The first task after site preparation was literally the construction of those "good fences." With five prime contractors and complex lay-down and site logistics problems, most owners in this situation would have hired a PMC to keep track of everything and manage the interfaces. A PMC was considered but ultimately rejected because the PMC candidates wanted part of the execution. The owners decided to hire a sixth contractor on a reimbursable basis with very clear rules about behavior—the reimbursable contractor was barred from hiring anyone who had ever worked for one of the lump-sum contractors on the project. The reimbursable contractor was assigned any tasks that "fell between the fences," such as logistics, canteen, safe and timely movement of construction workers to and from the site, and so on. The reimbursable contractor also served another purpose: if one of the lump-sum contractors submitted a change order that the sponsor team thought was significantly overpriced, they refused the change, saying that they would have the reimbursable contractor do the work when the lump-sum contractor was out of the area. This had the beneficial effect of significantly moderating the prices on change orders from all five lump-sum contractors. The result was a highly successful project that could easily have become a nightmare.

The best EPC lump-sum projects had the characteristic of a hands-on sponsor team that would not let the contractors fail. In all of the lump-sum megaprojects, I cannot find a single instance in which the basis of a contractor claim was that the owner interfered when the contractor got into trouble on the job. There were cases of claims based on owner interference, but they were around issues such as the owner taking responsibility for managing the lay-down yard, not intervention. Interference between contractors is one of the major sources of contractor claims.[4] Strong interface management, like that described in the preceding example, is what prevents those claims from materializing.

Interface management is one of the most critical jobs on any complex megaproject. The interface management effort needs to start as part of FEL-2 and continue through the execution of the project. As discussed in Chapter 9, interface management is not a job for junior engineers; it is central to the success of the endeavor. One of the key mistakes made in EPC lump-sum projects is to imagine that because the contractors "are responsible for the execution of the project," the owner team size can be small. Owner team size on successful megaprojects is quite insensitive to contracting approach. What varies with the contracting approach is the content of what the team is doing, not the numbers of people required.

The Illusion of Wholesale Risk Transfer on EPC Lump-Sum Contracts

→ only in Japan

Most adherents of EPC lump-sum contracting for megaprojects argue that the contracting strategy effectuates significant transfer of risk and responsibility from the sponsors to the EPC lump-sum contractor. The facts, however, suggest that this really is not the case. Some lump-sum prime contractors did indeed lose significant amounts of money on megaprojects in our set. However, those losses for the contractors did not translate into gains for the sponsors. Instead, those losses translated into facilities with an endless stream of operating problems.

Significant risk transfer from sponsors to contractors is structurally impossible. Contractors, including the very large contractors that take leading roles in megaprojects, are too thinly capitalized to survive wholesale risk transfer on large projects. During the period of overcapacity of EPC services between the mid-1980s and the early years of the twenty-first century, the contractors that had to take on significant EPC lump-sum projects to have enough work mostly failed to survive. Many of those that survived were badly wounded, and all learned an indelible lesson: The failure to be carefully risk averse will surely result in bankruptcy. The only cases in which major losses were sustained and high-quality projects resulted for owners involved large Japanese contractors. Those contractors were supported by large commercial banks that were part of their business consortia. They were in effect losing other people's money.

Risk transfer is possible on smaller projects because the contractor in a loss position can afford to complete the project with reasonably good performance without destroying its business. The value of preserving its reputation and the hope of future business make that calculation reasonable. On a megaproject, however, the losses are too large. Furthermore, because there are very few contractors that are capable of taking on megaproject leadership, industrial sponsors have very few choices. Every project, in effect, becomes a "one-night stand" because the downside consequences for the contractors are minimal. If industrial companies banned forever using contractors that have performed very poorly on megaprojects, they would quickly find themselves without contractors to hire. Even when contractors have behaved in utterly unethical ways toward an owner on a large project, they can be quite sure that more business will be forthcoming anyway. I can think of only a couple of cases in 30 years in which a major contractor has been effectively banned by an owner for poor performance. Those were by large national oil companies.

The simple fact that major risk transfer cannot take place on megaprojects should not lead sponsors to automatically abandon EPC lump-sum contracting. EPC lump-sum arrangements have some important advantages in terms of project organization. EPC lump-sum contracts reduce the number of interfaces that the lead sponsor has to manage. Often, the lead contractor in an EPC lump-sum strategy has developed working relationships with the organizations that will act as subcontractors for the project. The major contractors are often highly proficient at procurement and can orchestrate getting all of the various pieces of the project fitted together. EPC lump-sum contracting may be the only realistic way in which sponsors with weak project organizations can have any hope of executing a megaproject successfully.

However, our findings have some important implications for how EPC lump-sum arrangements should be approached by sponsors. If a sponsor is hoping for a bargain-basement price by using a lump-sum strategy, that hope will lead to trouble. Even when all works well, EPC lump-sum contracts do and *should* cost more than other contracting approaches. This is simply because the lead contractor is being asked to take on more work than in other forms. Also, there is some chance that an EPC lump-sum contract will result in a substantial loss to the contractor. (Remember, that does not necessarily mean a gain to the sponsors!) From the contractor's viewpoint, taking on a large EPC lump-sum contract is a bit like playing Russian roulette. Usually, there is no bullet in the chamber, even if the project seriously overruns, because most significant overruns on lump-sum projects are accompanied by lots of changes that largely render the lump-sum nature of the contract moot. Once in a while, however, there is an unlucky spin and the contractor might get stuck with a catastrophic loss. The contractor wants, reasonably enough, to do everything possible to insure against such a loss.

As a result, large EPC lump-sum bids will carry a risk premium over and above normal contractor contingency, except when the market for their services is in a prolonged slump and they face the prospect of extinction without winning the project. Some owner companies, especially national companies in the Middle East, take a very hard "no change orders accepted" approach on their EPC lump-sum contracts, even when they, as the owner, have clearly made changes that should normally cause an increase in the contract price. Often, the courts of jurisdiction in any disputes are the home country courts and hence viewed as a home playing field advantage. In those cases, the companies are paying risk premiums of 25 to 40 percent over a "fair" contract price to the low bidders on the projects. Some of our "failure" projects in the Middle East came in on budget, on schedule, and started up appropriately but paid 40 percent more for the project than they should have.

Often, the underlying purpose of using an EPC lump-sum approach to contracting for megaprojects is not risk transfer but *blame* transfer. Under an EPC lump-sum arrangement, especially with a single contractor taking the responsibility, that contractor can become the designated scapegoat when problems arise. Government preferences for lump-sum contracts are rational when one considers the traditional weaknesses of government project organizations. Competitively bid EPC lump-sum contracts are also perceived to be less subject to corrupt practices than are other contractual forms (although for practical purposes, I find it difficult to see any advantage in that regard). Many companies, especially in the Middle East, cling to EPC lump-sum approaches because of very unhappy experiences with reimbursable contracts in the past. A good many of the megaprojects built in the Middle East in the 1970s by Western contractors on reimbursable contracts overran hugely without any ability of the host governments to control. It soured the countries and their national companies on reimbursable contracting for a generation.

The Pricing of Risk in EPC Lump-Sum Contracts

The period of oversupply in EPC services for the global industrial megaprojects market came to an abrupt end in early 2004. The period of oversupply had extended over the prior 20 years, and that 20-year period significantly upset the power balance in contracting, with a strong tilt toward the buyers. The effect of the imbalance was that owners could get almost any terms they wanted from contractors, many of which were struggling to survive. Many, of course, did not. As shown in Figure 11.6, this period saw a substantial concentration of the market for large industrial projects. By 2003, the top 10 international contractors controlled about 75 percent of the major projects market, up from roughly 50 percent a decade earlier.

During the long period of oversupply, contractors were forced away from pricing risk as they bid on EPC lump-sum contracts and accepted more and more onerous terms for all types of contracts. During this period, it was common for contractors to have to finance substantial portions of the project because the terms allowed owners to withhold payments for relatively trivial reasons. Liability clauses were rewritten to make contractors liable for almost all mishaps, often even including cases in which the owner was found to be primarily responsible or even negligent!

When the market turned in 2004, contractors had accumulated 20 years of grievances. Those that survived had become very adept at avoiding potentially catastrophic risks. And as soon as market

Figure 11.6
Concentration of EPC Market Has Increased

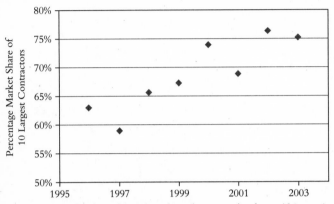

Market share of the industrial/petroleum sector that the top 10 international design firms hold

Source: Engineering News Record, The Top International Design Firms, July issues, 1996–2004

balance was restored, the major contractors started pricing risk back into their bids.

By examining the bids against the situation of the projects, we have isolated seven risk areas that contractors started to price in 2004. As the decade progressed, the risk premiums for these areas rose and peaked in 2008. They have subsided some, but still are priced and will likely be priced more aggressively once again as the megaproject market is slated to accelerate in the first half of this second decade. I will define each area and the rough amounts that have been added to base bids to account for the perceived risks associated.

Onerous Local Content Requirements   As discussed in prior chapters, local content requirements are nearly universal, even in areas that pride themselves as fully world open market. As I have also mentioned, getting local content into projects is simply business smart. Local content is associated with building local support for projects and with fewer hassles from opportunistic politicians. Local content is often considerably less expensive than alternative supply.

The problem with local content surfaces when there is a requirement that appears difficult or impossible to fulfill. In places without an industrial supply infrastructure, such as structural steel, pipe manufacture, high-quality equipment vendors, and engineering firms, relatively few inputs into industrial megaprojects can actually be supplied. The inputs tend to be restricted to nonengineered bulk materials and construction labor. Often, the local labor is not qualified for many of the key crafts, such as alloy welding. For example, we had one megaproject in Central Asia that stipulated an astonishing 80 percent local content requirement for a petroleum development project and pipeline. There is not even a basic line pipe manufacture in the country!

Often, the host governments are trying to push the limits of feasible local content, which is understandable, but they have trouble figuring out where that feasibility point becomes very expensive in terms of risk pricing. Not surprisingly, international company complaints are viewed as whining. In these situations, the local content requirements should be understood by the sponsors as a perceived major risk to lump-sum bidders. When local content is viewed as difficult to meet, contractors have added a premium of 30 to 40 percent above the base bid for onshore projects. This added premium has been so large that it has pushed many sponsors away from EPC lump-sum contracting. For offshore petroleum development projects, the added premium has been around 15 percent.

Civil Unrest in the Immediate Area   For some obscure reason, contractors believe it is difficult to build a megaproject and dodge bullets at the same time. When there is shooting in the neighborhood, contractors are adding an average of 25 to 30 percent to their bids.

Harsh Physical Environment or Climate   Contractors are perceiving projects in difficult climates as posing unknown risks that need some degree of cushion in their bids. Projects in remote desert areas, very mountainous areas, arctic areas, and tropical jungle areas are carrying risk premiums of 20 to 25 percent. What the contractors are in effect saying is that there are so many unknowns in these areas that rather than trying to build the problems into the base estimates, they will simply put an added premium on top. This is reasonable when one considers that developing a solid bid for a megaproject is an expensive proposition for contractors. In a period when they are receiving a substantial number of ITBs, the added time needed to explore all of the logistical challenges of harsh climates doesn't make economic sense. The failure rates in our data in very remote locations suggests that the added premiums are founded in sound logic.

(4) *Political Instability*   Political instability translates into logistical nightmares for contractors. They find that goods cannot be moved across ports. Visas are not being processed. Staff are being arrested by local authorities. Some nationals are now persona non grata. These sorts of hassles make getting a project completed in a timely way very difficult. Although they may be the source of legitimate claims, this is not a welcome route for the contractor because the claims process is also risky. Areas of political instability are adding 15 to 20 percent to bids.

(5) *An Unstable Regulatory Regime*   Politically unstable areas also have unstable regulatory regimes, but I counted them under the prior category. Many quite stable political areas have regulatory problems. As discussed back in Chapter 4, regulatory problems may be symptomatic of a weak institutional environment. In such environments, permits are highly political acts. But many areas with stable institutional environments have problematic regulatory regimes. In some cases, the regulators find themselves simply overwhelmed with the workload and cannot get permits issued in a timely or predictable way. In some areas, there are so many interveners allowed in the regulatory process that the timing of permits is utterly unpredictable. When contractors under EPC lump-sum contracts are tasked with permitting, they look at this area as a source of delay and therefore risk and are adding 15 to 20 percent to the bids to cover.

(6) *High Potential for Craft Labor Shortages*   During the middle of the last decade, craft labor shortages sprang up in a number of areas, including some that had never before seen them. Western Canada, West Australia and then all of Australia, the Middle East, Central Asia, the U.S. Gulf Coast, and selected parts of Asia all found themselves unable

to find enough qualified labor to complete large projects on time. Labor shortages are a real and present danger to projects. Contractors were adding about 15 percent to bids in areas of labor shortage, which was probably not enough. In some of these areas, the contractors stopped bidding on EPC lump-sum contracts altogether.

Currency Exchange Risk Essentially every industrial megaproject spends money in a number of different currencies. Many contractors found themselves seriously hurt by currency exchange rate fluctuations in the 1990s as financial crises caused very sudden changes. Therefore, when risk pricing again became possible, the contractors attached a premium to accepting the currency risks associated with their lump-sum projects. The size of the premium averaged about 8 to 13 percent.

I find two things astounding about this. First, the premium bid is far more than the amounts actually needed to go into currency markets and forward buy the currencies in question and thereby fix their values. And second, why in the world are industrial companies passing currency risks to their contractors? The kinds of companies sponsoring these projects are sophisticated financially, certainly more so than many of the contractors. They should either accept the risk themselves or hedge the risks themselves rather than attempting to pass the burden along and get charged a hefty premium.

Other Areas of Priced Risk Transfer

The seven risk areas just cited are not the risks that contractors evaluate. There are a host of contractual provisions that carry perceived risks for contractors that are routinely priced into their bids. Among others, these include:

- Uncapped liability provisions
- Responsibility for consequential damages
- Payment provisions (and especially provisions that make delay or withholding of payments easy)
- Provisions for processing change and schedule extensions, and
- Broad definitions of gross negligence

These provisions are contained in the terms and conditions in the contracts and apply to all contract types. Although we have not measured the bid premiums from such onerous provisions, contractors do factor them into their bid decisions. In some respects, harsh terms and conditions are insidious; one common reaction of contractors to such provisions is to decline to bid without explanation. Harsh terms and conditions also start the contractors out in a defensive mode, which is not conducive to successful projects.

The Myth of the "A Team"

I was once having a conversation with the chief executive officer (CEO) of one of the top international contractors and the subject of incentive contracts came up. He asked me why so many owners seem to prefer them. I answered, "Because they believe they will get the 'A team,' that is, the best people the contractor has to offer."

He laughed and said, "If they can figure out what the 'A Team' is, they are welcome to them. But they have to tell me because I have been trying to find them for years!"

I asked another contractor executive if he could name the "A Team" in his organization, and he said, "Sure, they retired two years ago."

There is an almost magical belief within the owner community that there are a set of much stronger project teams among the major contractors, which if they can be secured, will guarantee success. Although there is, of course, variability in the competence of contractor teams, just as there is for sponsor teams, the A Team is a myth. As a sponsor you are much more likely to find yourself with an A Team if your FEL has been excellent and all the owner functions were present and accounted for during FEL.

There are some attributes of contractor teams that do make a difference. First, all of the contractor lead participants should have worked for the contractor on at least one prior major project. If they have not, it is likely that they cannot actually operate the contractor systems because they are not sufficiently familiar with them. One of the most common shortfalls of contractors is not that their systems are poor; it is that the people on the project don't actually know how to run those systems. Second, you would greatly prefer a group from your leading contractors that have worked together before as a team. The contractor project manager, lead engineer, disciplinary leads, lead cost estimator, lead planner/scheduler, and construction/fabrication manager, if they will be responsible for construction, should have experience together. The search for the mythical A Team is a distraction from asking the right questions as you qualify the contractors. The issues are whether a potential contractor can and will field the right team for this particular project and whether the contractor will give reasonable assurances that the team selected will stay in place.

REIMBURSABLE CONTRACTS ARE FOR HIGHER-RISK PROJECTS

Reimbursable EPC and EPCm contracts were used for a quarter of the projects in our sample. This contract form was used by every industrial sector and in every region in the world. Reimbursable approaches are most appropriate, and may even be essential, when a project is subject to significant uncertainties that will carry well into execution. For example, reimbursable contracts were twice as likely to be used in highly remote locations. Reimbursable contracts were associated with greater use of innovative technology, and reimbursable forms were a little more common when projects were schedule driven. Reimbursable contracts were much more common when local project markets were overheated. For that reason, reimbursable forms have been the predominant megaproject contract type in Australia, Canada, and Central Asia during the first decade of this century. Projects with inherent risks are tilted toward reimbursable forms because sponsors and contractors are much less likely to be able to agree on a lump-sum price when execution is uncertain. Because of the economic inefficiency associated with risk transfer, real or imagined, from owners to contractors, the risk premiums contractors want for lump-sum contracts are too large for owners to swallow.

Straight reimbursable EPC contracts are difficult for most sponsor teams to control. Very few owners have the strong skills needed to prevent the reimbursable contract from becoming an open wallet that enables the contractors to charge many more than the budgeted hours for engineering and construction/fabrication. Most owners do not know, for example, what is an appropriate number of hours for various parts of the design. Most owners lack even basic understanding of megaproject construction management that would enable them to know if the field is being properly managed or not.

The Use of Incentive Schemes

This lack of expertise has led many owners to attempt to mitigate the open-ended nature of reimbursable contracts through the introduction of incentive schemes. These schemes involve extra profits to contractors if the project underruns its budget, schedule, or other objectives as desired. Sometimes the schemes involve extra payments for meeting the sanctioned objectives. Sometimes, they involve some form of penalties for disappointment such as "fee at risk" or "pain-sharing" approaches. The incentive schemes almost always applied to the prime contractors, which were the engineering and procurement organizations, and not specifically to the subcontractors who were used for construction.

None of the incentive schemes associated with reimbursable EPC contracts had any detectable effects on project success. They are a complete random walk. The success rate with incentives is actually lower than that without, but not statistically significant. The only relationship that I am able to detect is that cost target incentives were associated with *greater* schedule slippages, and that finding is statistically marginal. Our findings flatly contradict case study findings by researchers such as Berends.[5] To be sure there are some successful incentivized megaprojects. There just are not very many of them.

The incentive schemes suffer a number of defects. Most of these schemes were put in place with contractors that had also executed the FEED on the projects and had therefore had a primary role in the development of the sanction estimate. Knowing (or at least hoping) that the execution contract will contain incentives for underruns, these estimates characteristically overstate the bulk material quantities that will be needed to construct the facilities. Even slight padding of the bulk material quantities translates into a significant "cushion" in the estimate because the bulk material quantities are the primary drivers of engineering hours and construction hours. If all goes well, which is actually determined by fundamental things, the project then underruns, the contractor has "earned" a sizeable bonus, and the sponsors are pleased because they believe they have gotten a bargain. This leads some researchers and project directors to believe the incentive scheme has worked as well, when, in fact, the result was created via creative estimating and the project is actually a bit more expensive than it needed to be.

Those are the good incentivized outcomes. In the much more typical case (about four times as likely), the project runs into difficulties. Those difficulties were usually due to the project fundamentals not being good. Then, instead of generating better outcomes, the incentives get in the way. Imagine yourself as the prime contractor expecting to make profits largely by earning incentives. You are now three months into execution, and it is clear that the project is headed for an overrun. You see this simply by observing the number of changes coming through the system. Now you are looking at three years more of an unprofitable project. How do you respond? You may demand that the incentives be rebaselined. But if the sponsor agrees to that, the entire premise of incentives is undermined. More likely, you view the best route to profits to be cranking in as many hours and as many change orders as you possibly can. You will try to make profits on field hours via hidden profit there. You are feeling ill-used and abused and therefore entirely justified in finding profit opportunities wherever they crop up. The relationship between owner and contractor sours, and the project becomes harder due to the contract provisions, not easier.

Incentive schemes suffer an inherent logical problem: they implicitly assume that there is a great deal of money to be saved below the owner estimate during the execution of the project. But unless the estimate was padded, that just isn't true. Unusually efficient execution can save a bit if all goes well. But the idea that efficient execution can normally produce savings large enough to compensate contractors fairly is absurd. Execution is all about trying to hang on to the value that has been created. It is not about generating new value.*

---

*Those familiar with the project management literature will be reminded of the "influence curve," which dates at least back to the 1950s, despite those claiming more recent paternity. The influence curve shows that the ability to shape the value of a project is high only when the rate of expenditure is low.

I also have a nagging philosophical problem with the use of incentives in contracts, which goes beyond the simple fact that they don't work. I believe the offering and taking of incentives fundamentally disrespects the professionalism of contractors. What incentives are really saying is, "Because you, the contractor, won't do a good, honest job just for your fee, I need to bribe you with some contingent money based on whether you actually show up for this job." Incentive schemes may reflect the broken state of relationships between sponsors and contractors in the process industries, but because they do not work and have so much potential for abuse, they have made and will continue to make the relationships worse rather than better. The perceived need for incentive schemes was created by sponsors squeezing contractor fees during the 1990s down to a point where many of the contractors were no longer viable. Realizing that contractors with no hope of making a profit were without much incentive to do a good job, owners started to incentivize the contracts. The more appropriate course in a professional relationship would have been to simply restore a reasonable fee.

Controlling Contractor Hours and Fees on Reimbursable Contracts

Contractor hours can be effectively controlled by means other than lump-sum contracts or incentives. The most effective is the systematic reduction and then elimination of all profit potential as hours become excessive. The approach works in the following way:

1. Negotiate target hours for the major work tasks: detailed engineering, project management (if any), field engineering support, and commissioning and startup (if any). This will be a difficult negotiation, and the sponsor needs to bring as much data from prior projects to the process as possible.
2. The target hours, plus approved change orders (with hours, of course), will earn full overhead contribution and fees. Fees will stop when the target hours are reached in any category. Alternatively, fees will stop when the total ceiling is reached, unless that ceiling is raised by sponsor-generated change orders.

3. Another increment above the target, say 10 percent, will earn full overhead.
4. Above 110 percent, no overheads whatsoever will be paid. The contractor will be paid only for out-of-pocket costs.

This provides the contractor with:
- A guaranteed fee
- A cushion above the target on which no loss is taken
- An incentive to never go more than 10 percent above the target because at this point he or she is foregoing other opportunities in order to complete your project

This approach provides fair and balanced protection to both parties.

On reimbursable EPC and EPCm arrangements, the owner should want the contractor's profit to be made only in the contractor's fee. Unfortunately, that is often not the case, and unless the owners are careful, the fee may be but a small portion of the contractor's profit. Allow me to share a blatant example.

The project was a large onshore petroleum development project in a remote area. The project was technically straightforward. The big issue was going to be logistics and labor supply. Virtually all labor was going to have to be imported. The EPC contractor, as is often the case, executed FEED on the project. The project was estimated at $1.2 billion. When IPA evaluated the project prior to sanction, two problems were identified. First, there was very poor granularity in the estimate, so it was difficult to conduct a sensible evaluation of the cost competitiveness of the project. Second, the EPCm contractor was asking for only a $10 million fixed fee. That was less than 1 percent of the total project! It was particularly surprising to us because the contractor is well known throughout the industry for demanding high fees, so we were perplexed at the low fee and told the owner something was amiss. We were told, with a pat on the head, not to worry. Indeed, they were quite proud that they had managed to secure such a low fee.

The project was completed on time and on budget and had a smooth startup. It was apparently a very successful project. When we conducted the closeout evaluation, however, nobody could produce a coherent breakdown of the total cost of the project. The first breakdown made no sense at all; five iterations later and it still made no sense. The lead sponsor had hired a third-party controls firm to keep track of the costs but had failed to ensure that the key people would remain with the project through closeout. We strongly recommended a complete audit of the EPCm's costs. And here is another problem: The sponsors had standard audit clauses in their contract with the EPCm for reimbursable contracts, but they had not actually used those audit rights throughout the project. When confronted with the demand for an audit, the EPCm contractor said, "Well, you can try, but because you didn't exercise any of the audit rights throughout the project, we didn't really keep a lot of the 'stuff.'" The attempt to audit the project was utterly hopeless.

That would have been the end of the story except that about a year later, I ran into the EPCm contractor's chief estimator and controller on the project, who was now working for an owner client of ours. I asked him how much the contractor cleared on the project over and above that $10 million fee. He chuckled and said, "Just over $250 million free and clear." They had made money on just about everything. Materials were marked up and every field hour generated a "fee" from the construction organization to the EPCm.

I would like to say that this story is genuinely exceptional, but I strongly suspect that it is not. If a sponsor is not in a position to carefully audit expenditures on a reimbursable contract, then sometimes money will disappear without a trace. Unexercised rights are lost no matter what the language of the contract says. Finally, third-party controls organizations can be very good, but they provide no benefit if they leave the project before the cost closeout reports are completed and all the loose ends cleaned up. Pay the contractors a good fee; audit to ensure that is all you pay!

WHY MEGAPROJECT ALLIANCES FAIL

There are a number of features of alliance contracting that are quite problematic for industrial megaprojects. Industrial megaprojects are quite complex from a technology perspective. This means that they are necessarily engineering-intensive—much more so than, for example, most infrastructure projects. Many of the projects examined in this book are also inherently risky vis-à-vis operational safety. A majority of the projects involve huge hydrocarbon inventories that pose inherent safety risks.

This technical complexity means that quality in engineering, materials procurement, and construction is essential. However, quality in industrial megaprojects is often difficult to gauge in real-time without an extensive effort on the part of the sponsors. Engineering errors can render a plant unsafe or inoperable while being completely invisible to the naked eye. Equipment fabrication errors and incorrect or fraudulent metallurgy can do the same. To the extent sponsors believe that alliancing enables them to withdraw from very close and active supervision of quality, alliancing is very problematic.

If multiprime EPC lump-sum contracting thrives on the notion that "Good fences make good neighbors," alliance contracting believes in no fences at all. Alliance contracts are an extreme form of incentivized reimbursable schemes. The basic form is EPC reimbursable, so the same set of contractors stay on the job throughout. The twist is that all of the contractors share in the incentive scheme, usually proportionately to their slice of the entire project's estimated cost. The underlying rationale for this approach is actually rather elegant. Most megaprojects necessarily involve a large number of contractors, subcontractors, specialty contractors, and vendors. As I mentioned earlier, negotiating all of the interfaces among so many players is a major headache for sponsors in reimbursable formats and is even a major problem in multiprime EPC lump-sum arrangements. So, if we put everybody into a "shared destiny" pool, surely they will cooperate and manage the interfaces themselves. Even the sponsors will share in this pool. We are all in this together!

Unlike the rationale, the real world of megaprojects turns out to be quite messy. I have spoken to a great many contractors involved in alliance arrangements, and they have one thing in common: they privately but passionately despise the form. They believe that it completely breaks the relationship between what they do and what they get paid, rather than the opposite. Their point is simple: I may do everything right but end up with nothing because some idiot somewhere else on the project made a mistake! Some specialty contractors, such as heavy lift and installation, will categorically refuse to participate in these schemes. It is the norm rather than the exception that the agreement on the incentive scheme in alliances was not finalized until well after the start of execution and sometimes long after the start of execution.

The designers of alliances also thought that they would get the best features of EPC lump-sum contract with none of the drawbacks. The advantages of lump-sum contracting are that (1) the contractors manage their own interfaces, (2) the contractors will put that legendary A Team on the project because it is their own money, and (3) the sponsors don't have to field as large of a controls staff as on reimbursable projects because the contractors have no incentive to crank hours. The downsides of lump-sum contracting are that (1) quality is always a problem, (2) we have to pay a premium for risk transfer that we usually never manage to actually effectuate, and (3) the contractors rather than the sponsor get to keep any savings. With an alliance contract, the reasoning goes, (1) we will get the A Team because the contractors have the possibility of making a lot of money, (2) the contractors will manage their own interfaces—just like lump-sum contracting—but we will get to share underruns, (3) we don't have to pay a risk premium because the basic form is reimbursable, and (4) quality will not be a problem. (I have never actually heard the exact rationale of this last bit on quality.)

So what do we actually get with alliance contracts? We actually end up with some of the worst features of lump-sum contracts combined with the worst features of reimbursable contracts: *is worst of Both worlds*

- There is no evidence whatsoever that contractors assign more highly skilled and experienced people to alliance contracts than to other reimbursable contracts.
- We have, in fact, created exactly the same incentive structure to skimp on quality that exists in lump-sum contracts, which is evidenced by the fact that alliance-contract projects suffered the worst record of operability failures.*

---

*The early burst of enthusiasm for alliance contracting ensued before the operability problems of many of the alliance projects were understood. Operability data are almost never made public voluntarily, especially when they are poor.

- The interface management hypothesis is debunked by the fact that the contractors are actually *more* prone to fight among themselves, not less.
- As the data make very clear, there are rarely any underruns to divvy up. There were no underruns to share in more than 85 percent of the alliance projects!

The role of contracts is to:
- Define who is responsible and accountable for what. Good contracts define responsibilities very clearly. By defining responsibilities clearly, good contracts facilitate interface management, which is one of the most difficult areas of project management on megaprojects.
- Establish a useful mechanism for conflict resolution if difficulties arise.
- Provide a way that all parties working on a project can be *fairly and transparently* compensated for their work.

In a perfect world, having agreed on the contract, the document can be put in a drawer and never seen again. As we have seen, however, in industrial megaprojects, things rarely go entirely according to plan. When problems occur and it becomes necessary to pull the contract out of that drawer, the contract should help resolve the difficulties.

Alliance contracts tend to do none of the bulleted items listed above. Responsibilities and accountabilities are shared among all participants. But in practice this means that no one is actually responsible. The contractual approach was supposed to "dissolve the interfaces." But the interfaces between contractors, and between contractors and sponsors, cannot be eliminated and when poorly defined become entirely unmanageable.

The worst feature of the alliance contract form is that it actually makes it more difficult, rather than less so, to resolve problems when they occur. Megaprojects are messy. There will be problems, even if everything possible has been done to prepare the project. When a problem occurs, the contract should be pulled out of the drawer, dusted off, and read for assistance in resolving the problems. Alliance contracts, because we are "all in this together," do nothing to help us understand who is responsible and needs to step up and who is not. Alliance contracts are the epitome of "shared risk." *Shared risk* is shorthand for "it's nobody's responsibility." The typical alliance contract is so complex that it cannot be used to help settle disputes.

The alliance–contract projects were understaffed by owners; in nearly two-thirds of the alliances, the project director described the project as insufficiently staffed. The alliances also had another feature characteristic of failure: "stretch" targets. More aggressive cost and schedule targets were set for the alliance projects than any other contract type. Part of the ethos of *alliancing* was that great things could be done via this new contract form.

The alliancing approach is becoming more popular for commercial buildings, especially health care facilities, and public sector contracting of infrastructure projects in the United States and Australia respectively.* This contracting approach results in "multiparty" agreements executed by the owner, architect, general contractor, consulting engineers, and specialty trade contractors. There have only been a handful of projects executed on this basis in the United States and the verdict is out as to its overall effectiveness. If enough money is stuffed into the estimates the projects can appear successful because very few alliance projects outside the process industries are benchmarked for cost. Likewise, for buildings and transportation infrastructure quality problems are not nearly as obvious as they are for industrial projects that fail to start up.

It may be that the use of alliancing in other industry sectors is less problematic than alliancing on industrial facilities. Nonindustrial projects are not only less technically complex, but the lead construction contractor self-performs very little and the lead designers are not part of the construction contractor's organization. However, given the sorry track record of alliances for megaprojects and for process facilities in general, I have to wonder if the successes of alliances in other areas are not more apparent than real.

---

*See Department of Treasury and Finance, Victoria, Australia, *In Pursuit of Additional Value: A Benchmarking Study in Alliancing in the Australian Public Sector,* October 2009. The approach is sometimes called "Integrated Project Delivery" in the U.S. context and "alliancing" in the Australian context.

WHY MIXED CONTRACTING SUCCEEDS (Hybrid)

The orphan child of megaproject contracting is the mixed form, sometimes also called the hybrid approach. It involves separate contracting of engineering and procurement services on a reimbursable basis followed by lump-sum construction or fabrication with a construction organization. This approach was least used, but it was used at least once by every sector and in every part of the world. It was employed most frequently in petroleum development and in chemicals. As discussed previously, projects using this approach to contracting were much more successful than the average megaproject.

To discover that the mixed form was more successful was hardly a surprise. Prior research involving more than 2,800 processing facilities and petroleum developments around the world had established that the form was, by a substantial margin, the most cost-effective approach to contracting. Why does it work?

I believe there are several compelling reasons why the mixed contracting strategy is more successful than other forms. The mixed form breaks the contractual links between project engineering and construction or in the engineering and procurement world between engineering and fabrication, installation, and hookup and commissioning. Severing this link has a number of advantages. It reduces the engineering contractor's span of control, making the project more manageable. The focus is on engineering and engineering alone. It also prevents the engineering contractor from devising his or her project strategy so as to make extra profits from nonengineering activities.

The mixed form removes any incentive of the FEED contractor, who is usually the engineering contractor on non–EPC lump-sum projects, to pad the estimate or otherwise manipulate the incentive scheme. That frees up the use of incentives, if the owner so chooses, to be used for instrumental goals, such as low engineering error rates and appropriate sequencing of design. It also frees up the use of instrumental incentives for the construction firm as well around issues such as quality and proper sequencing of construction completion so as to facilitate turnover and commissioning.

The mixed strategy improves the quality of the construction management because construction management must stand alone and not be subsumed by the engineering contract. It forces owners to know something about construction management because they are going to be selecting the constructor/fabricator rather than relying on the engineering contractor to either provide that skill set in-house or contract it with minimal owner input. Many of the world EPC firms are much better at engineering and procurement than they are at construction or construction management. Most of the EPC contractors are engineering-centric organizations that have relegated construction to second-class status. Projects, however, are done better when engineering is construction driven. The mixed form does not ensure that will occur, but it does prevent engineering from simply dictating how the project will be executed.

A mixed strategy makes it much more likely that construction or fabrication will not start until the engineering and procurement effort has progressed far enough and well enough that construction will not be slowed by late, inaccurate, and out-of-sequence design and late and out-of-sequence materials. I return to this important subject in Chapter 12.

Finally, a mixed strategy is associated with much better front-end planning. The FEL index for the mixed projects was far better than any other contract form $(P\,|t| < .001)$. In particular, both engineering and execution planning elements were far superior when the mixed strategy was going to be used. The reason for this link is simple: the mixed strategy must be planned early. The construction or fabrication contractors have to be prequalified, which forces the sponsor team to know (or learn) something about construction management.

Mixed Contracting and Understanding
Construction Management

EPC contracting, both lump-sum and reimbursable, has one very dubious virtue for sponsors: It enables them to contract their megaprojects while being almost entirely ignorant of what constitutes effective construction management. When contracting EPC, sponsors usually get whatever constructors their engineering firm wants or can manage to get. Often, the construction arm of that engineering firm we really wanted is far from first rate.

This book is not the place to discuss the intricacies of excellent construction management. But sponsors must realize that excellent construction management may be the difference between success and failure, and in regions with labor shortages, it is the difference between success and utter disaster. If a sponsor is going to be capable of using the mixed contracting strategy, the ability to select effective construction managers is essential.

I consider the following areas of knowledge to be the backbone of effective construction management.

- **A modern safety system**

   Ideally, the construction management on a megaproject will employ a modern, positive-reinforcement–based safety program and will work with the sponsor team to ensure worker safety. What we are actually seeing on too many sites, especially in low-wage regions, are systems designed to minimize accident reporting.

- **Sequencing of design and materials delivery**

   The excellent construction management organization can examine a project and explain in detail the sequences that must be followed in the delivery of design and the ordering and delivery of equipment and materials to the construction site. Proper sequencing will drive field labor productivity more than any other single item. The quickest way to depress field productivity is for workers to have nothing to do.

- **Materials management**

   Megaprojects usually involve billions of dollars' worth of equipment and materials. One of the most common problems on megaprojects is not being able to locate materials when they are needed for construction. Many projects end up ordering items more than once because they can't be located, only to end up with millions of dollars' worth of surplus material at the end of the project. At some sites, material walks off the site at the end of every shift because the lay-down yards are not secure.

   Materials management and all of the logistics that go with it are very complex systems for megaprojects. They may require modern technology such as radio frequency identification (RFID) and global positioning system (GPS) location finders. Whether low tech or high tech, a great deal of skill and experience is essential.

- **Hiring of craft**

    The construction management organization on a megaproject absolutely must know how to acquire craft for the particular site. They must know the local norms. They must know what kinds of craft can be brought into a country or an area and which cannot. They must know where to source first-line supervisors. Conflicts between local labor and imported first-line supervision can shut sites down. In one of our projects, the animosity actually led to murder of first-line supervisors.

- **Productivity measurement and problem identification**

    The effective construction management organization must know how to monitor productivity down to the gang level. Their systems must enable rapid aggregation of productivity so that the construction management organization itself at a minimum knows what productivity looks like on a weekly basis. The effective construction management organization has a system that signals immediately, not months down the road, when an area is falling behind and identifies the problem as materials availability, changes, or craft skill immediately.

- **Construction management staffing**

    The construction management staff above general foremen should be at least 50 percent from the permanent staff of the construction management organization. If more than half of the construction management organization has been recruited from the street, you are not hiring a competent construction management, just a collection of people.

- **Construction management systems**

    The sponsor needs to understand what systems will monitor and report progress; how system completion and turnover will be ensured; how materials management will be done; how tools quality, appropriateness, and availability will be ensured; and how work package planning will be done, including safety planning and backup task planning.

THE USE OF A PROJECT MANAGING CONTRACTOR (PMC)   — *DISTRUST AMONG CONTRACTORS*

The PMC arrangement involves hiring a contractor that will act for the owner team or augment the owner team in managing the execution of a project. PMCs were employed by 15 percent of the projects in our sample and were used with every contract type, in every region of the world, and in every industrial sector. Projects with PMCs were not substantially different than other projects. They were a little more likely to be onshore projects, but a good many of the PMCs were in petroleum development.

The projects that used PMCs were considerably more likely to fail than those that did not $(P > |\chi^2| < .03)$. Their schedule performance and production attainment success were average, but their cost and cost growth performance was terrible. Projects using PMCs averaged a 40 percent real overrun and were highly uncompetitive in capital cost ($+38$ percent). They were a little poorer in FEL completeness at authorization, but that can account for only a small portion of the very high costs.

They were especially expensive when the execution contracts were EPC lump-sum and when alliances were used. I believe the reasons for these results are similar. The use of a PMC arrangement is met with great skepticism by the other contractors working on the project. The PMC is in a very powerful position to shape the destinies of the other contractors. If you believe that contractors don't trust owners, you are right. But they *really* don't trust other contractors! And if the PMC was also given part of the execution work on the project, as they were in a majority of cases, the distrust among the other contractors goes off-scale.* They believe the PMC will use its close ties to the owner and its position at the top of the project to make the execution of the project easier (and more profitable) for the PMC and harder (and less profitable) for everyone else. As a result, on EPC lump-sum projects, the lump-sum contractors are bidding higher than you would otherwise expect.

---

*There were even cases in which the PMC was contracted on a reimbursable basis for PMC work while executing work on an EPC lump-sum basis on the same project at the same site! This, of course, violates the first rule of sensible contracting.

Is this distrust justified? At least some of the time, the answer appears to be "yes." On some projects, the PMCs routinely disparaged the work of the other contractors to the owners. There were a number of complaints from other contractors about control of the laydown areas for construction. And in some cases, the PMC was quick to encourage the owner to replace execution contractors who were struggling . . . with themselves!

I am not sure that PMC arrangements can ever be used cost-effectively on large projects. I realize that this creates a real problem for some owners who simply do not have sufficient personnel to staff their megaprojects. If you have to use a PMC, I would make the following suggestions:

- Never allow the PMC to take any portion of the execution and make it clear to every other contractor that under no circumstances will the PMC be allowed to take on their work.
- Call the PMC something else, owner support services, for example.
- If at all possible, seek to blend the PMC into the owner team, with the owner team taking the key lead positions, such as subproject managers.
- Rather than using a tier 1 international contractor for this role, seek out second-tier contractors or large contractors that do not take on EPC lump-sum international work. What is needed is a source of skills to support the understaffed owner team, not an organization that will take over the project.

OWNERS AND CONTRACTORS LIVE IN DIFFERENT WORLDS

Despite the fact that many owners and contractors spend large portions of their careers seated right next to one another, I am convinced that most owners and contractors fundamentally do not actually understand one another. In particular, I think owners imagine that contractors are like owners. I suspect most contractors think that owners are from another planet.

This was brought home to me a few years ago during a conversation I was having with the director of capital projects for one of the major international oil companies. This was no newbie; he had 30 years of project experience in petroleum development projects all over the world and a well-earned reputation for being deeply cynical. He said to me, "I just don't understand why these darned contractors won't take on any risk, and when they do, they can't manage it. It really irritates me!" I was so amazed at his naïveté that I was struck dumb. Those who know me will testify that doesn't happen often.

When it comes to perceptions of risk, owners and contractors live in completely separate worlds. As the expression goes, where you stand depends on where you sit. Owners complain that contractors don't want to take on any risk, which they equate to responsibility, and that when contractors do, they want inordinately high prices for taking the risks on. Contractors believe that owners are pushing them to bet their business on every project and would push them into bankruptcy without a second thought.

The different views spring directly from the differences between industrial companies and contractors as economic entities. Owner/sponsors look at the world from the viewpoint of assets. Each project involves the creation of a new asset or the expansion and enhancement of an existing asset. How much cash flow the asset can generate relative to its cost determines the value of the project. Owner companies are judged in the marketplace by that calculus overall. Their balance sheets are "asset heavy."

By contrast, contractors are at the other end of the spectrum. They are almost devoid of physical assets. Their balance sheets are asset light and are asset light by design. Very few major contractors even own their headquarter buildings. Contractors earn primarily by the sale of services. They are judged in the marketplace by how well they avoid taking large equity risks as they earn fees from their services.

The difference between contractors and owners with respect to risk taking can be illustrated with a simple mental experiment. Let's take as an example the average failed megaproject in our database. The project was estimated to cost about $3.1 billion (in 2009 U.S. terms). That average failure suffered a 33 percent overrun, roughly $1 billion. Now let's suppose that one of the world's major contractors took the entire project on as an EPC lump-sum contract. If successful, it might have hoped to earn about $100 million from the project, but it wasn't successful and they suffered a $1 billion overrun. If the sponsors were careful, the contractor's hope of recovering the losses via claims will be dim. Where does the $1 billion come from? It is deducted straight from the company's balance sheet. What would the effect be on a very strong contractor such as KBR, JGC, or Aker? It would remove every bit of cash from their balance sheets and more![6] The loss would exceed the net operating cash flow of Fluor or Technip for 2009. It would do the same to most other major contractors around the world. They would find themselves scrambling to find credit to avoid insolvency.

Now, let's suppose that the owners had to "eat" that $1 billion overrun. What results? The return on that asset would decline from about 15 percent to about 5 percent. That is a very disappointing result for the investment, but not catastrophic, unless it was a very small owner. The $1 billion overrun, however, would be *added* to its balance sheet as an asset.

The economic differences between owners and contractors generate fundamental disagreements about how project risks should be priced by contractors. But in this regard, the contractors surely have the better of the argument. The first principle of risk pricing is that the price attached to a risk will be a function of the bettor's wealth vis-à-vis the size of the bet. In these bets, the contractor is almost always the poorer of the two parties to the contract and therefore *should* attach a significantly higher price to the risks that it takes on. Moreover, when taking on risks, it is economically rational for the contractor to seek to find ways of mitigating those risks.

Contractors equally do not understand owner's needs around creating operating assets. In my experience, contractors focus too narrowly on meeting targets on cost and schedule and attach little value to turnover sequencing and successful turnover of the asset to operations. These shortcomings should be expected given their orientation. Interestingly, construction organizations often appear more sensitive to the needs of turnover and commissioning than the engineering contractors.

Some "new and improved" approaches to contracting are based on the premise that with the proper contractual structures, the differences between owners and contractors can be bridged and goals aligned. I believe, and the data strongly support, that the differences cannot be bridged. The contractual platforms such as alliancing are actually highly unstable because they cannot actually ensure that contractors will be fairly and routinely compensated for their work. Similarly, most incentive schemes are transparently easy for contractors to game or again end up failing to compensate contractors for their work.

Both owner personnel and contractor personnel come to work each expecting to do their best on their project. Both need to be compensated for what they do. At the end of the day, it is not at all clear that we should want contractors to "think like owners" or owners to "think like contractors." Owners need to focus their attention on asset health and quality. Contractors need to focus their attention on execution excellence. Owners and contractors are different. Understanding, appreciating, and supporting those differences are essential for successful projects.

CHAPTER 12

THE CONTROL OF
EXECUTION RISK

You are about 90 percent through this book, and I am just now getting to project execution. Project execution is where 95 percent of the money will be spent, and typically execution will occupy about 60 percent of a mega-project's total cycle time as measured from the start of scope development through startup. So why am I giving it short shrift? The answer should already be apparent: because very few projects actually fail due to problems that originate in execution. This is not to suggest that execution of a megaproject is easy; it is not. Rather, it is testimony to how good contractors, especially fabricators and constructors, have become at doing their work when it has been properly prepared.

If a project has been prepared well, execution is about maintaining the value that has already been created. It is about *active* vigilance and the willingness and preparedness to intervene. If a project has been poorly put together on the front-end, execution is all about damage limitation. Victory is snatched from the jaws of defeat in fairy tales, not in megaprojects. Although it is possible to do everything right on the front-end and then snatch defeat from the jaws of victory, it is quite unusual.

CONTROLS MUST START EARLY

The work that will become controls in execution starts back in front-end loading (FEL). The choice of the basic contracting strategy in FEL-2 starts to shape the kind of controls that will be needed in execution. Starting to shape the controls approach toward the

305

end of FEL-3 is too late, but it's the norm. I believe sponsors start to think seriously about control only in FEL-3 because they relate controls with construction or fabrication activities. In fact, it is far more important to be carefully monitoring engineering than construction! When problems start to show up in engineering, it actually may be possible to do something about them that will save the project. If the problems are not seen until construction, it is usually too late.

One essential element of planning how to control the project is to establish the project management information technology (IT) system and approach that will be used. Of highest importance is to plan for as much interoperability of IT systems as humanly possible. The IT systems requirements should be incorporated into the invitations to bid (ITBs) for EPC lump-sum projects and into the requests for quotation from all of the key vendors of equipment. Ideally, it would be possible to conduct all design reviews electronically, including reviews of vendor drawings. It is essential that the cost and schedule information provided by the contractors during execution be in a form that the sponsors' systems can use effectively. It should be mandatory that schedule updates be provided in their native electronic form and be archived by sponsors for purposes of claims defense later.

The sponsors' rights to data and to audit must be established in the ITB and in the contract terms and conditions. Some owners believe that if they are pursuing an EPC lump-sum strategy, they cannot secure rights to data, to receive detailed reports, or to audit. That simply isn't true. Stipulate clearly what is desired in the ITB and in the resulting contract, and the rights are established. If (and only if) you exercise those rights immediately after the start of execution will you keep them. It is the sponsor team's responsibility to articulate the behaviors that it expects from the contractors and all others involved in the execution of the project. Those expectations should be communicated early and driven consistently. Getting the information that is needed to control the project is just one piece of that overall puzzle.

Full rights-in-data for reimbursable contracts are absolutely essential. Occasionally, a contractor argues that cost data are "proprietary" on reimbursable contracts. This is understandable, and it does facilitate larceny. That any owner would ever acquiesce to those arguments, however, is utterly astounding. Without full rights-in-data, the sponsors will never know where the money went, only that there was an awful lot of it.

The owners' key roles in execution are to be constantly aware of exactly how the project is progressing and to be prepared and willing to intervene constructively when problems occur. The only prudent position for sponsors is to assume that the contractors may not know how the project is going and may not tell you if things are going badly even if they know. Sometimes, the contractors' systems are not adequate to effectively monitor progress; sometimes, the people operating those systems are not operating them well. (Recall that this problem is to be expected if a large portion of a contractor's key people are "from off the street," that is, not longtime employees of the contractor.)

It is common that when contractors find themselves in trouble, the last person to be informed is the sponsor team's project director. The contractors usually attempt to work themselves out of a problem before finally asking for help. To be forced to call the fire brigade when you have set your house on fire is embarrassing. It is often six months or more after the first signs of trouble actually appeared that the sponsor project team is informed. It is then certainly too late to fix any major problems.

We had one case in which the contractor had gotten crosswise with the government officials on securing work permits for personnel to enter the country to work on the project. Rather than bring the mess to the project director, the contractor attempted to get higher-ups in the ministry to "fix the problem," which made it worse. Only when the owner finally started to see positions going unfilled did the contractor admit the problem. The sponsor then worked with the government (with lots of apologies) to resolve the issue. By that point, the project was already falling behind.

On the positive side, as I mentioned in Chapter 8, we had a contractor with big problems with the neighbors in an onshore petroleum development project. The sponsors' controls organization saw the problems immediately and stepped in to completely change the project's approach to environmental considerations and clearly saved the project.

PRIORITIES FOR MONITORING AND CONTROL

Priorities are, in part, a function of the type of contractual arrangements. For example, the emphasis required on cost is high for reimbursable contracts and less for EPC lump-sum contracts. The level of quality checking is very high for EPC lump-sum contracts and for cost-incentivized EPC and EPCm reimbursable contracts. Quality control (QC) is less urgent when nonincentivized reimbursable and mixed approaches are taken, although this is not to say that it is unimportant.

The variation in emphasis does not mean that concern and attention go to nil on any contract type. For example, with nonincentivized reimbursable contracts, quality is still an issue. However, the incentives to cut corners are not as strong. One of the (many) problems with alliance contracting is that sponsors have not realized that the incentive structure in those contracts create exactly the same situation in terms of QC as EPC lump-sum contracts do.

After studying these projects for many years, I am convinced that once execution starts, which is really during FEED, not postsanction, the priorities overall and independent of contract type should be:

1. Safety
2. Schedule and especially whether the project is *on schedule*
3. Quality and how quality interacts with schedule
4. Cost

Safety must be number one for several reasons. Safety is an ultimate value, not an instrumental one. The reason to be safe is a matter of human dignity, not a matter of saving money, having better morale, having fewer labor disruptions, or having a better construction or fabrication schedule. Those things happen too when safety programs are strong, but they are serendipitous, not the underlying reasons. Holding safety as a core value is essential because the contractors will be watching carefully to see whether the sponsor is willing to shortcut safety to serve an immediate purpose. Experience has taught contractors that too many owners don't really care about safety when it doesn't suit them. The sponsor team's dedication to safety sets the behavioral standard for everything else. The sponsors' requirement that all accidents, injuries, and near-misses be fully and openly reported reinforces the transparency that is needed for effective controls.

After safety comes schedule, not cost, even if the project is fully reimbursable. That order may surprise some readers given the emphasis I placed on capital cost in Chapter 5. After all, as Figure 5.2 shows, the first determinant of profitability is production attainment, followed by cost, followed by schedule as a distant third. Schedule is important in execution because, if the sponsor is watching it carefully, lagging schedule is the key leading indicator of trouble ahead. Slippage in the progress of detailed engineering should raise alarm throughout the sponsor team.

Every project director knows that as execution proceeds, all projects become driven by schedule. Cost comes to depend on meeting schedule because there is an optimal schedule that is an indicator of being on budget. Being rushed on the back end leads to quality problems as well. Too often, however, the careful watch on schedule begins too late in execution because controls were not ready. Monitoring of engineering progress really needs to start in FEED and be fully mobilized at the outset of detailed engineering.

Whether detailed engineering is likely to slip should not be a mystery to project teams. Figure 12.1 shows the relationship between the completeness of FEL at sanction and slippage in the detailed engineering schedule. If FEL is anything other than best practical, substantial

Figure 12.1
Engineering Slips when FEL Is Not Best

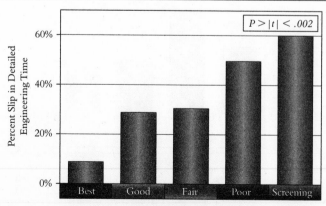

Front-End Loading Index

slippage in the completion of detailed engineering is to be expected. (We define detailed engineering as complete when demobilization of the full design team occurs, usually about 95 percent complete. Slippage is measured as the ratio of the actual period from mobilization to demobilization divided by the planned time.)

Other factors contribute to slippage in detailed engineering as well. Those factors are shown in Figure 12.2 and are all calculated with FEL controlled statistically. Not surprisingly, lack of team integration results in changes during engineering, which in turn, slow the process. Late receipt of permits is associated with a very large slippage in the engineering schedule. This reinforces my earlier admonition to get the permits as part of FEL or stop until the permits are received. Even after controlling for permitting problems, which were more common among petroleum development projects, oil and gas production projects experienced more engineering slippages than did other projects. For onshore projects in any sector, failure to complete the soils investigation as part of FEL was often damaging to engineering progress. And finally, a surprise: The use of substantially new technology was associated with *less* slippage, not more. That result is an artifact of sponsors being smart enough to set longer engineering schedules when technology is new.

Figure 12.2
Drivers of Slippage in Detailed Engineering Schedule

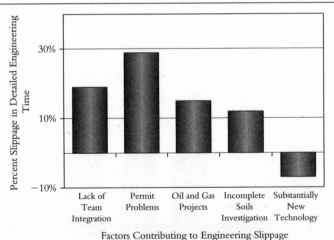

Factors Contributing to Engineering Slippage

There was another surprise result as well. Projects based in Australia, both onshore and offshore, suffered very severe engineering schedule slippages during the past decade. All of the values in Figure 12.2 were calculated with Australia controlled to prevent exaggeration of the slippages for non–Australian projects. The average Australian project suffered engineering schedule slippages of 60 percent! This reflects the dire situation in Australia for engineering resources over most of the past 10 years.

Although we did not systematically record it in the data collections, we know that late drawings from equipment vendors were another source of delay in detailed engineering. The problem with late drawings is particularly acute when the equipment is not standard. I encourage projects procuring difficult long-lead items to take a "coengineering" approach to procurement. This entails separately paying the vendors for their engineering work and even paying a premium for that engineering if the drawings are on time. This approach appears to ameliorate this problem. Also, one consideration in the selection of vendors should be the compatibility of their IT systems and their willingness to provide engineering work in a compatible system.

Schedule slippage during detailed engineering is an excellent indicator that the project is in the process of failing. In my view, it is also the last indicator that is still early enough to have much chance of being useful in changing the outcome markedly. *Even after controlling for the FEL index,* engineering slippage is a predictor of success ($P \mid \chi^2 \mid < .01$), cost growth ($P \mid t \mid < .001$), cost competitiveness ($P \mid t \mid < .0001$), production attainment failure ($P \mid \chi^2 \mid < .03$), and, of course, execution slippage ($P \mid t \mid < .0001$) and schedule competitiveness ($P \mid t \mid < .01$). Clearly, if engineering is slipping, the project is being lost. If the slip in engineering is discovered early enough and if there are contingency plans in place, engineering schedule can sometimes be recovered. More often it cannot, and then what's important is saving the project, not the engineering schedule per se.

It appears that most of the time, the sponsor team did not realize in real time that engineering was slipping. Several factors contributed to this problem. Sometimes the owners' controls organization was still in formation when detailed engineering was already underway. For this reason, as well as control of front-end work, I strongly recommend that controls start at the beginning of FEED. By the time FEED is completed, the controls organization should be fully operational and its tools calibrated. If the FEED contractor is going to stay on as the prime contractor for engineering, then the controls are set. If not, the controls approach to engineering and the data that will be required of the contractors must be spelled out in the ITB.

Most owners' controls organizations are better at monitoring construction progress than engineering progress. With modern design tools, the old-fashioned approach of counting drawings has no meaning. Unless the owner has set up the measurement system as part of the owner design reviews process, engineering progress is difficult to establish. Another very common problem was that reports of engineering progress from the contractors were not accurately discounted for design that had to be reworked because of engineering errors and omissions. When engineering quality was poor, progress was grossly overstated. Only design that has been reviewed, approved, and issued as final should be counted toward design complete. This is one of the ways in which quality control and assurance interact with schedule.

If engineering is late, the procurement of equipment and engineered materials will also be late. This in turn means that either construction will have to be delayed and possibly delayed quite substantially or the cost of the project will fly out of control. *If the engineering is slipping, the sponsors must be willing to rework the schedule so that work in the field or in the fabrication yards and shops does not start prematurely.* The actual loss of time is not as bad as it looks because (1) the project would have slowed down in fabrication or construction anyway at a time when slowdown was really expensive, and (2) with more material and engineering available, construction is faster than normal. If the project has weather windows, a longer planned engineering period is just plain prudent.

Our experience with megaprojects says that sponsors fail to slow projects even when they realize that engineering is falling behind. What that actually means is that they had no backup plan ready for that event. Concrete plans on how to intervene in the event of trouble are what we call risk management! You must be willing to stop early because stopping later doesn't work. The need to slow a project when engineering slips is absolutely mandatory when the region is short of construction labor, a subject to which we now turn.

MEGAPROJECT SURVIVAL IN LABOR-SHORT ENVIRONMENTS

Almost a third of our megaprojects were executed in environments that were short of the craft labor needed to do the construction. In this respect, offshore projects are more fortunate than onshore projects. Except where local content requirements forbid it, offshore projects can move their fabrication site to where the labor is available. Onshore projects have the option of adopting modular construction, but modules go only so far in reducing the local labor requirement and introduce a new set of challenges in design and logistics.

We describe a locale as labor-short if craft labor cannot be obtained and brought to the site in the numbers the project requires given the schedule it has established. Almost all onshore megaprojects strain available local labor resources, but generally labor can be brought to camps to supply the project. About a third of the time, that proves impossible; in these cases, only 16 percent of the projects succeed. Some of the most spectacular failures among our megaprojects occurred in these projects.

During at least parts of the past decade, we have seen severe labor shortages for large projects in Alberta, Canada; parts of Australia; the U.S. Gulf Coast; Central Asia; and much of the Middle East, especially along the Arabian Gulf. As the number of megaprojects is increasing again, we expect to see shortages recur in most of those areas in the next decade. In some areas the labor shortages may even be worse than in the past decade as rapid economic growth in India makes surplus labor from the subcontinent less available.

Labor shortages make the project environment especially fragile. If something goes wrong that bumps up the labor requirement, even modestly, the projects can go into a downward spiral in the field from which recovery is usually impossible. It is important to understand that the labor situation does not in itself cause projects to fail. But it does make failure easy.

The trigger that causes failure is the realization during field construction that considerably more labor will be required than expected. This situation is usually caused either by late and shoddy engineering that creates field inefficiencies or, in a few cases, by a misestimation of the labor requirements in the authorization estimate. When engineering deliverables are late, defective, or seriously out of the needed order, field productivity declines precipitously, which means that progress slows.

One reason this situation occurs is that owners have largely abandoned a decision gate in their work process just prior to committing to field execution of the project. Owners often do not know that engineering has fallen seriously behind because they have no effective independent measure of engineering progress. They are, instead, relying on the engineering contractors' submissions of progress. The problem is that sometimes the contractors publish misleading numbers, provide assurance they can catch up in time, or simply don't know themselves how far behind they have fallen.

The problem of late engineering became very widespread in the first decade of this century, and it's likely to continue to be a problem for megaprojects going forward. The problem was exacerbated by the use of low-cost engineering centers in developing countries with ample supplies of engineers. Those centers are now essential for rendering at least part of the design for the great majority of megaprojects around the world, and they frequently do an excellent job. The problem we have seen with the use of the low-cost center, however, is that once engineering schedule has been lost, the time cannot be recovered. There are two reasons for this. Recovering schedule places a lot of stress on the interface between the contractor's home office and the center. Also, the work processes at most of the centers are quite linear. Doing work out of the planned sequence, which would be needed to recover schedule, would threaten to bring the whole process to a standstill.

Late engineering usually results in orders for engineered material, such as pipe spools, being late as well. This results in late and out-of-order delivery to the site. If the field is already mobilized, the situation usually goes from bad to worse. Because engineering is delaying field progress, engineering is progressively rushed as the constructors demand design so they can keep their labor busy. To save time, engineering quality control is often bypassed, which enables shoddy design to reach the field. Shoddy design in the field leads to field rework, which slows the project even more. Rework in the field is associated

Figure 12.3
Depiction of the Downward Labor Productivity Spiral

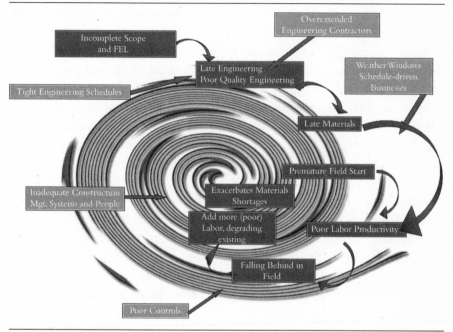

with safety problems, slowing work even further. And round and round we go. My attempt to illustrate this downward spiral is shown in Figure 12.3.

Of course, the most common reason that engineering falls behind right from the start of production design is that the FEL engineering was not complete. When the FEL engineering was not progressed sufficiently, the bulk materials (pipe, conduit, concrete, structural steel, etc.) cannot be measured accurately because the design will not support material take-offs. It is the bulk materials, not the equipment, that are the principal driver of required craft labor and the primary driver of engineering hours required. So we get growth in the bulk materials. There is more engineering to do than we had thought, so it falls behind; then when we get to the field, we discover that we never estimated enough field labor to start with. Things are often also complicated by seasonal weather windows that make the rescheduling of field start very difficult, and, of course, businesses want to see "progress on the ground." On many projects, there is no float in the schedule that can be used because it was removed in the hopes of meeting the overly aggressive schedules with which we started the project.

Late engineering is also more common on large projects today because large engineering contractors are short of skilled and experienced personnel. The aging demographic profiles of the major megaproject engineering contractors mirror the industrial owners in the OECD. Because the workload was light for many contractors for much of the 1990s, they did not hire and train young people during that period who would be today's experienced professionals.

The way we respond to late engineering or to the realization that we need a lot more labor than we estimated is usually not very creative. What project directors usually do actually makes the problem considerably worse; they hire more craft. When in a labor-short environment to start with, the craft available for hire are of low quality and often have to be brought in at hourly rates that are higher than the more productive craft already in place. Introducing less productive craft to a site tends to depress all craft productivity, which makes the problems even worse. So, we hire even more craft and so it goes. Many of the megaprojects executed in labor-short areas over the past 10 years have experienced some form of the downward labor productivity spiral.

A Truly Classic Example

Let me offer an example that is almost a checklist of what not to do in a labor-short environment. This was a difficult, complex joint venture project in a semiremote area. It required a good deal of highly skilled labor, especially for high alloy welding. I will start with the outcomes and then trace through how they got there. The total project was estimated to cost $5 billion. The project suffered a 50 percent (real) cost overrun and poor operability, although they finally did get everything up and running for the most part. The overall execution schedule, by contrast, slipped by only six months. Field labor hours grew from just over 10 million hours to just short of 30 million hours, in a high-wage environment! How did they do it?

The business was clear from the outset that the project was to be cost driven. As a commodity-producing project, that is almost always the right choice. As the project developed, however, the business pressure on the team to reduce costs not only continued, it increased. The team cut scope in one part of the project, but all of the cut scope came back later during execution as it became apparent that it was indispensable to functionality. In response to the cost pressure, the team made a classic error: it changed all of its estimating assumptions from average to "best in class." They assumed that equipment would be purchased at rock-bottom cost due to volume buying. They assumed they would be able to attract labor with minimum overtime. And they assumed that field labor productivity would be world class. The ratio of field hours to bulk materials was a full standard deviation below industry average. Their project management contractor (PMC), who was executing much of the FEL-3 work, must have known better but went along with the charade.

FEL-3 was declared complete with less than half of the piping and instrumentation diagrams (P&IDs) completed. As a result, the authorization cost estimate underestimated the bulk materials hugely because take-offs of the materials from the design were not possible. With no significant scope changes, concrete increased by a quarter, pipe by more than a third, instruments by more than two-thirds, and electrical quantities by more than a quarter. Now, the field hours-to-bulk materials ratio that had been merely heroic, was totally unachievable. The team did resource load the schedule at authorization, although exactly how they did that without quantities data is not clear. In any case, resource loading a schedule based on a gross underestimate of quantities is a waste of effort.

The engineering was late; it had to be in that so much more work was required than estimated. Another project in the region had been counted on to provide a good portion of the project's craft labor supply, but it slipped, just as megaprojects have a tendency to do. The field started to fall behind almost the moment it was mobilized. Nonetheless, labor productivity at that point was reasonably good.

Then the business and the project director made a fateful decision: they decided that they would not give on the schedule. In all fairness, this is a really difficult decision. Sometimes, salvaging the schedule is exactly the right move. Those are situations in which there is additional labor available and the logistics and the materials available to install make it possible to add labor to the site.

In this case, however, the labor was not available. It had to be recruited from thousands of kilometers away and its quality was not good. Productivity collapsed. For one large part of the project, welding productivity fell to more than 20 hours per linear foot of pipe installed (70 hours/meter) versus a norm of less than 4 hours per foot. Overall productivity was much worse than industry norms for the region, and by our estimate, about 10 million craft hours were wasted. But they completed the project, and it sort of worked. However, $2.5 billion in shareholder wealth vanished in the process.

How to Survive

So what is the antidote to the poison of a labor-short environment? I have found only two practices, which are intimately related, that reduce the odds of this situation developing. The first is to deliberately set more realistic execution schedules that reflect the actual field and labor supply conditions. The projects that were successful in labor-short environments set schedules on average that were 23 percent longer than a benchmark schedule for projects of their type and size. The failed projects set schedules that were 9 percent faster than the benchmark schedule. The difference is clearly statistically significant ($P > |t| < .003$). The second practice that counted was that the successful projects were much more likely to have developed detailed schedules as part of their FEL. More than 80 percent of the projects that succeeded in labor-short environments had resource loaded their engineering and construction schedules as part of FEL, versus 29 percent of the failures ($P > |\chi^2| < .01$). None of the successful projects had only higher-level milestone-type schedules.

Figure 12.4 shows how developing more detailed schedules affects the chances of success when in labor-short situations. The projects that resource loaded their schedules in labor-short environments succeeded 37 percent of the time. Those that did not almost always failed. Although it is reasonable to protest that 37 percent isn't very good, it actually is a little better than megaproject average!

Figure 12.4
Scheduling Detail Is Critical in Labor-Short Environments

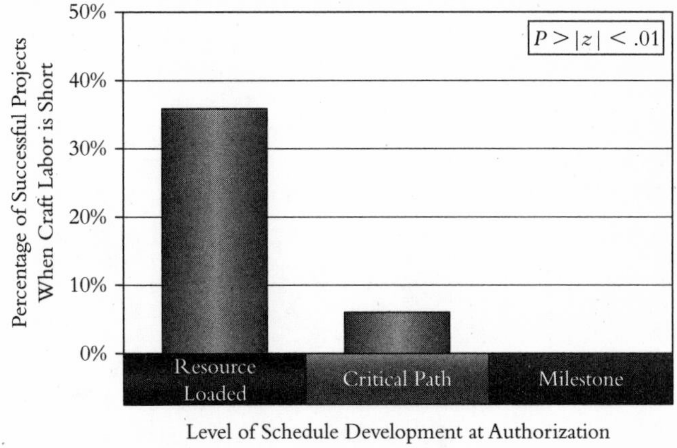

Level of Schedule Development at Authorization

The Criticality of Complete Scheduling

Unfortunately, of all the execution planning tasks, the one that is most likely to be left undone is the fully integrated, networked, resource-loaded schedule. The push back that we hear is primarily directed at the resource loading of the engineering and construction or fabrication schedules as part of the FEL. The usual complaint is, "Why should we resource load the schedule when that has to be done by the execution contractors anyway? It just duplicates work!"

No, it really doesn't. First, some EPC contractors create excellent resource-loaded schedules, and many do not. They often do not resource load the engineering schedule, and the engineering schedule turns out to be critically important for reasons discussed earlier. Second, the reason that the sponsors need to resource load the schedule is to be able to evaluate whether the project is actually feasible as planned and whether the contractor they will be selecting to execute the project actually understands the job. Too many megaprojects fail before they ever start execution because the schedule put forth by the sponsor is not achievable, even in principle. When an honest procurement schedule and the labor resource requirements are included

Figure 12.5
Resource Loading Is the Best Curb on Schedule Optimism

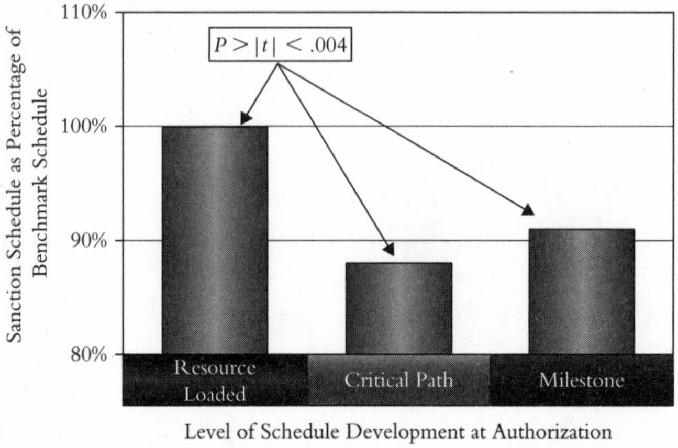

Level of Schedule Development at Authorization

in many megaproject schedules, it becomes apparent that the targeted schedule is unachievable.

As Figure 12.5 shows, only resource loading the schedule makes denial go away. Merely defining the critical path, which is a good deal of work, is not enough. When schedules are resource loaded, the project director is armed with facts when trying to push back against schedule pressure. Remember, the businesses don't want these projects to fail any more than the project professionals do. They just expect that the engineers will want to be too conservative. When confronted with the facts, they can usually be trusted to respond reasonably. Without the facts, it is just "our view versus their view."

Unlike many smaller projects, the schedules of megaprojects are typically noncompressible. For most projects, the execution schedule can be shortened significantly by addressing a relatively small number of items on the critical path. Usually, acceleration involves expediting a small number of major equipment items. If we are really in a hurry, labor can sometimes be profitably added to speed execution.

For megaprojects, however, the situation is very different. At any particular node in the critical path, there will not be just one or a few items on or very close to the critical path; there may be 10 to 20. To achieve any acceleration at that node, all of the items will have to be successfully expedited.

A little mental experiment shows why this is unlikely to happen. If there is a (generous) 90 percent chance of expediting each item and there are 15 items on or close to the critical path at that node, the probability of gaining any schedule acceleration is 0.9^{15}, or about 20 percent, provided that the expediting of each item is independent of all others. That means I will spend a good deal of money and have only 1 chance in 5 of actually gaining any speed. (Note that if the chances of expediting 2 of the 15 items were actually 50 percent instead of 90, the probability of gaining any speed falls to 6 percent.) Of course, I can simply remove all float in the schedule and pretend it will be faster, but given the fact that 78 percent of megaproject execution schedules slip, more float is needed rather than less.

Going the other route of trying to add labor to most megaprojects is a nonstarter. Most megaprojects struggle to accommodate physically and logistically the labor they plan to have and are in no position to add bodies. Megaproject schedules are solids; they cannot be compressed.

The situation with offshore projects that slip their fabrication schedules is often even more dire. Often, the tow-out and installation of new production platforms must be scheduled more than a year in advance. The situation is often complicated by weather-window restrictions as well. When fabrication slips, tow-out and installation cannot be allowed to slip and fabrication work is transferred offshore. Figure 12.6 shows what happens when construction work cannot be completed in the fabrication yard and work is carried offshore.[1] The cost of commissioning the platform explodes as soon as work must be carried offshore. That is because, on average, each construction hour offshore costs four times what it would have cost back in the fabrication yard. If the execution of the project starts to slip in early engineering, there is often time to juggle the tow-out and installation dates to save a great deal of money. The projects that were forced to carry work offshore ended up with an average total facilities cost overrun of 47 percent.

Figure 12.6
Carrying Fabrication Work Offshore Is Expensive

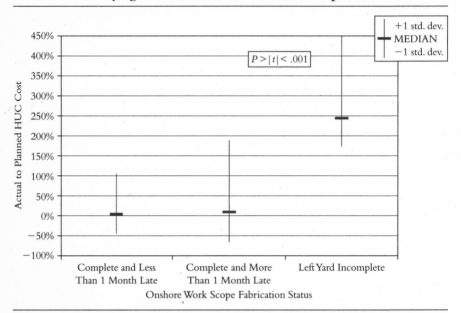

RISK MANAGEMENT PRACTICES

Almost all of the projects in our sample were subjected to a series of
risk management exercises, starting in FEL. Because so many practices
were applied to so many of the projects, it is difficult to explore the
effectiveness of the practices statistically. Our research on the use of risk
management practices on smaller projects suggests that there is value in
things like brainstorming sessions for risks; structured brainstorming of
strengths, weaknesses, opportunities, and threats (SWOTs); and so forth.
Our research around the use of peer reviews on smaller projects suggests
they are of very limited use and may even cause harm by injecting too
much conservatism into cost estimates.

Exercises that sensitize team members to potential problems
down the road must surely be worthwhile. But we all must remember that the very basis of risk management is sound basic practice
around things such as clear business objectives, team staffing and
integration, and thorough FEL. In the absence of those things, layering
on risk management practices is a futile exercise.

What I do not see in most risk identification, mitigation, and management exercises is a process for identifying the leading indicators of trouble and then working through exactly how the project team will respond in the event that the problem starts to materialize. For example, very few projects had a backup plan for how to respond if the detailed engineering started to fall behind. Virtually none of the projects that needed to be ready to shift the start of construction, for example, were actually ready to do so. The right to intervene when engineering is falling behind must be stipulated in the contracts with the engineering and construction/fabrication firms.

I believe the way we approach risk management on megaprojects needs to be different than standard technique. I believe it needs to focus almost entirely on "what if" planning. Using real examples, how will we, as an owner team, actually intervene in the process in the following situations, and others:

- The contractor is in violation of government rules around bringing people into the country.
- The businesses make a significant scope change during _____. (Fill in the blank.)
- The government makes a rule change around _____. (Fill in the blank.)

The focus traditionally is on identification of potential problems, entering those problems into a risk register, assigning a (usually junior) person as a "risk manager," and forgetting about it. Too often when a previously identified problem actually occurs, the project director and team are not prepared to respond because the response has not been worked through in advance.

RISK MODELING: A TALE OF TWO PRACTICES

Two types of modeling are routinely practiced on large projects:

1. Monte Carlo simulation of cost risk, usually with an eye to setting the appropriate contingency
2. Probabilistic analysis of the authorization schedule to assess the reasonableness of the forecast time requirement

Although these practices appear similar, they actually have very different efficacy. Monte Carlo (and variations) simulation of cost is less than worthless; it actually does harm. Probabilistic schedule analysis is very useful.

Monte Carlo Cost Risk Simulation Does Not Work

Of the projects in our sample, 61 percent used Monte Carlo simulation to model the probability that the authorization cost estimate would overrun (or underrun, but that is rarely an issue). Monte Carlo is a simulation technique for aggregating a series of distributions of elements into a distribution of the whole. It was developed to shortcut the cumbersome mathematical task of summing distributions. There are several underlying assumptions for the accuracy of the technique, the most important of which is orthogonality; that is, every distribution must be independent of every other distribution or the interdependencies must be accurately modeled and incorporated into the simulation.

When Monte Carlo is used to model cost risk, the procedure is first to develop the estimated cost of the project using normal practice for sanction estimates. Then, using a combination of team members and experts, a distribution is assigned around each element. For example, the cost of field labor (or any of its subelements) would be assigned an amount above and below the estimated value. The distribution might incorporate risk around both changes (increases) in hourly cost and productivity. An interdependency with the distribution around bulk material quantities might also be introduced.

After all of the distributions around all the elements in the estimate have been assigned, the simulation routine is run with samples randomly from the distributions as a function of the density of each distribution. The result from several thousand runs then forms the new composite distribution of cost risk. The contingency is set based on the probability of not overrunning that is desired, usually about 60 percent of not overrunning.

So does it work? For a risk modeling technique to be said to work, it must relate in a systematic way to the things that are first principle drivers of risk. As we have established, team integration, adequacy of team staffing, and most especially, FEL are the primary drivers of cost

TEAMS / FEL

overrun risk on projects. So if Monte Carlo simulation is working, it should result in contingencies that correlate well with those factors. We would also hope that Monte Carlo simulation results would correlate better than when the technique was not used, or one might conclude it is a waste of time.

Lacking an integrated team adds to risk. When Monte Carlo simulation is not used, project teams are reflecting that risk with higher contingency $(P\ |t|\ <\ .0001)$. When Monte Carlo simulation is used, contingencies are actually *lower* but the result is not statistically significant $(P\ |t|\ <\ .08)$. There is no relationship between Monte Carlo use and contingency when team staffing was not adequate. The real killer for Monte Carlo simulation comes from the relationship between contingency and FEL with Monte Carlo simulation used. That is what Figure 12.7 shows.

Three relationships are shown in the figure. The first is the actual relationship between cost deviation (the ratio of actual to authorization estimated cost) and the FEL index. The relationship is very strong and remains so no matter what other factors are introduced. It is a true driver of risk. The bottom line is the relationship between

Figure 12.7
Monte Carlo Generated Cost Contingencies Are Unrelated to Risk

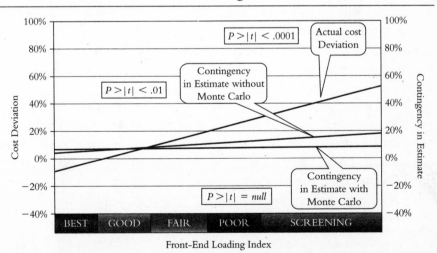

FEL and contingency when Monte Carlo simulation is employed. The line is flat. Monte Carlo simulation is producing an average contingency of 9 percent, with a standard deviation of less than 4 percent, independent of any first principle elements of risk. Remarkably, that distribution is normally distributed when we would fully expect it to be sharply skewed to the right. The average megaproject cost estimate when Monte Carlo simulation was used overran by 21 percent, with a standard deviation of 26 percent and a sharp right skew.

When Monte Carlo simulation was not used, teams were actually more sensitive to basic risks as they set contingency. A slope that is statistically significant at less than 1 chance in 100 does exist between contingency and the FEL index when Monte Carlo simulation is not used. This is why I have to conclude that Monte Carlo simulation actually does harm; it is not merely worthless.* The use of Monte Carlo simulation has no relationship to success of megaprojects or any of our other five figures of merit of projects: cost growth, cost competitiveness, schedule slippage, schedule competitiveness, or production attainment.

So why is Monte Carlo simulation so widely used? I believe it is because it seems so plausible. The Monte Carlo simulation results have, to use Stephen Colbert's wonderful word, the feel of *truthiness* about them, that is, the sense of being true without any of the burden of actually being true.† After all, a "scientific simulator" generated these results, not mere humans! Monte Carlo simulation is also easy to use and has given birth to a substantial cottage industry that is deeply invested in the approach.

The reasons that Monte Carlo simulation fails are basic to the tool itself and its application to the problem:

- Monte Carlo simulation is merely a simulator that does an excellent job aggregating distributions. The problems start with the distributions themselves. Cost estimates rarely overrun because there were errors in getting the distribution around any individual element in the estimate right. Cost estimates overrun because

---

*These results hold for smaller projects as well.
†Until truthiness came along, I referred to the Monte Carlo simulation results as a thin gloss of scientific verisimilitude on pure BS. Truthiness is more succinct.

the scope was not all defined, which means that the central value of every element in the estimate was wrong.

- The distributions used in the Monte Carlo analysis are fabrications. By that I do not mean they are lies but that they are made up—fabricated—by a group. They are not based on historically observed distributions of outcomes, nor do they have any first principles basis. They are opinion. Behavioral research dating back to the mid-1950s and Ward Edwards' Engineering Psychology Group at the University of Michigan has shown that when experts are asked to posit a distribution around some event, they will tend to make the distribution much more peaked and normally distributed than it actually is. That means that the distributions used in Monte Carlo simulation will actually tend to be systematically biased toward less variance. This is exactly what we observe in the data. Instead of a mean of 9 percent contingency with a near-normal distribution, we observe a 30 percent (9 percent plus the actual 21 percent overrun) mean with a sharply skewed distribution. Instead of a standard deviation of 4 percent, we should have seen a standard deviation in excess of 25 percent.

- The orthogonality assumption, which is absolutely central to the mathematical integrity of Monte Carlo simulation, is grossly violated by the real world of projects, large and small. In projects, bad things tend to happen in groups, not individually, because projects are so tightly woven. Events that affect projects in major ways, such as scope changes, engineering errors, erratic business decision making, or poor FEL, tend to go together. Even when one of those things occurs individually, it tends to trigger a cascade of problematic effects. Defenders of Monte Carlo simulation will sometimes respond to this criticism by saying that the interdependencies can be modeled. That is pure fantasy.

PROBABILISTIC SCHEDULE ASSESSMENT DOES WORK

If Monte Carlo simulation of cost risk is a complete flop, probabilistic evaluation of schedule has proved a useful technique for megaprojects. Probabilistic schedule assessment (PSA) involves examining the elements on or near the critical path for a project and testing how varying the durations of critical elements changes the overall schedule duration. PSA is asking the question, How likely is it that everything will go according to plan?

The use of PSA at project authorization is associated with a 27 percent decrease in the amount of execution schedule slippage by the projects ($P |t| < .001$). The use of PSA is helping project teams see that their chances of achieving the schedules that have been established are very poor. That then causes them to insert float at various points that are defined as low probability of achievement. Setting realistic schedules is associated with better overall results. The use of PSA is associated with a lower probability of production attainment failure as well as lowered schedule slippage. More realistic schedules improve quality. Improved quality plays out in better operability.

READING THE TEA LEAVES: KEY WARNING SIGNS OF TROUBLE AHEAD

The period from late FEL through early execution is a very busy period for project teams. It is easy for them to be too busy to begin thinking about risk surveillance. But this period is about the last chance during which an impending disaster might be averted. To see if any telltale signs of trouble could be seen, I reviewed the project histories for any events that recurred from very late FEL through the first few months of execution that might have provided early enough warning of trouble to come that changes could be made, especially changes in schedule. I list an event only if it occurred in three or more failed projects and did not appear more than once in successful projects.

Changes

- Were any scope changes made during FEED? Scope changes in FEL-3 are strongly associated with detailed engineering being late.
- Has a change in the nameplate capacity occurred that was based on using up design margins in equipment? This is not really a scope change because it does not involve new equipment, merely

using up all of the spare capacity in the specified equipment. This was strongly associated with startup problems.

Basic Data

- For engineering and procurement projects, are the seismic data (imaging of the reservoir) being reprocessed, even if there are assurances that "no changes will result"?
- Is a pilot facility still being run as execution is getting started? This is a killer.

Procurement

- Were the long-lead items actually ordered on time?
- Did the vendors provide a firm contractual commitment for delivery or a "target date"?
- Have any changes to long-lead items been required due to design development?

Contracting

- Was the licensing fee or contractor fee a "bargain"? For example, if a licensor is offering the technology for $1, it is because you are the guinea pig, not because the developer is generous. If the contractor fee request is abnormally low, it is because he or she knows something you do not.
- Is the prime (or one of the prime) engineering contractors being asked to do something in a way that is not usual for them, for example, not subbing out part of the design or using an office that would not normally work on projects at your location?
- Are any of the engineering contractors balking at the terms and conditions (T&Cs) for the contract? Remember, they all saw the T&Cs as part of the ITB, so if they are not accepting them now that you are in negotiation, something else is going on. In most cases, it is wise to keep the second bidder "warm," even to the extent of some payment, until the deal with the bid winner is signed. (Keeping the second bidder warm also increases the chances that acceptable terms will be reached with the bid winner.)

Shaping and Partner Issues

- Has an old and "put to bed" shaping issue resurfaced at sanction time, for example, royalties, sharing of proceeds, environment, and local content?
- Is a partner balking at sanction for whatever reason?

Early Execution

- Are the engineering contractors having difficulty mobilizing?
- Is the sequencing of engineering progress as planned, taking rework into account?
- Have all the permits arrived?
- Is engineering having a high rate of rework?
- Are drawings from the equipment vendors arriving on schedule?
- Is there agreement and understanding between engineering and construction/fabrication contractors about exactly what the design submittals to fabricators will look like and how detailed will the drawings be?

If the answers to any of these questions are discouraging, then engineering is probably going to slip and the contingency plans that were made for that eventuality need to be put in motion. It is all too easy to hope that things will sort themselves out, but they almost never do. Now would be the time to slow the project by design rather than have it slow by default later on.

MAINTAINING VALUE

As the project progresses out of engineering and into construction or fabrication, the task of the controls group shifts almost completely to preventing seemingly little things from becoming big problems. For onshore projects, the next critical juncture will be field mobilization. Some projects were tripped up by an inability to move workers in and out of the site each day. Long queues would develop outside the gates, with waiting times of more than an hour to get in. This problem is most likely to occur in low-wage environments where the numbers of people involved may be many thousands. But it has also occurred in

Alberta, Canada, and in the United States in the past decade. In high-wage countries, the labor absolutely must be paid for their waiting time or they will leave the project.

As construction progresses, the achieved labor productivity should be checked against the estimate basis continuously. If productivity is not as high as expected for the civil crafts, which are first on the job, it is very important to understand why. If the quality of the labor draw is not as good as expected, then there may be problems with labor quality throughout the job.

Often when there are labor productivity problems on a project, I hear both owner and contractor managements complain that the labor is unmotivated. Even if it happens to be true in a particular case, to frame the problem in that way is to lose the project. Labor productivity problems must be viewed solely as management problems. To do otherwise is to play the victim while the project suffers. In fact, most problems with labor productivity are problems of organization, materials management, first-line supervision, and basic labor skill. All of these problems are subject to management mitigation. It has been my observation that labor is often unmotivated at sites that are poorly run with insufficient materials available and hostile first-line supervisors. Before even considering adding labor to the site to attempt to recover schedule, be certain that you understand the problem and that additional labor will fix it rather than make it worse.

Finally, as construction or fabrication passes the halfway point, attention should turn to ensuring that the systems are being completed in the proper sequence for turnover to the commissioning and startup teams. This requires that the construction management organization begin to switch its attention from maximum rates of materials installation back to the master schedule that dictates when various systems must be completed to have an efficient startup process.

The turnover sequences should have been fully developed during FEL with the operating organization that will eventually take over the facilities. As construction/fabrication proceeds, operator training and manual preparation must also be progressing on the venture side. Ideally, the same people who will lead the startup and initial operation of the facilities will be involved in the drawing review process in early execution and will be present as commissioning activities begin.

Megaprojects often take many months to commission and start up. Often, at remote sites the utilities are needed as early as possible to support construction. The utilities are almost always required to be fully operational and reliable before startup of any processing units begins. Waiting until mechanical completion of all units before beginning the commissioning effort will stretch out the total cycle time at a point that causes maximum economic damage because all of the investment is in place but not earning revenue. Unfortunately, that is often what actually happens because the utilities are often among the last units defined, engineered, and ultimately completed.

CHAPTER 13

FOCUS ON SUCCESS

As we move into the second decade of the twenty-first century, we need a real sense of urgency about the quality of our most important industrial projects. The projects discussed in this book are very difficult, and that difficulty is reflected in disappointing outcomes for too many of them. So many problems contribute to these disappointing results that it might be tempting to despair of ever getting things put right. I don't agree with that assessment. One of the conclusions the reader should reach from our discussion is that sponsors actually have an enormous amount of control over the risk on these projects. But, if we are going to exercise that control and markedly improve the outcomes of these projects, sponsors will have to make some basic changes to their approach. Allow me to summarize those that I believe are most important.

ADDRESS THE BUSINESS-TECHNICAL DIVIDE

The first and clearly most important challenge is to address the deep chasm of misunderstanding between business and technical professionals about how these projects should be developed, governed, and executed. The need for improvement lies on both sides of the divide.

Project and technical professionals generally are too reluctant to speak up when they see problems from the business side that will likely cause failure. When they do speak up, they too frequently do not articulate their concerns in a way that the businesses can readily assimilate. I often get the feeling when doing postmortems of the bad megaprojects that the technical professionals are more satisfied with having been right about an issue than getting the issue successfully addressed. Project professionals need to learn how to communicate in language that is clear and persuasive to their business colleagues. The attitude of "I could have told 'em if they had asked" is not acceptable.

The business professionals have to accept more than half the blame for this situation because it is the businesses that are genuinely in charge. To put it bluntly, too many businesspeople making key decisions about these projects do not understand what they are doing. These big projects are very unforgiving. They must be prepared extraordinarily well, which takes skill and patience on both the business and technical sides. Once set in motion at the closure of shaping and scope development, they cannot be fine-tuned, sped up, slowed down, or redirected.

I am concerned that the businesses in some companies, especially big oil companies, will be convinced that none of these messages are aimed at them. They consider themselves project savvy and far too successful to imagine that they are at fault. However, one does not achieve a 78 percent failure rate in petroleum development projects without a lot of large company projects included. Indeed, large company projects lead the way. And let's be candid, at $80+ per barrel, a lot of very bad projects make money. But they are still bad projects. And those bad projects are still eating away at the shareholders' capital and returns as well as the long-term sustainability of the firm.

The first step to bridging the divide between the businesses and the project professionals is for the businesses to be far more inclusive of key project people in their initial development of the projects. Deals should not be struck without fully understanding the project consequences of how the deal is shaped. Much more dialog between businesses and project professionals is needed at every stage. The aura of distrust that now surrounds so many of the relationships between the businesses and the technical functions must be dispelled. Dialog is the only way to do it.

Some observers of this dynamic between business and project professionals believe that the problems originate with the decline in the numbers of technically trained businesspeople in industrial firms. I am not so sure. I see at least as many problems when the businesspeople started as technical professionals as when they did not. Sometimes I think former technical people need to be seen as being as "tough on those project people" as anyone else.

I believe that some of the problems originate in and are reinforced by business education curricula that emphasize financial savvy and deemphasize the role of the technical functions in industrial firms. Surely a balance must be struck, but running a successful commodity-producing business is at least as much a series of technical problems around how to achieve the lowest possible cost of production as it is a series of financial issues.

The often covert hostility that has developed between business and technical professionals in industrial organizations is the first-order driver of poor megaproject outcomes. Bridging the divide will help restore a spirit of cooperation not only in the development and execution of the projects but more generally in the way the owner companies operate. The failure to bridge this divide threatens their existence.

FORMALIZE AND INSTITUTIONALIZE THE SHAPING PROCESS

The need to shape megaprojects is one of their nearly unique characteristics. Most sponsoring companies lack a systematic approach to shaping that helps them ensure that the right things are getting done for every project. The shaping process is what binds the project together from the corporate boardroom to the production floor.

Every industrial firm has a strategy for how it will gain comparative advantage in a competitive world. That strategy includes technology, supply chain, and production assets. In successful firms those elements are tightly woven together. The corporate strategy informs the businesses what sorts of assets in what areas of the world will be acceptable and desirable. The business goals for the projects define how the corporate goals around generating comparative advantage will be manifested in this project. And finally, the detailed business objectives define the project objectives that the team must meet to be considered successful.

Businesses need to think about and prepare for megaprojects differently. The shaping process is how the sponsors' quest for comparative advantage is married to the messy real world of capital project opportunities. The shaping process defines and then allocates the value of the project to stakeholders in a way that should be intended to create a stable platform from which the project can be developed and executed while bringing enough value to the sponsors to make the project economically worthwhile.

Shaping is clearly an art, but even art requires disciplined skill, practice, and process. Companies that develop the skills and processes to be able to shape projects well will generate comparative advantage. But the ingredient that is most often missing is discipline. When it comes to capital projects, and especially to large capital projects, undisciplined is a fair characterization. Discipline is every bit as needed on the business side of these projects as the technical side, but we are not seeing it. The decentralized nature of many modern industrial firms, especially in minerals and petroleum, adds to the tendency to approach each new project with a new and hastily generated game plan.

The solution is not difficult, but by the nature of the problem, must come straight from the top of the corporations. Establish a standard work process for the shaping of large projects and then hold senior leaders in the businesses accountable for meeting the requirements that the work process entails.

DEVELOP THE TEAM STAFFING STRATEGY

One of the big issues facing industrial sponsors going forward is how to staff the many projects that we would like to do. If the projects are too thinly staffed by sponsors, the data clearly indicate they will fail. Every company that hopes to sponsor megaprojects in the next decade needs to establish the approach they will take to staffing. There are several alternatives, none of which are truly ideal.

The first step is to take a complete worldwide (for global companies) inventory of the resources available. Most large companies that are even slightly decentralized do not really know what they have because important human resources that might be best employed corporately are locked up in business units. Highly decentralized companies usually are altogether in the dark.

The next step, obviously, is to compare the resources available and deployable to the intended large project portfolio. When matching the portfolio to the skills available, it is important to be realistic about the staffing levels that will be required. Planning for skeleton staff is planning to fail. When the resources are insufficient to adequately staff the projects, some creative alternatives will have to be considered.

The first and most obvious alternative that should be used, regardless of whether other alternative staffing models are considered, is a robust training program specifically aimed at the difficulties associated with megaproject management. The curricula should include training for *business directors and megaproject project directors together,* as well as material for subproject managers and their reports, procurement/supply chain, and finance and legal. (Finance and legal might best be trained with business and project directors.) The goal of a megaproject training program should be to take staff who have large project experience ($100 million) and prepare them for the special difficulties they will face on megaprojects. If a training program cannot bring enough people up to speed, then other possibilities might be explored as well.

A few companies have elected to develop long-term relationships with major international contractors to do their major projects globally. This approach has been used for smaller projects many times with mixed success. When used for large projects, these "partnership" arrangements have generally been disappointing. These arrangements tend to create very strong temptations for the contractor to use the partnership arrangement for purposes of developing people they have just acquired or to dump people who are not productive.

A few companies have established engineering centers in places like India to support their projects around the world. The idea seems sound in principle, but there is not yet enough history to see how well these centers will work. They do, however, address the critical shortages of project management skills.

Some of the critical skills, such as controls, quality assurance/quality control (QA/QC), and planning/scheduling might be acquired from other industries, such as transportation and infrastructure, because those skill sets are largely transferable across industrial sectors. Third-party providers are also available for some of these skills, but with the caveat that they must be "tied up" for the duration of the project.

One alternative that needs to be fully considered is to trim the weakest elements of the large project portfolio to match the skill levels that can realistically be made available. Although sponsoring companies are understandably reluctant to go this route, it would be far preferable to drop some projects that cannot be staffed properly than to thin out resources from across the portfolio and have a much higher large project failure rate. Decentralized companies, that is, companies organized with strong separate business units, struggle to rationalize their portfolios. But they are precisely the companies that need it most. Decentralized companies suffer a disproportionate number of disastrous megaprojects.

Finally, all megaproject sponsors need to understand that there will be no bailouts of projects by contractors. The big contractors that can do this work are facing many of the same constraints as the sponsors.

FEL = 3-5%

REMEMBER, FRONT-END LOADING IS STILL THE WORLD'S BEST CAPITAL INVESTMENT

The investment needed in front-end loading (FEL) is about 3 to 5 percent of total capital cost and about 30 to 40 percent of total project cycle time. The value of that money and time is huge; the projects with best FEL averaged more than four times the net present value (NPV) per dollar of investment of all the rest of the projects. The projects that did not achieve at least good FEL were usually NPV negative.

If the FEL on your projects is other than best practical, you need to ask why. The most common answer is schedule pressure, but there are other major contributors as well: unclear business objectives that fail to articulate what the business needs for success, the failure to secure cooperation from the nonproject functions such as operations, and the lack of enough knowledgeable staff.

FEL is, above all else, a matter of discipline. In the best situations, that discipline is driven from the top of the organization through the businesses to the projects. Because the stage-gated FEL work process is a core business process, the businesses should insist on it. In any case, a technical authority sitting high in the corporate hierarchy needs to be in a position to stop poorly prepared projects before they incinerate shareholder wealth.

FEL is a matter of good corporate governance as well as a matter of project excellence. Without the level playing field that FEL provides, a corporation's portfolio of projects can never be truly coherent.

Corporate main boards of directors must insist on equally good preparation of all major projects.

RESTORE PROFESSIONALISM (AND SANITY) TO THE OWNER-CONTRACTOR RELATIONSHIP

The major international contractors are essential to successfully executing megaprojects. They are professional services firms, but they are not treated like professional service firms in today's marketplace. A normal market for professional service providers is that they are paid a fee for their services. If they are reputed to be extraordinarily good providers of services, they can command a higher fee than those considered mediocre. The highly skilled surgeon will have a more successful practice than the less skilled surgeon.

The owner community has deprofessionalized the relationships between owners and contractors. The owners, through the ignorance of the businesses and purchasing organizations, have attempted to describe engineering and project management services as a commodity business that should be purchased primarily on price. In fact, however, only a small part of the engineering and project services, detailed engineering, even approximates a commodity. Indeed, EPC services should be purchased primarily based on quality, not price, because of the huge variability in quality among contractors and among projects.

The misguided attempt by the owner community to deprofessionalize EPC services has resulted in pathological behavior that seriously damages major projects. Some of the contractors responded to the change in owner behavior and coherence by becoming almost nakedly predatory. Some have responded by becoming primarily defensive in their posture toward owners. Owners have responded by seeking to play incentive bribery games with the contractors, which cannot possibly work in the long term because the incentives will be gamed or the measures taken to prevent gaming will induce still worse problems.

Owners need to return to the basic notion that contractors should be paid for their work. If they do a good job, they need to be rewarded with a better chance of securing the next project. If they do a poor job and do so systematically, they should disappear. To make that work requires a return to institutional coherence on the part of the sponsor community.

TOWARD MORE SUCCESSFUL MEGAPROJECTS

The industrial megaprojects executed over the past decade or so have, taken as a whole, been disappointing. It is important to remember, however, that there were also some genuinely brilliant successes. But those brilliant successes were not generated by geniuses; they were developed and executed by men and women who were careful, patient, cooperative, and committed to excellence.

The second decade of the twenty-first century will see more very large industrial projects than at any time in history. The challenge for all stakeholders, sponsors, and contractors alike is to see that we generate many more successful projects in the next decade than we did in the past. I hope that when it comes time to review the history of the next decade of megaprojects, we can have a much happier story to tell.

GLOSSARY AND ABBREVIATIONS

Basic Data   Also sometimes referred to as Basic Data package, the body of scientific information that underlies the design of facilities. The Basic Data for a megaproject would require many hundreds of pages to compile. The term is used in a number of places in the text and is the subject of Chapter 7.

Bias   Used only in its statistical sense in this book. An estimator is biased if it systematically overpredicts or underpredicts the true distribution of results.

EPC   Refers to engineering, materials procurement, and construction—the three principal activities required to create a capital project. EPC also refers to the industry that provides these three services to capital projects. The firms in the EPC industry are called contractors. In addition, EPC refers to a form of contracting for engineering, procurement, and construction services that has all three activities performed by a single contracting company or by a single consortium of contractor companies.

EPCm   Stands for engineering, procurement, and construction management. EPCm is a contract approach in which a single contractor (or consortium) executes engineering and procurement and then manages, but does not perform, construction or fabrication.

FEED   Stands for front-end engineering design. This term is used primarily by the oil and chemical industries for the third phase of FEL.

FEL   Stands for front-end loading. This term refers to the work process needed to prepare a project for execution. FEL is generally organized into three phases: business case development, scope development, and project definition and planning.

Forward sold   Refers to selling the output of a megaproject before the project starts. Forward selling is very important for liquefied natural gas (LNG) and in some cases for metals. Forward selling reduces some risks for the project sponsors on the commercial side but often increases project risks because most forward selling involves "take-or-pay" contracts. Such contracts obligate the seller to provide product to the buyer regardless of whether or not the project is operating at the agreed-upon price. Conversely, the buyer is obligated to accept product at the agreed-upon price.

IPA Stands for Independent Project Analysis, Inc., a global research and consulting company devoted exclusively to the understanding of capital projects and capital project delivery organizations in the petroleum, chemicals, minerals, pharmaceutical, and power industries. All of the data on megaprojects in this book resulted from IPA evaluations of the projects for their sponsors.

NGO Stands for nongovernmental organizations, including a range of public interest organizations usually devoted to particular causes that are often politically sensitive: environmental protection, protection of vulnerable native peoples, anticorruption, and the like.

OECD Stands for the Organisation for Economic Cooperation and Development, an organization of countries with market-based economies, almost all of which are economically highly developed. Much of Western Europe, Japan, Canada, and the United States are among its 50 member states. The OECD designation is used as a shorthand for developed economies.

Project teams Refers to the groups of owner, individual contractors, and contractor personnel that develop and manage projects. In most cases, I refer to the sponsor.

Resource holders The owners of natural resources that will be developed by the megaproject. Resource holders are usually governments.

Sponsors Interchangeable with owners. Sponsors are entities, usually private firms or government-owned, that are seeking to develop and benefit from a megaproject. In most cases, the sponsors were also the monetary investors in the projects.

Stakeholders Individuals and organizations, including governments, that claim some part of the project's value. Sponsors are stakeholders but not all stakeholders are sponsors. NGOs and local communities, for example, are often stakeholders but rarely sponsors. The claim on value does not have to take the form of monetary payment. For example, environmental organizations may "take payment" in the form of a reconfiguration of a project that is (or is perceived to be) less damaging to the physical environment.

NOTES

Chapter 1

1. G. R. Castle, "North Sea Scorecard," *Society of Petroleum Engineers Paper 15358* (October 1986).
2. Estimates of world reserves held by national oil companies range from 75 percent to more than 90 percent. See, for example, *Wall Street Journal,* May 22, 2010.
3. Peter Morris and George Hough, *The Anatomy of Major Projects* (New York: John Wiley, 1987).
4. Roger Miller and Donald R. Lessard, *The Strategic Management of Large Engineering Projects* (Cambridge, MA: MIT Press, 2000).
5. Bent Flyvbjerg, Nils Bruzelius, and Werner Rothengatter, *Megaprojects and Risk: An Anatomy of Ambition* (Cambridge, MA: Cambridge University Press, 2003).
6. Miller and Lessard (2000).

Chapter 2

1. See Edward W. Merrow, Kenneth E. Phillips, and Christopher W. Myers, *Understanding Cost Growth and Performance Shortfalls in Pioneer Process Plants,* Santa Monica, CA.: The Rand Corporation, 1981; and Edward W. Merrow with Lorraine McDonnell and R. Yilmaz Arguden, *Understanding the Outcomes of Megaprojects: A Quantitative Analysis of Very Large Civilian Projects,* Santa Monica, CA.: The Rand Corporation, 1988.

Chapter 3

1. Peter Morris and George Hough, *The Anatomy of Major Projects* (New York: John Wiley, 1987). Morris and Hough defined *success* and *failure* along three dimensions: "functionality," which is only partly captured by my measure of production versus plan; "project management," which they define as delivery on cost, schedule, and technical specification; and contractors' commercial performance. I consider their final criterion irrelevant. I believe that my criteria for success and those of Morris and Hough would come to the same conclusion in most cases. Their project set included some very difficult to deal

with projects such as the Concorde Supersonic Transport, which I consider a prestige or monumental project rather than a commercial venture.

2. When a company has a bad megaproject, it is not uncommon to see a glowing article in the trade press about what a wonderful project it was. Perhaps the most amusing example of this was in *Offshore Magazine* touting BP's Thunder Horse as a "Top 5 Project of the Year 2009." Thunder Horse was supposed to be operational in 2005 and was about four years late and far over budget after suffering a series of technical problems, none of which were mentioned in the article. (*Offshore Magazine* 69[12], December 1, 2009.)

Chapter 4

1. I owe the term *shaping* to Miller and Lessard. Their ground-breaking volume is largely devoted to this subject. (Roger Miller and Donald R. Lessard, *The Strategic Management of Large Engineering Projects* [Cambridge, MA: MIT Press, 2000].)
2. Peter W. G. Morris and Ashley Jamieson, "Moving from Corporate Strategy to Project Strategy," *Project Management Journal,* 36, No. 4(2005), pp. 5–18.
3. Emery and Trist in their seminal article, "The causal texture of organizational environments," *Human Relations* 18 (1965): 21–32, explain the profound importance of the nature and stability of the environment (which they call "texture") to the difficulty inherent in organizational management. Projects are, of course, organizations as well and are quite sensitive to their context.
4. See www.Transparency.org.
5. This process was described nicely in Elmer E. Schattschneider, *The Semi-Sovereign People* (New York: Collier, 1962).
6. See William R. Jobin, *Dams and Disease* (New York: Routledge: 1999); and Richard T. Jackson, *Ok Tedi: The Pot of Gold* (Port Moresby: University of Papua New Guinea Press, 1986).

Chapter 5

1. In game theory, a game against nature involves dealing with threats that are random in character rather than a game against (or with) intelligent and purposive players. There is no requirement that the players be rational in any normal sense of the word. In fact, sometimes being (or being seen to be) irrational is a considerable advantage. See Thomas C. Schelling, *Strategy of Conflict* (Cambridge, MA: Harvard University Press, 1960).
2. I thank my friend, Judge T. Rawles Jones, Jr., for that dictum about contracts.
3. Roger Miller and Xavier Olleros, "Project Shaping as a Competitive Advantage," in Roger Miller and Donald R. Lessard, *The Strategic Management of Large Engineering Projects* (Cambridge, MA: MIT Press, 2000), 109 ff.
4. There are many good books on ROA. My favorite is Lenos Trigeorgis, *Real Options* (Cambridge, MA: MIT Press, 1996).

5. This is called the Averch-Johnson effect by economists. See Harvey Averch and Leland L. Johnson, "Behavior of the Firm Under Regulatory Constraint," *American Economic Review* 52(5) (1962): 1052–1069.

Chapter 6

1. Global Data, "Global Oil and Gas Capital Expenditure Outlook—2010"; T. Kevin Smith, "Outlook Improves for Chemical Industry Spending," *Chemical Engineering Progress* (July 2010); PriceWaterhouseCoopers, "Review of Global Trends in the Mining Industry 2010."

Chapter 7

1. *Design for Energy and the Environment* (Boca Raton, FL: CRC Press, 2010): 229. Used by Permission.
2. See E. W. Merrow, Kenneth Phillips, and Christopher W. Myers, *Understanding Cost Growth and Performance Shortfalls in Pioneer Process Plants* (Santa Monica, CA: The Rand Corporation, 1981).
3. See E. W. Merrow, *Bringing New Technologies to Market: The Process Industry's Experience* (Reston, VA: Independent Project Analysis, Inc: 1995).

Chapter 8

1. Robert S. Young, "Quantifying the Relationship between Project Performance and Team Functionality," Keynote Address to the Annual Meeting of the Australian Project Management Institute, 2010.
2. The insight that conflicts of interest are particularly acute in situations of team or joint production is hardly new. See Armen Alchian and Harold Demsetz, "Production, Information Costs and Economic Organization," *American Economic Review* 62 (1972): 777–795. The sponsors-contractors relationship is simply a variant of the principal-agent problem in economics. It is very difficult—some would say impossible—to structure incentives in a way that eliminates the problem. This fairly obvious insight seems to have been lost on many sponsors.
3. See Rob Young, "Quantifying the Relationship between Project Performance and Team Functionality," Keynote Address to the Annual Meeting of the Australian Project Management Institute, 2010. Young has developed a battery of questions that creates an index of team alignment. He finds that when teams are aligned and positive about a project during the front end, their views almost always turn out to be correct. When team members are in disagreement, those who are pessimistic turn out to be correct.
4. See Phyllis C. Kulkarni and Kelli L. Ratliff, "Best Practices for Joint Ventures," Presentation to the Industry Benchmarking Consortium Annual Meeting, March 2004. Available at www.ipaglobal.com.

Chapter 9

1. See Karl Sabbagh, *Twenty-First Century Jet: The Making of the Boeing* 777 (New York: Simon & Schuster, 1995).

Chapter 10

1. E. W. Merrow, Kenneth Phillips, and Christopher W. Myers, *Understanding Cost Growth and Performance Shortfalls in Pioneer Process Plants* (Santa Monica, CA: The Rand Corporation, 1981).
2. See Nick Lowes and Jean Paul van Driel, "Too Much of a Good Thing?" *Petroleum Review* (June 2004).
3. Paul Barshop and Chris Farrokhnia, "Best Practice for Alternative Selection in FEL-2," Presentation to the 19th Annual Meeting of the Industry Benchmarking Consortium, March 2009. Available at www.ipaglobal.com.
4. Paul H. Barshop and Christopher Giguere, "Improving the Effectiveness of the Scope Development Phase of Front-end Loading," Presentation to the 16th Annual Meeting of the Industry Benchmarking Consortium, March 2006. Available at www.ipaglobal.com.

Chapter 11

1. Roger Miller and Donald Lessard, "Public Good and Private Strategies: Making Sense of Project Performance," in Roger Miller and Donald R. Lessard, *The Strategic Management of Large Engineering Projects* (Cambridge, MA: MIT Press, 2000), 38–39.
2. T. C. Berends, *Contracting Economics of Large Engineering and Construction Projects* Delft: University of Delft (2009).
3. See James G. Zack, "Claimsmanship: Current Perspective," *Journal of Construction Engineering and Management* 119 (September 1993).
4. See Robert Frank Cushman and James J. Myers, *Construction Law Handbook,* Vol 2 (Aspen Publishers Online, 1999), 967 ff. For a discussion of how the courts have treated the obligations of owners versus contractors in their obligations on subcontractor claims, see Michael C. Loulakis et al., *Construction Management Law and Practice* (New York: John Wiley & Sons, 1995), 357 ff.
5. Berends (2009), 128.
6. Based on publicly available financial statements for 2009.

Chapter 12

1. The figure is from William Lamport and David Rosenberg, "Hook-up and Commissioning: The Last Step to a Successful Project," presented at the Upstream Industry Benchmarking Conference, November 2005.

INDEX